£6·50
16·00

Political issues and community work

This volume has been edited by Paul Curno in
co-operation with the Editorial Board appointed
by the Association of Community Workers:

It is no. 4 in the Community Work series.

Political issues and community work

edited by

Paul Curno

Routledge & Kegan Paul

London, Henley and Boston

First published in 1978
by Routledge & Kegan Paul Ltd,
39 Store Street,
London WC1E 7DD,
Broadway House,
Newtown Road,
Henley-on-Thames,
Oxon RG9 1EN and
9 Park Street,
Boston, Mass. 02108, USA
Set by Hope Services, Wantage
and printed in Great Britain by
Lowe & Brydone Ltd
© Routledge & Kegan Paul Ltd 1978

British Library Cataloguing in Publication Data

Community work.

    4: Political issues and community work.
    1. Social group work — Great Britain
    2. Community development — Great Britain
    I. Curno, Paul
    361'.941   HV245   78-40347

    ISBN 0 7100 8975 9
    ISBN 0 7100 8976 7 Pbk.

Contents

Introduction   xi

Part I   Dilemmas of Community Work and Ideology

1   Political values and community work practice
     John Lambert   3

2   Hard lines and soft options: a criticism of some left
     attitudes to community work
     Jerry Smith   17

3   CDP: Community work or class politics?
     David Corkey and Gary Craig   36

4   Ideology and practice
     Harry Salmon   67

5   Criticism and containment
     Martin Loney   85

6   Don't agonise — organise
     Jim Radford   106

Part II   Local Politics and Community Work

7   Brown rice or rice pudding: some dilemmas in
     community work
     Caroline Polmear   123

v

8 Politics and participation: a case study
Florence Rossetti   136

9 The Community Development section of Liverpool
City Council, 1972-5
Peter Clyne   159

10 Politics, conflict and community action in
Northern Ireland
Tom Lovett and Robin Percival   174

Part III   Three Perspectives for Development

11 Joint union—resident action
Jack Mundey and Gary Craig   199

12 Class, culture and community work
Laurence J. Tasker   219

13 Community work, social change and social planning
David N. Thomas   239

Contributors

John Lambert became interested in community work while doing research on housing and planning issues in Birmingham. From 1970 to 1976 he worked with the Sparkbrook Association in Birmingham, initially as Director and then on a voluntary basis. This placement made him interested in community work education and training, and from 1974 to 1976 he was Senior Lecturer in Community Work at Birmingham Polytechnic. He now teaches in the Department of Social Administration and School of Social Work, University College, Cardiff.

Jerry Smith worked as a neighbourhood worker for the Young Volunteer Force Foundation (now Community Projects Foundation) in Wolverhampton (1970–2) and Bradford (1973–6). Currently (January 1978) he is completing a community work course at Bradford University and looking for a job. He is one of the authors of the *Community Groups' Handbooks* published by CPF recently.

David Corkey is a tutor on the Community and Youth Work Course at Sunderland Polytechnic. Before that he worked in Londonderry as a Community Development Officer for the Northern Ireland Community Relations Commission, and in North Shields as Director of one of the national Community Development Projects sponsored by the Home Office and selected local authorities.

Gary Craig has worked for five years in Newcastle-upon-Tyne for the Benwell Community Project, part of the national Community Development Project, on housing and employment issues. He is a NUPE shop steward and Trades Council organiser. Earlier, he worked for YVFF in Stoke-on-Trent and Chesterfield for three years and taught in England and Ghana.

Harry Salmon worked from 1954 to 1971 in inner city areas, both as a methodist minister and as a community worker. In Coventry from 1971 to 1977 he was a fieldwork teacher in community work and during this time he helped to set up a resource centre to service working-class groups and organisations. He is now a tutor in community work at Westhill College, Birmingham. He is also Chairman of the Association of Community Workers.

Martin Loney is Senior Lecturer in Community Work at the Polytechnic of the South Bank, London. He has served as President of the Canadian Union of Students, General Secretary of the National Council for Civil Liberties, worked in race relations research in Bradford and Sheffield, evaluated social action programmes in the third world for World University Service in Geneva and taught at Carleton University in Ottawa. He was one of the organisers of the first private sector tenants' association in Ottawa. He is the author of *Rhodesia: White Racism and Imperial Response* (Penguin Books) and numerous articles.

Jim Radford is a long-term community organiser, and is currently General Secretary of Manchester Council for Voluntary Service; he was previously Director of the Blackfriars Settlement in London. He made dramatic use of direct action throughout the 1960s with positive results, particularly on housing issues, but uses different strategies for different situations and prefers persuasion and negotiation where possible.

Caroline Polmear is a tutor in Applied Social Studies at Bedford College, University of London. She previously worked for four years with the Camden Council of Social Service—first as a neighbourhood worker, and later, until 1976, as Head of the Community Development Department.

Florence Rossetti is a lecturer in Applied Social Studies at Bath University. She was previously team leader of the Southwark Community Development Project during its first two years. Earlier experience included community relations work in this country and community development in Italy and Africa.

Peter Clyne is Assistant Education Officer for Community Education and Careers with the Inner London Education Authority.
He was previously Community Development Officer for the City
of Liverpool and before that gained experience as a teacher, youth
leader and adult education organiser. His book, *The Disadvantaged
Adult: Educational and Social Needs of Minority Groups*, was
published by Longmans in 1973. He is currently a member of the
Advisory Council for Adult and Continuing Education.

Tom Lovett is currently the Director of CARE (the Community
Action Research and Education Project) at the New University of
Ulster, Institute of Continuing Education. This three-year project
is concerned with meeting the educational and research needs of
community groups in Northern Ireland. Prior to the establishment
of CARE, he was involved in community educational work with
the Community Studies Division of the Institute in 1972—7.
Earlier, from 1969 to 1972, he worked with the Liverpool Educational Priority Area Project concerned mainly with adult education
and community development. He has published *Adult Education,
Community Development and the Working Class* (Ward Lock
Educational, London, 1975), based on that work.

Robin Percival is an active member of the Bogside Community
Association in Derry, and was previously Secretary to the Association. He is a member of the Executive Committee of Community
Organisations in Northern Ireland (CONI). He teaches sociology at
the Londonderry College of Technology.

Jack Mundey is the son of an Australian farmer in Northern
Queensland. He was for a while a professional footballer (Australian
Rules) in Sydney, but since the early 1960s has worked in the construction industry in New South Wales. He was the first secretary
of the Builders Labourers' Federation to be elected under new
democratic rules for a limited period of office.

Laurence Tasker is Lecturer in Applied Social Studies at the
University of Surrey, formerly at Swansea and Birmingham
Universities. His fieldwork experience includes community organ-
isation and neighbourhood work.

David Thomas was a neighbourhood worker with the Camden Committee for Community Relations; he then joined the Southwark Community Project and since 1973 has been teaching on the community work courses at the National Institute for Social Work.

Introduction

Paul Curno, Marjorie Mayo and David Jones

The aim of this volume is to provide practitioners of community work with material for them to consider the implications of some of the more prominent political theories, exhortations and issues of a political nature with which they are constantly faced in their daily work.

The book is intended moreover not only for professional community workers, but also for those who are indirectly or tangentially involved in the community and local politics, whether as social workers, teachers, planners, lawyers or students; the issues are, of course, key problem areas too for both community activists themselves, and for local politicians.

Many of the authors are, or have recently been, field workers, and their contributions explore a number of broadly defined 'political' questions in the light of this experience. As a result, this volume does not offer a series of essays based on a clearly defined position of political consensus—indeed many of the papers are directly contradictory to each other—but rather a collection of views against which readers can question and reformulate their own positions and work. The unifying theme, then, is not the political ideology of the different contributions, but their relevance to the problems of community work practice.

This is the fourth volume produced by ACW in conjunction with Routledge & Kegan Paul.[1] Two further volumes are currently in preparation, and to some degree must be seen as complementary to the present book—these are on jobs and the community, and community work and public participation.

In the Introduction to *Community Work One* there was a reference to 'community work coming of age' with the publication of that volume. We would hesitate to be categorical about the degree of maturity which community work has now reached, but we do believe that this collection of papers reflects the outcome of the professional, not to say emotional, traumas through which so many workers have passed in the five years since that edition was prepared. Furthermore, it points to the emergence of a more realistic appraisal both of the problems to be overcome in bringing about greater community control of resources, policies and organisations, and of the likely contribution of community work to that process. The renewed attention to the needs of the inner cities, coupled with government initiatives as a result of high unemployment, offers community work a valuable opportunity to develop an effective practice based on this reappraisal.

Over these years community workers have been faced with fundamental dilemmas. Financial cutbacks have resulted in the loss of resources to services and to local communities (and to community work jobs). There has been high optimism but moderate gains. Community workers have reacted with a variety of ideological responses. One reaction has been to look inwards and to question the professional identity of community work, the significance or otherwise of training and qualifications, etc. It is perhaps hardly surprising that all this has given rise to confusion, sometimes paralysis, and even occasionally to political suicide on the part of workers and their projects.

To some degree this must be seen as the downward curve of the arc of optimism and enthusiasm with which community work and participation were greeted in the late 1960s and early 1970s. This enthusiasm has now waned, due in part to the realisation that many issues cannot be resolved at the local level, an awareness which has been driven home particularly hard in recent years by the cuts. Initially, community groups who made a strong case about their needs to the local authority were often successful. However, such local successes, while bringing about a change in people's perceptions of local government, also result in over-high expectations on the part of community workers. There was corresponding disillusionment when it was seen that the radical changes which had been expected or hoped for did not automatically follow. None the less, the experience helped to focus the attention of community workers on the relationship between local and national questions, and encouraged them to explore ways in which the inter-relatedness of economic and social issues could be perceived and influenced by local communities.

This growth of political awareness by community workers has been one of the most significant developments in the past five years.

Inevitably it has led to workers adopting different ideological positions. John Lambert in his introductory paper to Part I identifies four stances—conservative, liberal, socialist/Marxist, and anarchist or libertarian (although other contributors make a further distinction between socialist and Marxist). He suggests that there is nothing inherently radical in community work; different beliefs or positions, reflecting differing perceptions of government or the state, lead to different community work practice. As a result, the polarisation of ideologies has added to the confusion of community workers, and created anxiety for many about whether they were actually reinforcing systems and structures they were ideologically committed to changing.

This debate is the underlying theme of Part I; each contributor analyses the current and potential influences of community work in the light of his own theoretical standpoint. Thus Corkey and Craig, in outlining the history of the national Community Development Project (CDP), issue a challenge to community workers in stating that by undertaking traditional forms of community work they are acting as agents of social control, since they aim at the better social integration of those with whom they work; i.e. that they are socialising working-class communities into the existing economic system. Martin Loney, in focusing on the increasing interdependence of the state and voluntary organisations, lends support to this view by suggesting that as the state moves steadily to corporatism, it requires ever-increasing citizen participation to secure consent as an alternative to more extensive and overt coercion. Radical programmes *can*, he argues, be developed through the use of government money, but voluntary organisations and community groups need to be aware of the risks as well as the advantages involved.

While agreeing that dangers of co-option must be avoided, Jerry Smith regrets the 'radical pessimism which pervades community work', and urges that the opportunities presented by participation be fully exploited. He argues that the state becomes vulnerable to transformation by the incorporation of working-class groups within the structure, and particularly so at the weakest link in the system—local government level. Taking a slightly different tack, Harry Salmon argues that the vast majority of citizens are suspicious of political fervour and those who speak of class differences. Salmon sets out to demonstrate that the more radical the ideology, the greater the disparity between ideology and practice.

Suggesting that many Marxists underestimate the complexity of society, he stresses that community workers need to work in different contexts and at different levels, and that structural changes in society will be achieved not by community workers predominantly but through the contributions of a wide range of people—political activists, shop-floor workers, radical professionals and others. In the final paper in Part I, Jim Radford outlines his belief in the necessity for a 'piecemeal revolution' which must carry people with it at each stage. While welcoming the swing away from non-directiveness in community work, he warns that community workers, in developing anti-authoritarian solutions, should also develop an anti-authoritarian political theory, for 'it is clear that the threat to individual rights and freedom and to genuine participation is just as likely to come from the extreme left as it is from the right. A community worker . . . must be concerned to help people resist either brand of authoritarianism'.

Contributors to this volume were asked to develop their arguments within a broad focus of work at a local rather than a national level, since this is the arena within which community workers mainly operate, and because it is here that community groups can exercise most influence over those matters which are of concern to them. Although national politics set the wider framework for neighbourhood community work, the editors decided to concentrate upon local politics for the purposes of this volume. The four papers in Part II, which is concerned with the *practice* of community work, forcefully underline the issues facing a community worker, whatever the context. Thus Caroline Polmear, in a chapter about 'the minutiae' of neighbourhood work, describes the dilemmas faced by a worker when there are differences in values and political attitudes between residents, and between groups, in a locality. She stresses the importance of community workers being sensitive to the culture in which they work (a theme developed by Laurence Tasker in Part III). In a similar vein, Florence Rossetti urges that the complexity of the local authority machine should not be underestimated. In parallel papers, she and Peter Clyne present remarkably complementary perceptions of the 'hidden world between policy-making and policy implementation', from their own experiences of working with a local authority. They demonstrate that the machine, far from being monolithic, comprises political, administrative and professional conflicts. Added to this are the further problems which arise when initially sympathetic councillors alter their view of community work when confronted by its implications—leading Peter Clyne to conclude that 'it is very difficult for a City Council to put a progressive community development policy into practice'.

In very many ways the picture of community action in Northern Ireland by Tom Lovett and Robin Percival summarises and dramatically illustrates the ideological, practical and political dilemmas faced in some form by most community groups elsewhere in the UK—albeit without the added horror of armed conflict. The opportunities are there, and the groups have shown willingness to grasp them. Yet without clear and agreed goals, based on a coherent political analysis, inter- and intra-group conflicts, and the dangers of co-option by an efficient bureaucratic machine, can become overwhelming. None the less, they maintain that in Northern Ireland community action has become a social movement which offers the only radical alternative to para-military action or traditional politics.

After the early euphoria about the expected effectiveness of local participation, community workers appear to be reacting to their initial disillusionment in two ways. One response has been a renewed determination to develop knowledge and technical competence in areas not previously considered, together with the ability to pass these on to community groups. Local, regional and national resource centres are one logical outcome, existing as they do to provide people with both essential technical knowledge and more general community work support in using the information supplied.

In Part III, David Thomas goes further in support of this trend. He starts from Gilbert and Specht's view that the three values of participation, leadership and expertise are in competition and while one waxes the others wane. The implication, he argues, is that 'because of the complexity of social issues that face local authorities, and the scarcity of resources available to deal with them, the value of *expertise* will gain ascendency in the second half of the 1970s'. Drawing together a number of issues raised in this volume, he proposes that competence in analysis and techniques of social planning provides a means of linking political analysis and neighbourhood and organisational intervention and change.

A second response to earlier disillusion has been an increasing emphasis on the importance of picking realistic targets, and of making alliances with other relevant organisations—e.g. between trades councils and tenant groups. Laurence Tasker, after looking in depth at the causes and effects of 'negative socialisation' on many working-class communities, points out that the task of 'compensatory education' can be overwhelming for the lone community worker, and suggests that there should be a reconsideration of the potential in extending links with the social services. He also considers (as do Jerry Smith and David Thomas) that lessons can be learnt from the women's movement, with which they recommend closer connections. But it is around joint action with the trade union movement that there has been most speculation in community work in the past few years. Apart from the Coventry Workshop, however, there have been few serious attempts to explore what such co-operation might offer. The discussion between Jack Mundey and Gary Craig about the joint campaigns organised by Australian trade unions and residents' groups opens up numerous possibilities. This contribution is particularly timely, given the changing perspectives of community work.

The recent economic climate, with high unemployment and lower public spending, together with certain government initiatives (for example the Job Creation Programme and the Partnership Areas), has resulted in community workers gaining a different perception of problems. The social impact of changing employment opportunities has definitely arrived on the community worker's agenda. This shift of focus will be taken up in the forthcoming collection on jobs and the community. Certainly the implication for politics and community work can be expected to be immense. In particular, the discussion with Jack Mundey poses a whole new range of questions about alliances and strategies for community groups, and community workers.

Note

1 The first two, *Community Work One* and *Community Work Two,* presented overviews of the community work fields; the third book, *Women in the Community*, was the first of this series to take a more focused look at particular aspects of the work.

Part I Dilemmas of Community Work and Ideology

1 Political values and community work practice

John Lambert

Community work, as will be very apparent to readers of the volumes in this series, takes many forms, means many things, finds different sponsors, attracts different workers, and can claim a variety of achievements. No one definition will satisfy all practitioners and what are claims of success for one may be frustrations and failures for others. The growth of community work in recent years has been as a response to the persistence of poverty amidst relative affluence. Its popularity is no doubt because of its capacity to comprise so many broad practices involving practitioners whose values and purposes range widely across political, religious and ideological spectra.

If some competing explanations for the persistence of poverty in contemporary Britain are considered, it may become clearer how community work can be consistent with distinct assumptions or beliefs. It will be apparent that there is nothing inherently radical or progressive in community work *per se* unless those terms apply to any new mode or fashion of social action: but also it should be apparent that different political beliefs or positions provide different justifications for different styles or methods of community work practice.

There are perhaps some good reasons for trying to disentangle some of these differences. With the growth of community work opportunities and the rise of specialist community work courses and the inclusion of courses in social work training, it must be confusing to teachers and students to be presented with diverse actions and attitudes all seeking to be included within this new movement. Moreover, there are now current claims and counter-claims about community work's radical or change potential. For some there are activities which can be dismissed as *merely* community care, while for others community action is dangerously political. Nor should the diversity be presented merely as choices

3

which the individual student teacher or worker selects according to taste, for within the diversity are quite distinct conceptualisations of the world, of politics, of government, of what constitutes social change, and what ought to be done about all these.

Let's try and sketch the variety of political positions and attitudes toward poverty, and particularly to the persistence of poverty in a rich advanced industrialised welfare state society such as contemporary Britain. For the conservative there is a certain inevitability about poverty, since whatever is done about equality of opportunity, achievements, efforts and rewards will not, and ought not to, be equal. If we look at individuals we find some unwilling and incapable of effort, some who through no fault of their own have fallen on hard times, some suffering from severe individual difficulties and problems seemingly transmitted from one generation to the next—such that the poor will always be with us. Action is needed to provide opportunities for the deserving; and while help and sympathy are needed for the inadequate, care must be taken not to encourage the undeserving who will surely take advantage of any soft option.

For the liberal, the poverty which persists is a shame and a challenge, but it is undoubtedly less than in times gone by. It represents essentially a failure of government to ensure adequate distribution of goods and services. The need is to provide opportunities for all by ensuring the proper management of facilities. This necessitates active government involvement in some spheres where unrestrained market forces will not provide sufficient goods at prices within reach of the less well off. But by gradual reform and proper management, the remaining pockets of deprivation are being tackled by the mechanisms of the welfare state. For the socialist, the current mode of production gives rise to basic inequalities revealed through unemployment, large sectors of low pay, a continued dependence upon sub-standard housing, schools and other facilities. Although state provision has grown in recent years, control and planning is still only partial and so poverty and deprivation remain structural features of the contemporary order. What progress has been made has derived from political action by workers' parties to wrest some control from the bourgeoisie over the provision of some goods and services.

These three generalised attitudes and explanations—individualistic, governmental, and structural—can account very broadly for most of the established party-political accounts and activities to combat poverty. Ideas and theories such as the Cycle of Deprivation find favour on the right; within Conservative, Labour and Liberal Parties are many who would adhere to the view that managerial or institutional malfunctioning underlies the persistence of poverty.

From the left and 'Marxist' fringes of the Labour Party come the analysis and actions to tackle the structural dimensions of inequality—structural, that is, to modern capitalism.

A fourth view is worth consideration, since it would seem to influence no little part of the community work response: one that identifies the state, the corporation and the bureacracy as the source of our problems, and, if only man were genuinely free to live a life freed from their constraints, an exemplary life would follow. This attitude, which might be termed anarchist or libertarian, can *sound* like a Conservative response to the large institutions of state nationalisation or a left-wing response to the essentially *competitive* features of capitalist enterprise, is none the less a distinctive social analysis not merely 'a plague on all political houses!'

If we now consider some of the influences which have contributed to the growth of community work in the past decade, it may be possible to see how each distinctive political perspective suggests a different emphasis and priority for action. Three inter-related influences are worth noting:

(1) As part of a response by central and local government to the acute managerial problems posed by various forms of 'urban' deprivation. In the quest for more efficient use of scarce resources, kinds of community work may assist improved communication between providers and clients.

(2) As a response by the recipients of various government services in the face of increasingly larger and more bureaucratic forms of service delivery, a variety of more or less organised groups and associations have been established to assert their claims on the distribution of resources.

(3) As a response by those dissatisfied with the existing political machinery of government and parties for the articulation of a number of demands and grievances, a variety of groups and action efforts have sought to mobilise sections of the population on specific issues or in specific locations.

If a word is needed to link these influences, it is 'participation':

and it might be noted that in the late 1960s, as part of the 're-discovery' of poverty, three major government enquiries into the provision of services caught and amplified this quest for partici-pation—Plowden on education, Seebohm on the social services, Skeffington on town planning. Now it is surely significant that the growth of organised 'community worked' participation should relate to facilities and services provided by the state. If, in our 'mixed' economy, the control of production remains rooted in the private sector, there has been a growing range of goods whose pro-vision is increasingly taken for granted as part of a body of rights to which all should have access. Housing, a health service, educa-tional provision, transport and aspects of leisure facilities, are not provided by private enterprise but have been taken over by the state and are the main work of central and local government. The reason for their take-over can be found in the increasing demand for them as of right, and because their rising costs make them no longer a profitable sector for private investment. In a 'mixed' economy, private investment concentrates on elements of individ-ual consumption, where demand and profit is more easily manipu-lated. The state has responsibility for these more collective needs, these items of *collective consumption*. Their provision is essential not only to satisfy the demands and expectations of the people but also for the continuation of profitable private business—workers must be housed and educated adequately, they and the goods they produce must be able to move easily in the market place. It is precisely because their provision is at one and the same time essen-tial to the maintenance of the social order, an unprofitable part of ordinary capitalist investment and the focus of demands, that their management, provision and allocation is problematical. So it is in relation to managerial efforts related to these kinds of facilities that the growth of participatory community work has been so marked in recent years. And it is by virtue of this that community work efforts are a matter of politics, since the decisions about resources, priorities and recognition with which community work is essentially concerned are, quite simply, political decisions. So, returning to our four summarised accounts, what actions are suggested? Here it is necessary to examine different views of government and the state contained within the four points of view. For the Conservative and Liberal, the modern democratic state is essentially a benign institution—the means of ensuring fairness, justice, opportunity and equality. For the socialist and the anarch-

ist, the state is essentially repressive: for the socialist it is potentially something quite different—for the anarchist such a machinery
is inherently anti-human. So, for the Conservative and Liberal,
participatory community work seeks to enhance relationships
between government and the people: for the anarchist, participation aims to release people from their dependence upon controlling
institutions. Let us examine further these different views of the
state. It should be noted that the liberal democratic view is the
more common and widely accepted account. It is taught in schools
and universities, is taken for granted by most political commentators and analysts and underlies most public and popular views
of the world as it is. The significance of this being the dominant
explanation will be examined later.

In this account or theory, the modern state—that is government,
central and local, and the institutions which are answerable ultimately to Parliament such as the legislature, civil service, judiciary,
army and police—is the neutral arbiter of the diverse and competing
interests which constitute society. The state stands apart from the
above society, mediating the competing demands. The purpose of
the state is to prevent the domination of one set of interests and
to ensure the representation of all. The means whereby this is
achieved is by representative assemblies, central and local, comprised of popularly elected representatives establishing legitimate
means of access to a multiplicity of pressure groups. These groups,
organised to a greater or lesser extent, are not in competition with
political representatives but are complementary to them, providing
channels of communication to enable elected representatives to
represent fully and responsibly the interests of all constituents. In
this way, recognition is assured and sooner or later it is everyone's
turn for a share of the available resources. In this formulation, it
should be noted, the political sphere and its decisions are seen as
separate and autonomous—it is a sphere to which those seeking
resources need to gain access. It should also be noted that this
determining, defining and maintaining of means of access is a major
task of the state apparatus.

Within such a framework it will be apparent that the opportunities for community work are virtually limitless as a way of ensuring
that the means of access to government are exploited to the full
by organising neighbourhood-based interest groups to seek and
obtain their rightful share of the resources by participating in the
political life of their community. For the Conservative, such work

can be the means of promoting self-help and self-reliance, of avoiding dependency and of demonstrating the rewards and privileges which are available for the citizen. For the Liberal, the legitimacy of pressure-group activity allows for a variety of activities whereby those usually left out are represented directly or have their interests sponsored by those with knowledge about their situation.

The alternative critique of the liberal democratic state considers the state apparatus to be not neutral or autonomous but the means whereby the privileged, dominant or ruling class maintains its domination. For the Marxist, the dominant interests are those of the ruling class of the bourgeoisie—those who own and control the means of production and sustain a free market where demand for their goods can be maintained to enable profit to be made and capital accumulated. The role of the state is to manage the affairs of the bourgeoisie—crucially to reproduce the conditions whereby workers continue to make their labour available for the process of capital accumulation. So the critic draws attention to the predominance of representatives of elites in the ruling circles of the state apparatus and the extremely limited scope working-class interests have been able to achieve, especially when it comes to questions of power and decision-making. Within this perspective, extensive participation is undoubtedly a fact of life; but not as a means of effecting redistribution so much as a means of alerting the top to pressures and alignments among lower participants so that the problem of order—social control—can be effectively tackled. Within this model it should be noticed that there is achieved some change and redistribution but within controlled limits—limits set by the overall requirement to protect the profitability of the private sector. Real redistributional changes of resources and crucially of power (defining the means of access to decisions) is far more problematical. Typically, the gains made by interest groups will be found on scrutiny to be at another group's expense, for the availability of resources is limited—the economic instance is ultimately determinate. The social demand for equality, for the abolition of scarcity, is in contradiction to the quest of privately controlled capital for maintained profit through competition in a 'free' market or through monopoly means. Poverty is a structural aspect of this organisation.

From this model, what follows for community work? The basis for social change is class struggle to replace the existing relations between owners and workers with common ownership of the means of production and the eradication of competition and profit so that social goals can take priority over capital accumulation. Such a transformation will occur only when a class party can take power and such an opportunity will arise when the internal contradictions of the capitalist system and its mixed economy become too great. For some people, no doubt, until that day of revolution comes, there is precious little to be done. For others, though, it remains the case that the struggle for a just socialist society is made with and through the state apparatus whose control and legitimation are by no means absolute. In many respects the contemporary state promises what it cannot deliver—promises which are central concerns of a socialist programme: greater equality, rewards and opportunities based on aptitude not inheritance, a safe, clean, secure environment for family lives which promote creativity, skills, enjoyment, etc., free from competition and exploitation. The widespread acceptance of such values and the failure to achieve them provide a host of opportunities for work which maintains expectations and hopes and explores the means of their fulfilment; and which seeks to explain their non-achievement. For if there is to be a mass party of the working class to struggle for power and seize it when the capitalist mode breaks down, there must be a membership conscious of the class-dimensions of society and of the meaning and basis for class struggle.

So, for socialists or Marxists, there is no problem in working within a range of participatory endeavours, although their concerns will be with notions of power and consciousness and they will be likely to be sensitive to situations in which the controlling and diversionary potential of social and community work are especially marked. For the anarchist and libertarian, the state is something out from under which the road to freedom leads, and alternative modes of encouraging creativity and community are likely to be sought away from participatory and political endeavours to avoid the tentacles of control. Now it is quite consistent with both these sets of theories that there should have been an upsurge in community work in recent years. Within the liberal democratic formulation, as expectations rise so do participatory demands—and as the trend is towards more efficient, more bureaucratic and more technological forms of management—characteristically in larger units, so the problem of participation will loom larger on every organisational agenda whether it is a business or a part of local or central government. For the Marxist critic of liberal theory, the problems of management for the state are forever being magnified as the contradictions between the social demands and the underlying processes become more marked: greater participation sponsored by managerial elites is another twisting and turning for survival and legitimacy of a system incapable of delivering what it promises.

These different political viewpoints and contrasting theories of the state are of necessity simplifications and generalisations; but they can be of some use in explaining the diversity of claims and accounts of community work practice. Within the Conservative sector of thought and practice are many examples of community care where quite simply the notion of community of neighbour-hood is used to back up—or in more recent times 'front up'—the scarce resources of the social services departments in terms of contact and support for the frail or otherwise needy and isolated residents of an area. For the Liberal in search of managerial in-novation, a professionally competent social planning community work—detailing the need and scope for comprehensiveness and co-ordination in resource delivery based on full consumer participation —promises much employment. For party activists, community organising holds out hopes of a revival of interest in local politics. The Community Development Projects are providing a rich and varied source of examples of community work informed by the full range of political assumptions, and it is from this source that come both the clearest critique of community work's conservatism and the indications of the scope for a radical politically committed form of community work.

So the contemporary situation is one in which community work can appear to be a whole range of activities: its diverse practices can bring about changes in an individual's supportive network, changes in managerial practices at government level, changes in the types of organisations pressing for change, changes in the level of awareness about social conditions. These activities require rather different skills, will appeal to different sorts of workers, and will engage different kinds of sponsors and employers. Is it a matter of choice for the intending community worker which niche or style he ends up in? Or are some of these claims mutually exclusive? It may be instructive, perhaps, to explore further the nature of the radical argument against some forms of community work, partic-ularly at a time when community work is becoming a standard part of far from radical courses for generic social workers. What kind of evidence is there for the success or otherwise of what, for

want of better phrases, can be termed liberal participatory community work on the one hand and radical or socialist community
action on the other?

There is not a great deal of evidence that local government
appears to be particularly responsive to community-based pressure
groups participating in housing, planning or other kinds of resource-
centred issues. Such resources do appear to be stakes in a zero-sum
game whereby one group's gain is another's loss and redistribution
as a result of pressure-group activities is slight. Like so many of the
gains won for the working class by welfare reform measures, on
examination the measures benefit the already relatively privileged
and the overall dimensions of inequality are unscathed, although
absolute standards have improved.

On the other hand there are few accounts of successful community work achieving the radicalisation of a working-class community, and there is frequently some vagueness and uncertainty
about the activities involved in such politicising efforts. Might this
not demonstrate more than inadequate techniques but a mistaken
analysis? After all, do not working-class people experience not a
controlling repressive state apparatus but a situation not only of
very great material advantages but quite extensive provision of
good quality education, housing, health and social services as part
of a welfare system gained by the political party expressing their
interest?

Any analysis of the political opportunities for community work
has to look more carefully at the sorts of issues with which community work is typically involved: and at the ways ordinary people
account for the world of continuing inequality amidst relative
plenty which surrounds them. Earlier I noted that, in the liberal
democratic framework of the state, the political sphere is represented as autonomous: that is, the political 'centre' is in some way
the neutral arbiter of competing claims which lays down the
means of access for various pressure groups to influence essentially
political decisions about resource allocation. For a great many
community work projects this autonomy, this separation, breaks
down as increasingly the problems and issues communities face are
a direct product of the managing state: the need to participate,
the interest in participation, is not community generated but a
response to the activities of the 'political' centre.

In social work practice there appears to be a growth of interest
in how to work with clients whose main problem appears to be

not so much any individual failing but the tangled web of state provision devised to alleviate their situational poverty: simply to benefit according to the rules of access, many people now need the help and guidance of a worker who can fathom the mysteries of the welfare state. The issues which are the focus of community work in a neighbourhood, posing problems for organisation and participation, are frequently those of urban renewal—whether for large-scale development or for grant-aided home and area improvement where local government controls not just the means of access but the actual resources being distributed. Indeed, participation is increasingly something being 'written-in', as it were, as a requirement of management; not as something giving expression to the interests of some distinct pressure group. Increasingly it is difficult to discover 'bottom up' participatory action consistent with pressure group activity but 'top down' participatory action consistent with the 'control' perspective. The scope for an alternative politics or of community politics related to the provision by the state of these broadly defined neighbourhood facilities is extremely limited, because of the way participatory activities are part and parcel of the existing institutional order. Typically, any residents' group seeking to improve the process of redevelopment, for instance, finds no alternative open to it but to struggle to achieve legitimacy within the existing local political system: influence rather than power appears possible . . . but such influence also seems very limited. Yet there is little sign of concerted and organised quests for power.

The conservatism of many neighbourhood residents, their deference to authority, their resignation to 'things as they are' will be familiar to many community workers. Is this evidence of real contentment, a socially desirable consensus and the absence of far-reaching conflicts, especially of class conflict? Or is it evidence of a socialised acceptance of an unequal world? Or when community workers talk of or seek *change*, is it change within a consensus or change of some more structural feature whose very acceptance is part of the problem? Now some authors and commentators would note that the interests of a local *community* are essentially parochial, intensely conservative and antithetical to the development of a consciousness of class. In this view, community work which stays in the neighbourhood rooted in local issues as local issues can be equated to playing into the hands of the dominant class in whose interest it is to prevent the emergence of that broader view entailed in class consciousness. Others would argue that such a limitation is a danger but it need not be an inherent feature of community work. It is important that both viewpoints lay equal importance upon the role of ideas in social change: a person's understanding of the world shapes his political attitudes and actions. So it is important to consider what is the source of these ideas. It is perhaps useful and important for community workers to recognise how their efforts are a part of a continuous process whereby ideas and meanings about the world, and what to expect, are made available. Sometimes the hopes and claims for the change effects of community work appear unrealistic when related to other influences which are at work, making and shaping consciousness. Many, I suspect, would recognise among those with whom they work a 'hierarchy of credibility'—it being taken as given that any tale told by those at the top does define the way things really are: and very quickly alternatives to the higher account are termed utopian, unrealistic, only for an ideal world. Therefore, the suggestions and opportunities that might be taken are ruled out as inadmissible.

Is community work to accommodate to this dominant realism and reasonableness or can it be opposed to it without denying the sense and integrity of those ordinary people whose accounts of their real world are informed by that dominant realism. This, of course, is a problem for any political activist trying to change the way people think about their world so as to act to make it different. But for the Marxist the ideas which are current and part of that dominant realism are not free-floating random concepts for the taking or leaving, since the ruling ideas of every age are those of the ruling class. Certainly 'community' and the values that are associated with it need to be seen in that way: hence for the Marxist or socialist the expectation should be that community work will display its class features in the same way as do other social practices—social work, health care, education. But that does not mean that no 'oppositional' or alternative work is possible. If it is part of the Marxist analysis that ultimately what will bring about social change are contradictions between the social and economic demands of contemporary capitalism, and that ideas and practice are for ever undergoing changes reflecting the continuous state of contradiction, then it follows that consensus is not natural but imposed. In such a situation, democratic participation can never be merely controlling, it can and will demonstrate the imposed and controlling nature of the consensus. Whatever the intensity of managerial endeavours, despite the current enmeshment of local politics and local government administration into a powerful controlling force, despite the elaborate processes whereby the legitimacy of the existing pattern of inequality is sustained, despite the limited scope for community action either as pressure-group politics or as a source of alternative politics, each activity can illuminate the contradictions between claim and achievement in the contemporary social order.

Radical or alternative community work is involved in this social exposition of the limits of capitalism. It should be stressed that the situations for this exposition are identical very often to those where 'conventional' or accommodative community work is practised. It is only among the ultra-doctrinaire that developing consciousness entails solemn study of theoretical texts unrelated to active involvement in the world as it is.

So, I am optimistic that there can be a viable, worth-while, 'political' community work informed by a radical, socialist or Marxist perspective. I would also argue for the need to protect that form and perspective at a time when community work is becoming so common a part of the dominant conventional wisdom. Just when standards of living are no longer rising, when poverty is still common, when the plight of the over-taxed wealthy is higher on political agendas than that of those who are unemployed or low paid, and at a time when the twin evils of racialism and fascism are becoming strident in their appeal, it does seem important to define a mode of community work which avoids either that utopianism in which true consciousness is cultivated for the day when bourgeois society is smashed or that pragmatism which goes along in not too much discomfort with the world as it is. The focus for attention is not some alternative value system hard to imagine in real terms, but those commonly held values which bourgeois society fails to attain—greater equality, lessening poverty, a clean, humane environment, a cultivation of creative abilities, a fostering of political knowledge and of active participation, the openness of opportunities despite handicaps of birth or origin. With such an aim, community work and community workers can safely concentrate on short-term goals, be active in employment, in their home neighbourhoods, in a political party, even to translate the experience of work into political terms. Stanley Cohen, addressing himself to an audience of social workers, has commended the ideas of Thomas Mathieson, the Danish penal reformer and activist, for those in search of radical activity. From Mathieson, the advice is 'stay unfinished'—i.e. don't get committed to a total programme or be seduced into doing the authorities' work for them by devising alternative strategies and negotiating their inclusion in some compromise reform package: in that way you will be 'finished'. But, Cohen suggests, 'Stay in your agency or organisation, but don't let it seduce you. Take every effort to unmask its pretensions and euphemisms, use its resources in a defensive way for your clients . . .' For community workers, as for social workers, the advice seems sound. Such are the shortcomings, tensions and contradictions in the organisation and administration of welfare that there are likely to be more than a few practitioners sceptical, if not critical, of the official ideology of what constitutes practice. In many branches of professionalised local government, there are those in search of a better deal for those whose interests the agency is supposed to put first. The opportunities may not be very long term, and progress may be slow, but no socialist in the 1970s is likely to suppose that it will be otherwise. In this respect, community work is like other social practices—in the social services, in education, in health care, in planning, etc.—the presence of a majority committed to a dominant conventional form of practice does not mean that there are no practitioners with alternative critical views or that an alternative critical practice is impossible.

Note

The origins of this article derive from my having to teach community work to sceptical sociology undergraduates and to committed social and community workers. My former colleague, Nick Derricourt, will recognise many of his own ideas taken over and used unashamedly here for my purposes. It will be apparent to many readers that it is highly derivative and hardly original. I have not provided tedious and copious footnotes and references, but the reader may like to know the main sources for further study and reading. The sketch of alternative political ideologies comes from the Association of Community Workers booklet *Knowledge and Skills for Community Workers* (ACW, 1975). The Coventry CDP (1976) contains a fuller discussion of the links between theories about poverty and their practice outcome. *Ideology and Social Welfare* by Victor George and Paul Wilding (Routledge & Kegan Paul, 1976) provides an excellent sustained treatment of the broader issue for the serious student. Ralph Miliband's *The State and Capitalist Society* (Quartet Books, 1973) provides a highly readable and critical treatment of theories of the state. My view of 'collective consumption' derives from the

French Marxist school of urban sociologists whose key works are translated and discussed in C. G. Pickvance (ed.), *Urban Sociology* (Tavistock, 1976). The 'hierarchy of credibility' comes from Howard Becker, 'Whose Side Are We On?', in *Sociological Work* (Allen Lane, 1971). For accommodative and oppositional value systems, see Frank Parkin's *Class Inequality and the Political Order* (Paladin, 1972). For an example of committed and effective oppositional community work, consider Bob Ashcroft and Keith Jackson, 'Adult Education and Social Action', in *Community Work One* (Routledge & Kegan Paul, 1974). Peter Morris's Introduction to David Thomas's *Organising for Social Change* (Allen & Unwin, 1976) is an excellent and succinct statement of the influences leading to the growth of community work and the very different assumptions and practices, ultimately contradictory, contained within them. Stanley Cohen's article cited here is 'It's All Right for You to Talk: Political and Sociological Manifestoes for Social Action', in Roy Bailey and Mike Brake (eds), *Radical Social Work* (Arnold, 1975).

2 Hard lines and soft options: a criticism of some left attitudes to community work

Jerry Smith

I shall start on an autobiographical note, since what follows may best be understood in the light of a changing, and I hope developing, political career rather than as the stance of someone who believes he knows the precise nature of the problems and solutions. Like many colleagues in community work I am a product of student activism in the late 1960s, and for good or ill have never entirely rejected the cultural (as opposed to economic) bias and libertarian values of that period. Since then, perhaps because of a lack of any sound economic foundation to my socialism, I sailed for a time—in my first years as a paid, professional community worker—close to the gentle breeze of co-option; underwent a period of personal confusion; and then, hesitantly at first, later more deliberately, moved leftward again, towards a more Marxist position.

How far I shall continue to travel in this direction is uncertain. I tend, unfortunately, to take my political influences more from people and events than from books and theories. So far as I can tell, the only thoroughgoing explanation of the present condition of western society and how it has been arrived at which makes much sense is a Marxist one. The people whose thinking has impressed me most in recent years have also usually been Marxists. On the other hand, some of the biggest political idiots around at the moment, both generally and in community work, also claim to be Marxists. There are also a few brave intellects genuinely struggling in an open-minded way to transcend Marxist thinking rather than reject it. Whether they have a valid point or not I cannot tell; I know only it is very easy to jeer from the sidelines, from the comfortable position of feeling one is able to explain every social phenomenon from the point of view of class struggle and economic determinism.

I see myself very definitely as a fieldworker, but I do not draw the familiar distinction between practitioner and theoretician. It is a distinction which caricatures both sets of people rather grossly into those who think but do not do, and those who are relieved of the necessity of thinking about what they do. In so far as aspects of the argument which follows display the pragmatism of the field-worker, I regard the paper as a failure. In so far as many theoretical contributions don't lend themselves to translation into day-by-day objectives I regard *them* as failures, too. This last point applies to all ideological positions, but seems particularly to dog the Marxist perspective with its holistic philosophy and concentration on production, both of which are hard (but not impossible) to relate to the localised and domestic context of community work.

The current debate within community work is a polarised one, in which one is expected to enlist on the side of either the Marxists or the conservatives. It is true that the majority of those arguing against a Marxist perspective do put forward essentially conservative views, but the more salient point is the confusion of most such writing; it is by no means *consistently* conservative. I don't see this debate as a simple matter of two sides of a fence (on which I might be thought to be sitting), nor even as a straight-forward left-right spectrum (in which I might be thought to be claiming the good old-fashioned middle ground). The reality seems to be more one of a constellation of ideological positions. It so happens that one position, Marxism, is more consistent than any of the others, so that we are tempted to resolve a complex debate into one of Marxists *v.* the rest.

My point of view is one of sympathy with Marxism, then, rather than Marxist itself. It is not a popular position; the Marxist left is currently not keen on fellow-travellers, preferring out-and-out con-verts. I write as one who finds Marxism persuasive without being wholly convincing; who is at once impressed by practitioners and writers trying to fit Marxist theories to the experience of com-munity action, and dismayed by others of the same ideological hue trying to fit community action into predetermined theories.

Marx himself did not foresee with any clarity the growth of the welfare state and the public sector within a changed capitalist system of production; so appeals to 'the Marxism of Marx' cannot help us to explain community work, which is one small aspect of these changes. We are left, instead, with a variety of alternative Marxist explanations, some of them subtle and persuasive, others crude and nihilistic. This in itself is neither to be worried about nor wondered at. What does worry me is that so far it has been the 'nihilistic' school which has exerted the greatest influence on field-work.

Very probably, one reason for this is its simplicity (it can be stated, in its essentials, very quickly, as I shall try to show) and therefore its ability to offer a convenient 'explanation' for what most would agree has been a pretty uninspiring performance from community work to date. But I suspect that a more fundamental reason is that it gives us a good excuse for not trying too hard in the future. All it requires us to change is our rhetoric; the practice implications are limited in the extreme. Community work is portrayed as a means of social control and therefore doomed to fail the working class every time.

It is this kind of crude thinking, rather than Marxism generally, which this paper seeks to challenge. On a different level, though, there are problems with Marxist theory in many of the areas with which community work deals, as many Marxists readily acknowledge. The analysis of the state, family and domestic life, and changing class relations are all areas crucial to community work and which Marxists have only fairly recently turned (or returned) their attention to. If I add my own, I hope constructive, criticisms in these areas it is entirely in a fraternal spirit!

The people whose views I am criticising here are not an identifiable group or Marxist faction. Merely to describe them, as I have done so far, as 'nihilists' is to dismiss them with a pejorative label of my own invention. Within Marxism, these people adopt a Trotskyist approach and, while it is important to establish that not all Trotskyists see community work in their terms, it should also be pointed out that there are non-Trotskyist Marxist groups, usually containing a strong element of feminism in their thinking, who would certainly take a very different view. Big Flame is an example. Within community work, too, there is no identifiable group which I am criticising, but for the sake of concretising the argument at the risk of offending some people, I could perhaps point to most of the output of CDP over the past few years as an example of what I mean by 'nihilistic' Marxism.

The position I want to criticise is grounded in a theory of the state in advanced capitalist society. It holds that the state is not a neutral agent; nor is it an independent entity. It acts, first, in the economic interests of the dominant class, both through direct provision of the industrial infrastructure (roads, power, etc.) and through economic and land-use planning aimed at making the economic environment more predictable and profitable for big business.[1] Thus many community work issues such as planning, or road schemes, are a direct result of the state serving vested interests rather than the 'mistakes' of an insensitive bureaucracy. The other chief role of the state is that of social control; the maintenance of a stable social situation. This is accomplished not only through the coercive forces of law and order but increasingly through welfare provision and, especially in recent years, participation. Participation is a means of buying off working-class protest, while reforms in the fields of welfare and income inequality have the effect of removing protest without altering the power structure.

Community work, under this view, is located firmly within the processes of social control. It is argued, too, that community groups lack sanctions and a power base, and are forced into competition with one another for shares of the dwindling cake;[2] that experimentation with 'alternatives' of various kinds is diversionary; and that grass-roots action or 'community politics' clouds the real, the class issues. Critics of this persuasion generally point to a range of books and reports promoting a more or less conservative theory of community work, and stress its origins both in colonial community development and in social casework.[3]

The wholesale critics of community work are, understandably, sceptical about the possibilities of a radical practice, but commonly point to three ways forward. The first involves making links between community groups and the labour movement. The second asserts the need to fight on the real issues and to avoid compromises and diversions: mass protest about housing rather than tenant liaison committees, for example. But the mass protest cannot, of course, be expected to achieve short-term concrete results, and here the third approach comes in—the use of community issues as a means of political education about the class nature of society and the economic roots of the problems.

No summary as short as this can be entirely fair, but I believe this does bring out the essentials of the argument, and in the terms in which its proponents usually present it, rather than as a caricature. I don't take issue with all of it, by any means; the description of the economic role of the state, for example, seems an accurate one. The headings under which I would like to criticise the position are: the social control role of the state; the criticism of 'community politics', community power and experimentation with 'alternatives'; the specific criticisms of the origins and theory of community work; and finally the three action proposals which, to my mind, are not so much wrong as weak.

The notion that the state is not a neutral agency is hardly a startling one to anyone who has taken part in, say, the squatting movement. One doesn't need to be a Marxist to see that planners and policemen act in defence of the property rights of the wealthy. The mistake that radicals in community work have tended to make, though, has been to assume that the state had a great deal more independence of action than it has, and that many problems could be traced to a kind of bureaucratic value-system. What the Marxist analysis does, most notably in Ralph Miliband's book, *The State in Capitalist Society*,[4] is to make the connections which show just how the state is bound up with the economic system. The need to demonstrate the nature of the state and its machinery has, however, taken precedence over the need to suggest appropriate action. While Miliband clearly does not see the state as monolithic, or all its servants as willing ones, one is left with the feeling that the left has entered some very hostile and largely uncharted terrain as it attempts action which is not directly located in the sphere of production. It is not surprising, then, that some Marxists would prefer to restrict community action to those forms which relate directly to the more familiar area of industrial struggle, such as campaigns against the cuts.

Fortunately, not all Marxists are urging the retreat from the wilderness of community action. Cynthia Cockburn's book, *The Local State*,[5] represents an attempt to chart a way through the shifting sands of co-option. She continually stresses the point— which Miliband recognised but underplayed, and which leftist critics of community work usually ignore—that the increasing scope of the state and its involvement in reform, welfare and participation is also to be seen as part of the price paid by capitalism for its continued survival. The state, in short, is riddled with contradictions and hence contains possibilities for action. It contains, in fact, the seeds of its own future transformation; the form such a transformation takes will depend, inter alia, on the means by which working-class groups engage the state. In concentrating on the local state—principally local government—we are also able to examine what is probably the weakest link in the state system, both because of its greater proximity to the consumers of its services (its relatively high level of democracy) and because of the recent and continuing upheavals in its structure and organisation.

A growing body of Marxist literature points to a process by which new and more subtle forms of social control have been added to the original coercive forces of law and order. Socialisation goes hand in hand with repression, while reform and welfare provision suppress or divert dissent. This forms a recurrent theme in the literature of community work; thus for CDP the police are only 'the tip of the iceberg' of social control,[6] while Paul Corrigan refers rather extravagantly (in a way perhaps typical of the self-aggrandisement of community workers) to 'the two major symbols of control in capitalist society: the tank [and] the community worker'.[7]

The latest addition to the increasingly sophisticated tool-kit of the state is 'participation'. It is now de rigueur, in any Marxist critique of community work, to open with the ritual intonation of 'Plowden-Skeffington-Seebohm-CDP-CCP', the supposed 'experiments in participatory democracy' which, it is alleged, are just one more con-trick perpetrated on the unsuspected working class. But if one sees participation as *only* a method of social control and thus argues that it should be avoided, real possibilities as well as the obvious dangers of co-option are sacrificed. The truth is that, as Cockburn says:[8]

> This incorporation of the population is a two-edged sword
> for the state (and for the working class). Because the closer
> working class groups come to inclusion within the state
> system, the more dangerous is any disruptive behaviour to
> the equilibrium of the state. The state has reduced risk in one
> way but increased it in another.

The aim should not be to take the easy way out and shun 'participation', but to be alive to the dangers while trying to exploit the possibilities.

Community work itself is placed along with participation as no more than a new method of social control, whereas in fact it, too, represents a new, if presently marginal, risk to the state. But any analysis of the position of community work which is prepared to move beyond the purely doctrinaire must also recognise certain other peculiarities. It cannot be denied that community work performs (or is intended to perform) certain social control functions. Nevertheless, these functions are different in kind from those performed by other agencies of socialisation such as the education system or social casework. In particular, community work is not tied into a statutory framework; its objectives (no matter by whom they are stated) are diverse; its day-to-day operations are relatively loosely controlled. The key to an understanding of community work at present is the very fact of its small scale and marginal position. It is a profession (or semi-profession) which is relatively easily subverted but whose subversion achieves little. It represents one of the outer limits reached during a period when the state's 'soft' social-control functions achieved a new dominance—a period which ended, at least temporarily, a few years ago. The state is currently withdrawing from community work, and it was never wholly embraced by more than a tiny handful of local authorities. The prospects are either that community work will be reduced to the form in which it began as a paid activity—that of social experiment, largely within the voluntary sector and marginal at best—or that it will be revived by the local state in new and more circumscribed forms. But to pretend, as many of its critics do, that community work is doing a grand job for the state is to blind oneself to the obvious question of why, in that case, the state has paid so little attention to it. The state continues to invest rather more money in tanks than community workers.

The point needs making in another way, too. The function of community work is, we are told, to divert or to put the lid on working-class action which would otherwise take more threatening forms. Given that there is no shortage of towns and neighbourhoods which don't have the doubtful benefit of our presence, there ought to be some evidence of militant activity in these areas, but is there? There is certainly a sense in which community work has arisen as a response by the state to some very scattered and not particularly threatening direct action over the past decade or so, but for the most part what community work is intended to control is not incipient revolt but the breakdown of community life and the resultant heavy demand on the state in other spheres. The concerns which lead to state sponsorship of community work are only rarely militant working-class action; they are instead such things as juvenile crime and vandalism, growing numbers of single-parent families, or those forms of deviant behaviour which are usually subsumed under the heading 'problem families'. In other words, the inchoate rather than the organised working-class response to the changes taking place in advanced capitalist society; a response which brings misery for most of those involved in it as well as nervous palpitations for the state.

Which brings us to the thousand-dollar question. Social instability is bad for capitalism, right enough, but is that the same as saying that it necessarily advances the prospects of socialism? The implication of the critique of community work which I am attacking here is that the answer is 'Yes', though such a view may not be held explicitly. This simplistic and dangerous notion arises from some linear thinking: people who are anti-social, 'inadequate' or simply poor pose a threat to social stability. Attempts are made to socialise them, or 'alleviate their problems' under the guise of psychiatry, social work, community work. Since this can only divert their attention from the real causes of their misery, it is a form of social control and must be rejected.

This line of thought leads straight to the view that the possibilities of revolutionary change are enhanced by the presence of a growing mass of people who are disaffected, yes, but also incapacitated. It ignores the fact that if community work doesn't intervene, social work will; if social work doesn't psychiatry will. It ignores the profoundly socialising influences everyone absorbs from the mass media; and it ignores the immense normative powers of neighbours who can and do label people, perhaps even more thoroughly than state professionals. To shun community work as 'social control' when there is such a crying need for creative intervention in a situation where professional workers remain comparatively unconstrained is simply to take the easy way out of a complex problem. If we look at the question from the point of view of the people who are posing this threat to social stability and ask whether despair and confusion are to be preferred to the feeling that one can exercise some power over one's life through localised collective action, community work intervention may be seen in a more favourable light. It may reasonably be argued that this feeling of even very limited power is merely an illusion, a false-consciousness, and that to replace no-consciousness with false-consciousness isn't doing anyone any favours. I think, though, that we should at least keep an open mind on whether the particular 'false-consciousness' of community action is indeed that or is better regarded as a kind of 'transitional consciousness'. Impatient hard-liners rarely take the trouble to find out how people's consciousness changes, and too often seem to assume that, despite the all-pervading socialisation which they so deplore, it is possible to convince people of a revolutionary truth simply by putting it before them.

I have dwelt at some length on the social control role of the state in general and community work in particular because the central fallacy of the hard-line critique of community work is its simplistic and incomplete understanding of this area. Once the risks to the state, and the possibilities for socialist action, are recognised as well as the dangers, the main theoretical obstacle is passed. But not all the criticisms I want to deal with lie in this area; others attempt to take apart views which have often in the past been themselves regarded as radical within community work. Perhaps the most important of these is the attack on 'community politics' which is seen as a diversion from 'class politics'.

One of the founding concerns of community work, on which at the time there was a high level of consensus, was that a political vacuum existed at grass-roots level. Solutions ranged from participation schemes, to neighbourhood councils, to 'direct democracy', but all were agreed that there was a problem. The problem has by no means disappeared; it is merely no longer fashionable either on the left or among reformers of local government now preoccupied with corporate planning and area management. It has, indeed, been worsened with local government reorganisation. This political vacuum ought to concern us more than it does now. It is not *just* an inevitable result of the changing complexion of the state and the political system in particular; it, too, presents possibilities for action. A vacuum is usually filled quickly and the clear signs are that while the left concentrates on industrial struggle and community work deserts the neighbourhood for work on the wider issues, the right is stepping into the vacant spaces. The National Front is busy organising on council estates neglected by community workers and is concentrating on winning local government seats which the left sees as of marginal relevance. There is even a view gaining ground which suggests that 'community politics', because it is used by the NF and the Liberals, is somehow tainted—not to be touched lest we contaminate our ideological purity. The issue, however, is one of effective strategy, not ideology. So-called 'community politics' is currently helping the right to advance politically; a few years ago it was on the point of helping the Liberal Party too—until the party bosses got cold feet about all this populism and stamped on the radical Liberals.

The point is that to suggest the argument is between 'community politics' and 'class politics' (as though the two were mutually exclusive) is to indulge in a neat sleight of hand which again has the effect of paralysing action and pointing direct to the easy way out. 'Community politics', far from being a dangerous deviation, is in itself a politically neutral—almost meaningless—concept. I'm arguing here, if you like, not for 'community politics' but for an extension of 'class politics' to include a recognition of the value of neighbourhood work and, especially at the present time, a recognition of the need to fight fascism within neighbourhoods as well as in set-piece street confrontations.

A telling argument raised against neighbourhood work is that gains for one neighbourhood are made only at the expense of another. Such progressive redistribution as does occur takes place only *within* the working class, while the more usual story is that the crucial factor is not relative need but relative organisational strength. I have no doubt, from my own experience, that this is true. What I question is the conclusion that therefore we should all be working at the city-wide level except in those cases where an issue genuinely does affect only one neighbourhood. The alternative, which lies between isolated neighbourhood work and exclusive concentration on city-wide work, is that of simultaneous, or at least linked, neighbourhood work.

There are several arguments in favour of such an approach. One I have already mentioned—the threat from the right. Another is that the strength of city-wide organisations such as tenants' federations depends on the strength of their member (neighbourhood) organisations. It is ironic that those who stress the need to work at grass-roots level within the trade unions so often seem happy to work with what are frequently unrepresenative elites of working-class *community* leaders, thrown into city-wide issues by virtue of the community-work star system and often every bit as out of touch with their own constituencies as are the union leaders. A third reason for multi-neighbourhood work also derives from an analogy with trade union practice: the power of trade union or community groups is probably not maximised at the extremes of isolated, fragmented action and total unity, but in between, on the model of what one group successfully negotiates then becoming the demand of all. This would seem to be a better approach than out-and-out concentration on city-wide organisations and issues.

The final argument in favour of retaining neighbourhood-based work is more fundamental. Perhaps the basic underlying principle of community work—rightly, in my view—is that of starting from the perceptions of the people. If there is a contribution community work might make to a socialist cause it is one of gradually building up a popular movement over time, rather than exercising instant power. It does, and should, seek to involve the presently unpoliticised, starting at the level of their own perceptions. Neighbourhoods, even paradoxically including overspill deserts, do have meaning for the people who live in them, far more than do cities. People who would slip through the coarse-meshed net of class politics as it is presently constructed may be caught in the finer one of neighbourhood-based action and may go on to develop a deeper class consciousness. The point is certainly arguable but to suggest, as some Marxists do, that community action is *incapable* of generating class consciousness is to draw a highly premature conclusion out of some very sparse and patchy evidence.

Community work has a history of experimenting with 'alternatives' of one kind or another, from neighbourhood councils to free schools to food co-ops and urban farms. Such experimentation results from the heritage of radical theory in community work, which was put together largely by libertarians and pacifists optimistic about the possibilities of spontaneous change and of creating the new society subversively within the splitting chrysalis of the old. Subsequent events have progressively dampened this optimism. The first major problem was how to reconcile one's anarchistic beliefs with receiving a pay-packet, directly or indirectly, from the state. Some tried, half-heartedly, to convince themselves that this represented a kind of 'infiltration'. Others took the not too rocky road which leads from libertarianism to liberalism. But the experiments continued. Even though no one had any illusions now about their *revolutionary* potential, they were still seen as good-in-themselves. These experiments are now under attack from the left, as a deviation from action on the real issues. 'Tenant Co-operatives: A Diversion', howls *Community Action* magazine, for instance.[9] Any positive action, anything which dares to suggest how an alternative, socialist society might be organised in its details and which seeks in advance to locate and iron out some of its problems, is regarded as illusory. The 'real issue', it seems, is to squeeze as much blood as possible out of the capitalist monster before it dies—forget about what we'll feed on afterwards. Thus although very few of these socialists would see housing in a socialist society being organised along the same horrifyingly paternalistic lines as council housing is at present, they have no qualms about telling tenants to make demands which, if successful, would make them better off financially but still more dependent on the machine.

The final criticism of community work I want to deal with is that it is grounded in conservative and reactionary theories and traditions. A line is traced from colonial community development to community work in the UK, the implication being that community work represents an attempt to colonise the unexplored territories of poverty in our midst. (The fact that a few mad community workers 'go native' and identify with the poor is further evidence.) The theoretical founding fathers of the profession are held to be Batten, Goetschius and the Gulbenkian Group[10]—the list varies, but these three usually appear in it. Anyone who has read these hopelessly shallow works ought to find it hard to believe they could influence anyone. Their 'theory' may be used as a justification for conservative forms of community work by those in control of fieldwork, but that is not the same thing. On the other hand, a great many books, including those in the present series, testify not to the conservative origins of community work but to the great diversity of theoretical influences and traditions, including conservatism, on which it draws. It may be admitted that other radicals in community work are guilty of an equally narrow-minded concentration on the profession's libertarian roots— as though community work were somehow a combined brainwave of the Committee of 100 and the squatting movement—but there's no gain in understanding if one falsehood is simply replaced by another.

Out of what appears to be a total condemnation of community work, its critics usually draw three 'ways forward': making links with the labour movement, organising mass protest rather than small-scale action, and using community issues as a vehicle for political education. The last of these I have no quarrel with except to say that it too often involves a rather narrow concept of 'education' and that its proponents are usually concerned only with educating the already politicised. Courses on the political economy of cities are fine, but very few community activists are at the point where such phrases mean anything to them; such courses more often run for the benefit of left professionals (including community workers), with perhaps a couple of token working-class activists or trade unionists. The other, equally narrow, educational model is that of producing research reports, ostensibly for community groups. CDP has excelled in this, and some at least of their output has been valuable—to community workers, and maybe indirectly through them to community groups. But the idea that groups of working-class community activists might devour the kinds of reports CDP turns out with revolutionary relish only indicates either a lack of firm fieldwork experience on the part of their authors, or (more probably) an anxiety to put dogmatic correctness higher on the agenda than effective communication technique. I have worked in a project where such reports were on prominent display but, unlike some of the more mundane literature, were never picked up.

Only lip-service is paid, usually, to the concept of systematic learning through action. The ideas of Freire have influenced many people on the left, but these tend to be the ones who have in any case not given up hope for community work, rather than its wholesale critics. About the only example of 'education through action' in the field (or at least in the literature) is the work done around the Housing Finance Bill.[11] This was now some five years ago and, without detracting from it in any way, is beginning to wear a little thin. How long do we have to wait for another chance like it? It seems doubtful whether a future Conservative government will make the kinds of crass mistakes in its dealings with the working class which the last one did, while the issues are deliberately fogged under Labour. In short, this rather special and isolated example is of almost no use as a guide to action in the present.

There is a large and rather obvious question-mark to be put against the second proposal, that of organising mass protest rather than localised action and experimentation, in view of much of the foregoing discussion. Where is the mass movement going to come from? People who work in an essentially elitist way, interested only in a tiny group of politicised activists and disdainful of engaging the unpoliticised majority on their own terms, are not geared up to start mass protest. The truth is that the left, in Britain as in most other advanced capitalist countries, is seriously split and lacking in popular support, a point underlined by Ralph Miliband:[12]

> These [Communist] parties, whatever they may do, are
> bound to remain for a very long time political formations of
> secondary consequence—vanguard parties without the vast
> armies of members and supporters which revolutionary
> change in these societies clearly requires; and the same is even

more evident in regard to other groupings to the left of social democracy.

To suggest that one can build mass community protest without neighbourhood organising is tantamount to saying the trade union movement could have been formed without reference to any particular factory or industry. Once again it is the easy way out, the soft option.

The approach most strongly urged is that of making links between community groups and the labour movement. The need for such links has been argued for several years now[13] and can hardly, in itself, be criticised. But its place at the top of the agenda can and should be. Part of the soft option syndrome is that the left, while rejecting the last illusion, invents the next. The profound hope that the labour movement would provide the solution to the problems of community organising, that all community action needed was to plug in to the power source of the industrial strug- gle, has not shown much sign of being fulfilled. Those community projects which can afford to spend their resources on providing intelligence services for trade unions rather than community newspapers for neighbourhoods; newly-unionised community workers sit proudly on their local trades councils; and energy which once went into promoting *direct* action now goes into persuading those with the industrial muscle to take action on behalf of community groups. After a good three or four years of such work, some results ought to be showing. If they are, I, for one, have missed out on seeing them. There are three difficulties inherent in the approach which, I think, account for the results not matching the promise.

The first is that the public service unions, which tend to be the ones community groups deal with, are comparatively weak and have most to lose by taking action. Some are unions of the lower paid, while others are unions of professional and semi-professional staff who may well not be prepared to see an issue from the point of view of the 'clients'. The public sector unions generally have least economic power.

A second reason lies within the structure of the unions them- selves. The hope that something like the Australian 'Green Bans' movement would be repeated over here has not materialised, and we should perhaps heed the words of one of the organisers of that movement who said that the democratic organisation of the union involved was a major factor in the movements's success and that such action was less likely with the more bureaucratised British trade unions.[14] The only British 'community' movement which has so far shown any great sign of success in making links with trade unions is the middle-class environmentalist lobby.

The third reason runs deeper than the others. It is the possibility that the interests of trade unionists may not always coincide with those of community groups. Apart from the professional/consumer split already mentioned, which may operate in some·cases, there are major differences of interest to overcome in two main areas: the unemployed and those in work, and women and men. These real differences are not removed by pious appeals to class solidarity, even if in the final analysis they *are* less fundamental. An excellent example in the first area is that of the Newton Abbot Claimants' Union, whose self-help programmes were tolerated while confined to the realm of vegetable-growing but who quickly incurred the wrath of their local trades council when they tried to start a co-operative workshop.[15] The move has been criticised by one Marxist as alienating the very people whose support the CU most needed,[16] but this is to overlook the fact that the Claimants' Union movement (nationally) received almost no help or encouragement from organised labour. There is, in any case, the argument that possibly the demand of claimants for a productive life should take precedence over the restrictive practices of trade unions.

The central argument of the paper so far has been that concentration on the negative aspects of 'participation', 'self-help', 'alternatives' and community work itself denies the real possibilities presented by these developments. It represents linear and negative, rather than dialectical, thinking and unnecessarily constrains action. I believe that this is a problem on the left generally; I know it is a problem in community work. Rather than explore the challenges and risks involved in participation and so forth, the left prefers to stress only the dangers of these new situations and to refer the struggle back to the familiar realm of the labour movement and industrial action. Such views have readily found recruits within community work because they offer an 'explanation' for the disappointing performance of the profession. But the 'explanation' is a facile one and the proposals which stem from it are weak. It is important, of course, to recognise the structural position of community work within the capitalist state, but there are other areas, less traditionally 'political', which we should examine, too. I want to end by very briefly outlining these areas and to propose, in conclusion, that the main direction they suggest is that we should stress links with feminism rather more than links with the established labour movement.

After several years of debate, community work is still unable to face the transparent reality that it is a profession in all essentials. Professionalism (and I am using the term in its broad sense) implies limitations on practice, but far more limiting has been the stance of denying ourselves a professional status without saying what, then, we are. The result has been a kind of collective identity crisis which, I think, accounts rather more than community work's structural position for our lack of results. Harry Specht has suggested that the choice facing community work is between being a social movement and being a profession.[17] Only the most starry-eyed among us would still say that community work is a movement in itself. What it is, though, is a profession whose task is to contribute towards the creation of a social movement. For a socialist, that movement must be a working-class movement able to take on the political realities of advanced capitalism. It is a movement which exists at present only in the imagination of some socialists and concretely in two distinct and, by themselves, inadequate forms: the labour movement and the women's movement.

It is the women's movement, rather than the left, which has driven home the message that personal life, too, is political. Marxists generally recognise the socialising functions of the family, but too often only in terms which suggest that the family is *no more than* a part of the economic domain—specifically, the sphere of reproduction of labour power and of consumption. Under this economistic view, personal life is portrayed simply as a Punch and Judy show with the ruling class pulling the strings. But capitalism did not invent the family; what it did do, by socialising production, was to create a split between work and personal life and, with it, a whole new promise of personal fulfilment.[18] The inability of capitalism to satisfy the demand it has created for personal growth and development is among the contradictions of the capitalist system and is a major reason, aside from purely economic ones, for change and even disintegration taking place in family structure. These changes are every bit as much of a threat to the social order as industrial action or the 'profits squeeze', but almost without exception the analysis of such changes and attempts to direct them in positive ways have been left to the women's movement.

Community workers operate in the domestic sphere. We usually work with the people on whom the promise of personal fulfilment has gone the most sour. And we talk a lot about education and personal growth and development. Usually we talk about them in an embarrassed way, as a second best to excuse our failure to stop the last rent rise. Maybe we ought to accept, willingly, that community work is partly about such things and to take them on in a more systematic way. In this context the success of community workers currently trying to apply the concepts developed by Freire and others into the UK context is a very welcome development.

Community workers also work, specifically, with women more than with men. Ann Gallagher has pointed out that women seem more prepared to take militant action and to challenge their traditional roles in the poorest neighbourhoods (and, *a fortiori*, those with large numbers of single-parent families).[19] Just as a traditional Marxist analysis was suggesting that community work should concentrate more on the (male) labour movement and on the more solid and better-off working-class neighbourhoods, along comes a feminist justification for our continuing to work within the poorest neighbourhoods.

If traditional forms of working-class action are to be related to the new concerns of the politics of personal life, we need to develop organisations capable of linking the two areas, of reconciling the personal and the political. The hierarchical, male-dominated and often bureaucratised forms of the existing labour movement are clearly inadequate to the task. But the experience of both community work and the women's movement also suggests that the obvious alternative—the informal small group—cannot do the job either. Community work and the women's movement have invested a great deal of effort in such groups, for the very good reason that both are anxious to involve previously unpoliticised people, mistrustful or frightened of traditional, hierarchical and disciplined political organisations. The informal small group, however, has shown a tendency towards 'personality clashes' and domination by non-elected leaders, and no great ability to transcend itself either through the formation of 'networks' or by moving towards more structured forms. The women's movement has, in fact, had rather more success than has community work in achieving co-operation between small, independent groups through networks and national conferences, but at the expense of restricting its active membership largely to middle-class women. (It is this, rather than anything inherent in the demands of the movement, which I believe is responsible for the familiar (and unfair) allegation that the women's movement does not appeal to older and/or working-class women.) An example of the failure of this type of organisation in a community action setting is the National Federation of Claimants' Unions which, at national level, soon became dominated by middle-class claimants. There is a need to create organisations capable of steering a course betwen hierarchy and bureaucracy on the one hand and the 'tyranny of structurelessness'[20] on the other. British community work has paid almost no attention to this area; the women's movement has done rather more, but a fairly rich literature exists arising from the experience of community work in the USA.[21]

When static notions of oppression and control dominate the more dynamic notion of contradiction, Marxist thinking loses its essential dialectical nature and there seems nothing left to do but shout. I have tried to argue that the radical pessimism which now pervades community work might be lifted if we do three things. First, we should recognise the fact that community work is a profession and explore what that means. For me, it means working in a lighted, if enclosed, space, which is preferable to thrashing around in the dark, not knowing just where the boundaries are. Second, we need to appreciate that the kinds of developments which include 'participation' and community work itself offer possibilities as well as dangers. Third, and most fundamentally in the long run (though it has not been the main theme of this paper), community work has a role to play in the creation of a working-class movement which can reconcile traditional class politics with the politics of personal life. In this sense, the forging of links with feminism seems to me even more important than making links with the labour movement. In a more immediate way, it means being more systematic about the educational aspects of community work, and starting to think about the kinds of organisational forms which might be appropriate to this new political struggle.

References

1 J. Benington, *Local Government Becomes Big Business*, CDP, 1973.
2 Leeds Political Economy Class, *The Social Base of Leeds*, WEA (Leeds Branch), 1977.

3   M. Mayo, 'Community Development: A Radical Alternative?', in R. Bailey
    and M. Brake (eds), *Radical Social Work*, Edward Arnold, 1975.
4   Quartet, 1973.
5   Pluto Press, 1977.
6   CDP, *Gilding the Ghetto*, 1976.
7   'Community Work and Political Struggle', in P. Leonard (ed.), *The Socio-
    logy of Community Action*, University of Keele, 1975.
8   Op. cit., p. 101.
9   *Community Action*, no. 31, May—June 1977. See also the critical
    responses in ibid., no. 33, September—October 1977.
10 T. Batten, *The Non-directive Approach in Group and Community Work*,
    Oxford University Press, 1967; George Goetschius, *Working with Com-
    munity Groups*, Routledge & Kegan Paul, 1969; Gulbenkian Community
    Work Group, *Community Work and Social Change*, Longman, 1968;
    Current Issues in Community Work, Routledge & Kegan Paul, 1973.
11 B. Ashcroft and K. Jackson, 'Adult Education and Social Action' in
    D. Jones and M. Mayo (eds), *Community Work One*, Routledge & Kegan
    Paul, 1974.
12 op. cit., p. 246.
13 At least, for example, since R. Silburn, 'The Potential and Limitations of
    Community Action', in D. Bull (ed.), *Family Poverty*, Duckworth, 1971.
14 J. Mundey, *Trade Unions, Community Groups and the Environment*,
    Report of addresses to meeting organised by London Council of Social
    Service, LCSS, 1976.
15 B. Jordan, *Paupers*, Routledge & Kegan Paul, 1973.
16 C. Cannan, 'Welfare Rights and Wrongs' in R. Bailey and M. Brake (eds),
    op. cit.
17 H. Specht, *Community Development in the U.K.*, 1974 annual confer-
    ence of Association of Community Workers, pub. 1975.
18 E. Zaretsky, *Capitalism, the Family and Personal Life*, Pluto Press, 1976.
19 'Women and Community Work', in M. Mayo (ed.), *Women in the Com-
    munity*, Routledge & Kegan Paul, 1977.
20 The phrase is coined from a women's movement publication of the same
    name, published by *Rising Free*, 1973.
21 For those interested in going further into this area, see G. Brager and
    H. Specht, *Community Organizing*, Columbia University Press, 1973;
    C. Grosser, *New Directions in Community Organisation*, Praeger, 1976;
    J. Rothman, *Planning and Organizing for Social Change*, Columbia
    University Press, 1974. For an anarchist discussion of organisational
    forms, see 'The Forms of Freedom', in M. Bookchin, *Post-Scarcity
    Anarchism*, Wildwood, 1974.

3 CDP: Community work or class politics?

David Corkey and Gary Craig

In this chapter we put forward an alternative view of the action which is required to deal with social problems, a socialist critique of contemporary community work practice, because we believe that poverty and deprivation are a consequence not of the deficiencies and habits of the poor themselves but caused by, and maintained of necessity by, our present capitalist society; and that what is required is for tenants and residents to join in collective action with those in the labour movement active in the class struggle to bring the capitalist system to an end.

The first section of this chapter looks at community work theory since its early development in the 1930s. What this review of community work literature shows is that there is a common underlying basic assumption in all of these writings. However varied and intense the debate on the surface about whether or not community work is about problem-solving at grass roots level, about improving service provision through community participation, about community therapy enabling individuals to develop their potential, etc., the assumption is made that the problems dealt with by community work are somehow caused by internal deficiences in people themselves, which have to be removed in order for them to participate fully in society. One could equally substitute the word 'compete', as much of this writing emphasises what could be described as high Tory values of individualism, self-help or initiative which enable the individual to compete in society; and if one is unable to compete, to pull oneself up by one's boot-straps.

The extension of this is that community work aims at the better integration into society of those on whom the community worker operates; that is, that community work can be used as a mechanism of social control. Community workers, unless they understand this and choose to operate from a different perspective, are therefore in danger of becoming agents of a capitalist state effectively collaborating in maintaining the status quo.

We outline the history of the national Community Development Project (CDP) where many project workers have attempted to develop alternative strategies, with seemingly inevitable results; and describe a few projects and campaigns which have been developed by local projects in solidarity with the wider struggle of the working class.

Theoretical perspectives

Early community work theory in the 1930s, e.g. that developed by Petti and Steiner,[1] was clearly based on the belief that social work should be an all-inclusive activity, and that it should involve processes of grass roots democracy, as opposed to intervention by outside agencies, but by the early 1940s the idea of community work at grass roots level was being largely ignored in favour of an organisational approach which emphasised the bridging of gaps between service provision and social needs. In the late 1940s and early 1950s the emphasis changed again to a concern with problem-solving at a local level. Two writers of that period, McMillen and Murphy, both suggested that the focus of community work should be on solving local community problems, rather than meeting the inner needs of individuals and groups. But there appears to be a general absence of any alternative theoretical perspectives during this early period. Murray G. Ross was the first theorist to widen the whole scope of community work away from the specialist discipline of social work. For him, community work was a social tool to be used in a wide variety of contexts—agriculture, education, etc. For Ross, the primary objective was undoubtedly that of social control—what he called 'community integration'. Stability and equilibrium were the important things, to be achieved, he argued, through a strategy of consensus.[2]

Ross clearly ignored the realities of class society, and, even in community work terms, the importance of confrontation and conflict and the use of power. For him, community work was a process of the development of groups and community leaders which would be 'identified with, and accepted by the major sub groups in the community'. In other words, community work involved collaboration and co-operation with the existing power structures of society. It appears that, for these early community work theorists, the point at issue was whether or not community work was about problem-solving at local level, as opposed to organisational adjustment. There was never any discussion of politics, although they did veer occasionally towards this in discussions about values. These generally centred upon concepts such as the dignity and worth of the individual, self-determination and, to quote Friedlander (*Introduction to Social Welfare*), 'equal opportunities for all, limited only by the individual's innate capacities'. There seemed to be a widespread acceptance of the high Tory values mentioned earlier—of self-help and individual enterprise, and that if the individual failed in his struggle to improve his lot, it was because of inherent personal characteristics.

Irving Spergel suggested that there were corporate values implicit in community work. His examples included a high level of citizen participation, an acceptance of groups and organisations which support conflict and disagreement, and the structuring of equal opportunity into the institutions of modern society. Spergel recognises that class is a divisive factor which contributes to isolation and stigmatisation (p. 41), but he views this not in positive terms, i.e. that it is through collective working-class action that working people can struggle for better conditions, but rather as working people isolating themselves from the rest of society, and thereby suffering bad social conditions and a lack of service provision, which in turn exacerbates the situation.[3]

But George F. Thomason was in no doubt about the challenge which class politics exert on values implicit in community work. He writes that 'conflict which exists between the working class and others, [also] tends to lead to the recognition that in some circumstances the co-ordination of community effort will be impossible of achievement [and] . . . under these circumstances, it may be asked whether it is still possible to talk about community work.' Thomason also makes explicit the social control function of community structures, which 'lose power and control to factional groupings'. He suggests somewhat regretfully that the process of ordering society then breaks down—being polarised between the central organs of government, and networks of local groups.[4]

T. R. and Madge Batten write that the community worker (and, therefore, presumably community work) 'does not attempt to decide for people, or to lead, guide, or persuade them to accept any of his own specific conclusions about what is good for them.

He tries to get them to decide for themselves what their needs are; what if anything they are willing to do to meet them; and how they can best organise, plan, and act to carry their project through'. The Battens suggest that the outcome will usually be a project designed to produce some 'change for the better' in people's lives. They do not define what this means, and admit that, thus stated, this theory leaves a mass of questions unanswered. A clue to the Battens' answers is provided further on in their book in chapter 4, 'Developing Maturity'. The assumption here is that people's problems are caused primarily by what the Battens describe as a lack of maturity. They write: 'some, such as problem children and delinquents, may hardly mature at all, but apart from these and the problems they cause, many of our current political, economic and social problems, one might think, would have been avoided, or would be solved more easily if only more people were more mature.' With this as the basis of their political perspectives, the Battens then go on to discuss how people mature, and what the community worker can do to help. The method they suggest is by assisting individuals to form autonomous groups, and by working through their problems with them through a process of discussion, planning and action. There is no clearer statement than this of the basis of community work theory, i.e. that people are inadequate, and this is the primary cause of society's ill.[5]

These authors seem to have a knack of hitting the nail on the head, for in an earlier book T. R. Batten states quite clearly that in addition to introducing social change, community work must 'help people to adapt their way of life to the changes they accept, or have had imposed upon them.' One wonders how the Battens would deal with situations where there are changes people do not accept, and where they refuse to have them imposed upon them.[6]

These ideas are clearly based not only on problem-solving within a very narrow context but yet again on an assumption that there is something inherently wrong with people themselves, which must be put right by a therapeutic process.

Community work theory has been further developed by three publications associated with the Calouste Gulbenkian Foundation. The first, *Community Work* by Professor Leaper, describes an experimental course in the training of community workers funded by the Gulbenkian Foundation. Leaper selects three definitions of group work which again clearly emphasise participation in existing structures of society—the first by Wilson and Ryland (p. 148), that group work is 'the interacting process towards the accomplishment of goals which in our country are conceived in a democratic frame of reference', the second by Younghusband, that it is 'giving people a constructive experience of membership in a group so that they may develop further as individuals, and be better able to contribute to the life of the community', and one of his own statements of a UN seminar to the effect that in relation to youth work, group work is about 'helping the growth of good relationships within the group'.

The Calouste Gulbenkian Foundation Community Work Group contributed to a further solidifying of the values and assumptions described above. For this group of highly influential academics and administrators (they brought in five field-workers in 1971 just prior to the publication of their second book), the essence of community described in their first book is a 'sense of common bond, the sharing of an identity, membership in a group holding some things physical or spiritual, in common esteem, coupled with the acknowledgement of rights and obligation with reference to all others so identified'. 'The purpose of community work', they write, 'is concerned with affecting the course of social change through two processes of analysing social situations, and forming relationships with different groups to bring about some desirable change.' The aims of community work are described as community participation, self-fulfilment and the meeting of social needs.

In the section on values, the Community Work Group states quite correctly that community work is rooted in certain beliefs which derive from our culture and society. It lists these values, as so many theorists have done in the past:

> — a democratic society exists to enable all its citizens to develop their talents and interests to the fullest possible extent;
> — that the individual's capacity for growth and development depends on his active association with his fellows in a number of different groups;
> — respect for individual beliefs;
> — a balanced interplay between leadership, organisation and freedom.

The Group's fundamental belief in our present pluralist and capitalist society is summed up in the statement: 'variety in a society is a good to be welcomed in its own right'.[7] Does such variety, one asks, include the right of huge and powerful economic interests to prevail at the expense of working people, the private control and accumulation of capital, together with the state holding down wages and cutting back on social expenditure, leaving dilapidated schools, hospitals and appalling housing conditions?

The ultimate gesture which demonstrates the Group's liberal and pluralistic attitudes is their inclusion, in their second publication, of a chapter on Community Action. The Group recognises community action as a 'sector' of community work (p. 38), and puts forward a wide range of definitions—action in the community pursuing reform or changes,[8] mobilising groups which are powerless to promote their collective interest,[9] and suggests that the emphasis is on the poor taking action on their own behalf to overcome their political powerlessness. The Gulbenkian Group steers close to, but carefully avoids, an alternative approach in questioning 'the rationale of our existing power structure' and the assumptions underlying it. The chapter lacks a clear statement to the effect that relative deprivation is a consequence of, and functional to, our present capitalist society, and that community action must be an integral component of the class struggle if it is to be at all relevant. The Group seem to fall into the trap of which they urge their readers to be wary — 'viewing the action of local groups too exclusively from outside, or with the too facile assumptions of liberal middle class attitudes'.[10]

Some current writers on community work are arguing more forcefully that community work must become political (e.g. Griffiths[11] and Woolley[12]) but clearly what is meant here is political in a *general* sense, i.e. that there should be more awareness of local power structures, and of making alliances between community groups, trade unions, local political parties, etc. Professor Griffiths suggests that the objectives of community action are to 'promote, sustain and maintain' community development, and puts forward the proposition that 'community action is about power'. But he admits that there is a reluctance to develop this in ideological terms.

T. Woolley perhaps came closest of all to putting forward a class analysis when he maintained that the increased interest in community action in the 1960s must be seen as an attempt to contain and direct working-class discontent, and that it must be seen in the context of British reformist tradition whereby Britain has in effect avoided revolution for over two centuries by introducing just enough reforms to dispel protest without altering the power relationships which cause discontent. But he does not extend this apart from putting forward a political plea for people to have a 'realistic' political perspective, and not to be manipulated by either left wing or bourgeois elements.

Community workers are in danger of being misled into thinking that these recent theorists represent a radical development in community work, as much of this thinking is still within liberal and pluralist ideology. It is therefore equally important to clarify the distinction between 'community politics' and 'class politics'. Community politics was initially developed by the Young Liberals in the late 1960s as an electioneering technique which is now used widely by all political groupings, including the National Front, and is simply another name for raising local demands about local issues. It is a strategy which is as relevant to high-income middle-class areas faced with a local problem as it is to working-class areas. The development of class politics, however, is a recognition of the class divisions within society. A socialist approach to political and economic inequality implies the development of working-class politics in the context of an understanding that the problems of working-class areas are directly related to those of a capitalist society. This means being selective about the alliances which should be developed and supported, and working with rank-and-file workers such as the shop stewards movement, the left socialists in the Labour Party, and tenants and residents groups which are prepared to raise socialist demands about local housing conditions, social facilities, etc.

Action strategies now being promoted by many CDP projects include developments in these directions—campaigns around council house building, house improvements, and against the public expenditure cuts; welfare rights projects to show up the iniquities and injustices of the present system of means-tested benefits; the development of industrial research units for local workers; supporting shop stewards' working parties on industrial issues such as the Industry Bill; and campaigns on the unionisation of workers, women's rights, etc.

Many workers within CDP, in attempting to make sense of their position as professionals employed by the state to ameliorate the position of the working class, but not radically to improve it, have tended to support a Marxist analysis which sees the state as a system of institutions of the ruling capitalist class and which sees the basic conflict within society as being between the owners of capital and the working class. From this kind of analysis it follows that only through the collective efforts of the working class will a socialist society be achieved. In the last few years, these workers within CDP have been attempting to apply this analysis to organising projects in their area.

The professional working for the state in this way is faced with many contradictions, and it was more or less inevitable that action strategies based on this analysis would bring projects into confrontation with local authorities and the Home Office (those parts of the state system which were trying to exercise control over CDP), and, through CDP and other such 'experiments', over new forms of working-class organisation. The potential for such conflict is inherent in the position of anyone with the job description of 'community worker' or some such name who is employed by the state to improve the conditions of local people. In fact, disputes between community workers and their state employers, or the public airing of them, have been few, despite the fact that several thousand workers are now employed in this way. This, in part, is a testimony to the confusion in most such workers' minds as to what they should really be doing.

One conflict taken up by the media in a large way was the rather confused issue of Batley CDP and the Advice Centre for the Town (ACT), and this is referred to again below. The one other such dispute which was publicised recently was in Sefton, where two workers, one resigning and one being sacked, openly attacked their former employers, the Sefton District Council. This dispute led to a request to 'black' community jobs in Sefton, an investigation by the Association of Community Workers and a rather confused debate again. In neither of these disputes did workers mount a clear campaign which attempted to show the nature of state intervention. In addition, both the campaigns failed because workers were unwilling, or unable, to secure a political base supported by working people in their area or by working-class organisations. Many other workers face the possibility of this kind of conflict, but most local authority community workers are forced to 'come to terms' with their position or to resign, and nothing more is heard of them. Isolated workers in local authorities, with little ideological or political support, tend to turn, unsurprisingly, to non-contentious activities such as playgroups and luncheon clubs. Those conflicts which do emerge tend to be ones which are couched in pluralist or populist terms.

The state can, in fact, afford to allow some community workers and some areas of community work to extract small gains for the working class (or 'the poor' as it prefers to call them), and this is one further contradiction. However, while these gains appear to be achieving some small measure of redistribution of resources, they do not in fact challenge the basis of wealth and power in capitalist society. Similarly, local government can accept and almost institutionalise the apparently more radical rhetoric of community activists, for this again is frequently not informed by a socialist ideology but by anti-bureaucratic tendencies which manifest themselves as attacks on the failure of the impersonal Town Hall to 'deliver the goods'. On these terms, they mystify rather than clarify the real nature of the state. They rarely locate local government within the capitalist state or point to the need for a struggle which involves the whole of the working class. Indeed, by their focus on neighbourhoods, community workers and activists are often setting up groups and demands which compete with other working-class groups for the same scarce resources.

Much of the local detailed work, and the mistakes made in the early phases of CDP, have contributed to a feeling that community work, as it is generally understood, cannot produce a socialist society. It is rather a new means by which the state hopes to 'buy off' working-class protest. CDPs do not now on the whole see themselves in the business of community work but involved in supporting the political struggles of the working class, and a brief account of some of these initiatives is given at the end of this chapter.

A short history of CDP

The various strands which came together at the end of the 1960s in the establishment of the National Community Development Project are difficult to extract. The Seebohm Report, published in 1968, recommended that local authorities should establish integrated social services departments which would undertake the functions of the existing children's and welfare departments. Like the concept of local government reorganisation itself (and it was possible for a while that the implementation of Seebohm would be delayed till the local government reorganisation which eventually took place in 1974), Seebohm was informed by the notions of rationalisation, merger and productivity which were common coinage in the private sector. The early official descriptions of CDP make it clear that *cost-effectiveness* was a key concept. Here, for example, is the Home Office view of CDP in 1969, circulated to participating local authorities: [13]

> In the past, official efforts to analyse and meet social needs in the interlinked fields of employment, income security, housing, general environmental planning, health provision, social work, education, leisure facilities, and so on, were largely compartmentalised. Nowadays, however, the number of compartments is gradually diminishing (e.g. through developments like Seebohm); and their degree of separation is also lessening (e.g. through improvements in the techniques of planning and management). The CDP seeks to identify and demonstrate, by reference to the problems of selected small local communities, some practical ways of taking this trend further, through consultation and action among the separate departments of central and local government and voluntary organisations and the people of the local communities themselves.

The impetus of this view of community development came from the Children's Development Group, a Working Group (chaired by Derek Morrell) within the Home Office, and to a certain extent the development of CDP can be seen as an attempt to implement the ideas of the Seebohm Report, at least on a small scale. Shortly before CDP came into being on a practical level, Morrell died, and the Children's Section moved from the Home Office to the DHSS. CDP was left behind, and the grip of this particular ideology was considerably weakened.

The second strand might be regarded as the notion of '*positive discrimination*'. This has been taken up in a series of government reports and recommendations, most notably the Plowden Report of 1967 whose findings led to the establishment of Educational Priority Areas. By the time CDP was ready to move, EPAs were in operation and were available as a model with which CDP could readily be compared. It was not difficult to move from EPAs to the notion of community priority areas which would take a 'whole approach' to the problems of small area. This was in line with the growing emphasis on *community care*. This third strand, while in part reflecting a proper concern at the growth of institutional and impersonal welfare provision, was notable also for its cost-saving potential. Thus it linked back directly to the economic concerns of politicians and their professional advisers in the various welfare ministries.

These three strands are variously concerned with the economics of welfare provision, but the crucial factor which actually precipitated the foundation of CDP was probably a political concern. In a decade which has seen race riots on both sides of the Atlantic and a student/worker insurrection in Paris, there was a growing concern among politicians about social control, which was expressed in a number of ways. Traditional political processes had failed to integrate dissident groups into the smooth parliamentary machine, and the Labour government would have been particularly concerned at the virtual collapse of Labour politics in many cities.[14] Politicians of all colours were under pressure to meet the major threat to *social stability* which many people, drawing particularly on American experience, saw in terms of the collapse of the inner city areas. When Enoch Powell in April 1968 chose to translate this into a vision of 'rivers of blood' and linked the social threat clearly with growing coloured immigration, the government felt it had to act. Two week later the Urban Programme was announced by the Prime Minister, a programme of which CDP was to form a significant part.

The package which followed drew on all of these strands and thus had something for virtually everyone. From the politicians' point of view, although they appeared to be doing something (and, as the involvement of the Prime Minister might suggest, something very significant), the initiative didn't actually cost much (the cost of the Urban Programme as a whole was not expected to exceed £25m).[15] And while there was no commitment actually to act on the findings of CDP, it gave central government an opportunity to look more closely at the social problems of the inner city. For the civil servants and their professional social work advisers, although the politicians had required the delivery of the goods rather more speedily than had been expected, it did provide the opportunity (and perhaps money which might never have been available) to put current welfare thinking into practice.

CDP, then, developed in response to a wide set of political and economic circumstances some of which were concerned with social welfare and others with social control. In some ways the Urban Programme might be seen as a reformist gain by the labour movement in that it was an attempt, albeit a marginal one, to redistribute social resources through 'positive discrimination' in favour of poorer areas. What CDP actually did, though, was of less concern to the politicians who, having established it with the passing of the Social Needs Grants Act (1969), left it to the civil servants to look after. In terms of political expediency the establishment of CDP was more important than what it did once it had been established.

We have dwelt at some length on the origins of CDP since, in our view, it is helpful to see CDP in some general economic and political context. The remainder of this section will deal briefly with the history of the development of CDP which has led from the early consensus to the last year where workers in CDP were under considerable pressure from the state to curtail their activities.[16]

The Home Office, writing to local authorities in 1969, described the purpose of the project as 'a modest attempt at action research into the better understanding and more comprehensive tackling of social needs', by trying to 'help them [local authorities and voluntary organisations] and the communities they serve develop insights and channels of communication', and in particular 'to reinforce and not to damage the spirit and efforts of elective Local Government'.[17] The reaction of local authorities was mixed, reflecting local views of central government intervention, the attractiveness of further central government spending and the varying political complexions of local authorities. MPs took a hand: Richard Crossman in part persuaded the Mayor of Coventry to take CDP, whereas James Callaghan ensured that Cardiff did not. By 1970 the first four projects were planned for Southwark, Coventry, Glamorgan and Liverpool, and others followed at intervals through to 1972 in Newham, Batley, Paisley, Cumbria, Birmingham, Oldham, Newcastle-on-Tyne and North Tyneside. The final mix, which included one Scottish and one Welsh project, owed as much to political bargaining as to rational notions of comparability. The inclusion of two rural areas moved CDP some way from its concentration on inner city areas.

Local authorities and universities or polytechnics were encouraged to form teams of action and research workers. Their first job was to identify areas within their authorities suitable for the projects to operate in. As far as the Home Office was concerned, these teams would assist 'in the assessment of the localities' needs and of how they might best be met' and undertake 'continuous monitoring and final evaluation of the project teams' work and its lessons for feeding back to the Local Authority itself and to other local and central interests', and action teams would 'stimulate local residents to participate in this assessment', produce and encourage 'practical ideas of meeting the needs wherever it is realistic to seek to do so, e.g. through adjustments in policies, methods or priorities, with special emphasis on the development of contact and co-operation at all levels between the various local authority departments'.[18]

As projects developed their work, the day-to-day control of CDP passed further and further from the hands of central government. Thus, though from the government's viewpoint CDP aimed in part to integrate working-class protest within the project areas, the growing involvement of project workers in their neighbourhoods provided them with another perspective. It became clear to a number of workers in CDP that the initial assumptions behind CDP were incorrect. Coventry (August 1972)[19] reported that it was misleading to concentrate on small areas; Glamorgan (1973)[20] that the problems of Glyncorrwg derived from structural changes in the South Wales coalfield. Following these early reports, a new set of general perspectives emerged to which most projects gave support—that poverty and urban decline were a consequence not of the inadequacies of the poor themselves (a view particularly associated with the Tory government which was by now in office) or simply poor communication within local authorities requiring better planning and management techniques and associated cost benefits, but of fundamental inequalities in our present political system. The appalling housing conditions, high unemployment and low incomes of a large number of working-class people were a consequence, in fact, of *the private control of capital.* Projects slowly came to organise themselves locally and collectively at a national level to face this central problem.

The implications for practice of this perspective are outlined in the final section; the present section concludes with a description of the interaction between the Home Office and central CDP machinery on the one hand, and local projects on the other. The point illustrated by this interaction is that as long as projects were prepared to collude with the state's notion of what CDP was about, little control was exercised over projects' activities. Now that workers in local projects have radically challenged the Home Office and local authority perspective, the whole of the national project has been subject to continual harassment.

Originally CDP had, in addition to local project teams, a Central Research Unit established to identify possible project areas, produce a research design for local teams and to co-ordinate all research activities. Initially, with Action Teams under local authority management committees and Research Teams in the appropriate department of a local university or polytechnic, collective action amongst projects was difficult. The projects were faced with an unnecessarily complicated structure with an interlocking organisational hierarchy, having the Home Office at the pinnacle.

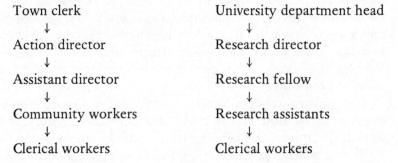

Home Office

Local authority	Polytechnic/university
↓	↓
Management committee	Department
↓	↓
Action team	Research team

and within each organisation there were internal hierarchies. At team level it generally was:

Town clerk	University department head
↓	↓
Action director	Research director
↓	↓
Assistant director	Research fellow
↓	↓
Community workers	Research assistants
↓	↓
Clerical workers	Clerical workers

Most project teams attempted to reorganise themselves internally on a democratic basis but it was only after considerable efforts on the part of the project teams that this pyramidal structure was generally broken down. The two joint meetings between projects and the Home Office in 1971 and 1972 led to criticisms of the Central Research Unit's failure to produce any help to the teams and its eventual disbandment, the establishment of a joint Consultative Council between project directors and the Home Office, and the removal shortly afterwards of the Home Office advisers. From these meetings also came the idea of cross-project research which became crucial later on. By the end of 1972, projects, meeting regularly at pre-meetings before the Consultative Council, had begun to think seriously about inter-project work. Various special interest groups looking at issues such as housing, unemployment and education were formed and there followed a joint project request to the Home Office that a central Information and Intelligence Unit (CDP IIU) should be established under the control of the projects to service the growing volume of inter-project work.

Following pressure from the projects, the Home Office agreed to an increased degree of local autonomy. Clearly, however, there was concern about control. Local autonomy meant greater freedom from day-to-day interference by Home Office civil servants and advisers, but the government needed to know what projects were up to. In the summer of 1973 the Minister of State at the Home Office demanded progress reports and the projects responded by not only putting these reports forward but also (sceptical of the view that the reports were for any purpose other than monitoring the projects or that they would get beyond the Minister's desk) collaborated in the production of an Inter-Project Report[21] for a wider audience, which began to spell out the shift in thinking within CDP. By this time (March 1974), the CDP IIU had been established and had begun to make a major contribution to the development and servicing of inter-project work. Groups representing a number of local projects began the process of working towards publications on employment[22] and council housing[23] directed at working-class audiences and informed by an increasingly socialist perspective.

The growing concern within government at the role of CDP began to show more clearly by 1974. After various hints about an uncertain future for CDP, the Home Office announced in June 1974 that a Management Review had been established to look at CDP's effectiveness and the need for new machinery (i.e. new forms of control over the projects).[24] Shortly afterwards the review began, but a number of workers within CDP further strengthened their collective position by forming a Political Economy Collective (PEC) with the aim of analysing and publicising processes in project areas through a Marxist political economy approach, and by replacing the Consultative Council, which by now was regarded as merely a token gesture at democratising CDP, with an elected CDP Workers' Organisation (CDPWO), which sent delegates to regular meetings and co-ordinated project initiatives on a national basis. In the event PEC published only three documents[25] and circulated a number of editions of an internal bulletin, but the tendency it represented was clearly a grave threat to the smooth running of the Poverty Programme. The Workers'

Organisation similarly had grave implications for the management of CDP, though its impact was weakened by the unwillingness of several projects to take an active part in it. The Home Office maintained even after the Workers' Organisation had been in existence for 15 months (and where all projects now were internally organised on a democratic basis) that the line of command continued to be through project directors, thus effectively refusing to accept the representative nature of CDPWO.

The conclusion of the Management Review, published after lengthy delays and prevarication, was that greater central control and co-ordination of the projects were required. Specifically, the Review proposed a central committee and a national co-ordinator and required forward plans from each project. Following complete opposition to the proposed central structure from local projects, supported in some cases by local authorities and universities to which projects were attached, the Home Office dropped the proposals. Projects were asked to provide individual forward plans for the Home Secretary and responded by co-operating to produce an Inter-Project Forward Plan which developed CDP's analysis further.[26] Immediately the long period of insecurity surrounding the Management Review appeared to be over, the Home Office announced that CDP would be subject to a public expenditure review and froze all new appointments for a period which they suggested would take 'several weeks'.

The period of the review lasted seven months, in fact, and its ending was prefaced by a well-timed leak to the *Sunday Times*,[27] which suggested that the Home Office would not be entirely unhappy if CDP were to end. This was followed by a highly ambiguous letter to local authorities which offered those in serious local dispute with the teams an opportunity to cut their losses. Kirklees, following the long dispute over Batley CDP and ACT (see below), and Cumbria, with a Tory-controlled council, both seized this opportunity and closed their projects prematurely by early 1976. The message was not lost on the remaining authorities.

Even then, the Home Office harassment was not concluded, but switched from action teams to research teams. Research sponsors were asked at short notice to submit forward plans, to further scrutinize expenditure and to provide extremely detailed breakdowns of the workload of research teams. Coming at a time when a number of research teams were about to negotiate an extension, it created further uncertainty and confusion. Following a further campaign of opposition to these proposals and a joint submission by research sponsors, extensions were granted to various research teams. The final blow fell in January 1976 when the Home Office, again without warning and following a dispute with the IIU over proposed censorship of forthcoming publications and the publication of the highly critical *Cutting the Welfare State*,[28] announced that the IIU would close as soon as the staff's three-month notice expired. Once again a lobby of *Tribune* MPs, trade unions, academics and newspaper coverage produced a reprieve, but only for a further four months and not, as projects had demanded, two years. The Unit finally closed in September 1976 after an unsuccessful attempt to find alternative sources of funding.

By the summer of 1976, the aim of the Home Office to create confusion and uncertainty and to weaken the ability of projects to resist collectively had succeeded to an extent. A number of individual projects had closed, some prematurely, or were about to close. The IIU, which had been the platform for a wide range of publications and publicity for the view of CDP workers, was about to close. Those projects which remained were increasingly isolated and, where local government elections returned Tory-controlled councils, under greater attack locally as well as from the government.[29] A number of further publications were planned by CDP workers. None of them was published before the IIU closed which made the bland assurances of the Home Office that it did not want to prevent the publication of CDP documents sound hollow indeed. (The editorial staff were later retained by the Home Office to complete four documents in the six months to March 1977: this apparent volte-face was explained by the needs of the Home Office to defend its position against the imperialism of the Department of the Environment and its new 'inner cities' initiative.)

Projects are now engaged in another struggle, over the question of evaluation. Project workers, both action and research, have asserted their right to complete the definitive evaluation of CDP, and there is no doubt that it would, if done this way, lead to further embarrassment for government and local sponsors alike. One way out for the Home Office would be to appoint a suitable institution with a liberal reputation to undertake the evaluation and to rationalise 'the failure of a social experiment'. What form the rationalisation might take is not particularly important, and it would depend in fact on the political perspective of the person employed (and several are known to be anxiously waiting in the wings for the contract). What it would not do is to highlight the real nature of inequalities. The Home Office has already shown itself to be quite prepared to ignore a wealth of experience from CDP by establishing the Comprehensive Community Programmes in 1975.[30] The conclusions of the fieldworkers in CDP for practice are radical in their implications and against the interests of the state. Little wonder, then, that the reaction of the state is to establish quickly another programme of further and more detailed enquiry which, by the nature of its management structure, offers less chance of 'things going wrong' and which can be given a central position in the government's social policy programme as CDP is (almost) quietly disposed of.

The positive involvement, as we have seen, of the Home Office began to diminish from about 1972 when the projects demanded— and got—greater autonomy for work at a local level and for inter-project work of their own choosing. From that time, the Central Research Unit began to be wound down and the close administrative links, although they remained formalised through the Consultative Council for two years, also began to be weakened. By 1975 the Home Office, continuing its withdrawal of commitment to CDP, felt free to cancel what would have effectively been the last Consultative Council, and subsequently the Home Office has not met local projects on a regular basis at all. Even the once regular Home Office observers at local project management committee meetings have been erratic in their attendance, and letters are replied to after considerable delays.

This latest attitude does not reflect a willingness to give complete autonomy to local projects but rather is in line with their decision, never made explicit, to encourage the demise of CDP by a succession of harassing actions. The Home Office recognised that, just as it had invited local authorities to take part in the experiment, so, in a sense, it had to invite them (as in the ambiguous letter of October 1975) to abandon it. The politicians in the Home Office felt confident about this strategy because, by now, most projects had been in serious disputes of one kind or another with local sponsors; in particular the local authorities.

The local projects in action

Most projects have had a number of disputes with local authorities. To a certain extent, local projects have also had conflicts with their sponsoring university or polytechnic. These, however, tended to be less serious in their effects than disputes with local authorities. Most of the disputes centred either on the nature of the action-research relationship or else differences about what issues and methods the university or polytechnic thought the project research workers ought to be looking at. Differences of this kind led Newcastle CDP to abandon Newcastle University's sponsorship and transfer to Durham University, and Newham's team to move from Brunel University to Oxford University via the North-East London Polytechnic. Although these differences were often fundamental to the nature of the work and of critical importance to the project workers—for example Newcastle University had suggested a research model which involved measurement of social indices 'before' and 'after', and felt it important that the research team should hold itself aloof from day-to-day intervention—they were not enough to threaten the stability of the project. For one thing, the research institutions had less political significance for the Home Office, and second, there were always other institutions if not anxious, then at least willing, to take on this strange animal and the extra resources and status it represented.

It was, therefore, the relationship of teams with local authorities that became more significant and critical to the future of local projects as the Home Office withdrew. From 1972 on, all projects with the exception of rural Cumbria, Newcastle and Tynemouth were administered by Labour authorities,[31] which might be expected to be more sympathetic to the general aims of CDP. However, despite a reasonably friendly political context at the local level, the tendency amongst a number of projects towards socialist critiques of the state at local and national level led to confrontations with authorities, the effects of which were felt in most project areas. And although national lobbying came to be significant in terms of attempting to rescue CDP as a national programme, or parts of it with a national element such as the IIU, there was little support individual projects could call on outside the project areas in times of conflict. The Home Office, as a spokesman put it in 1974, 'would not bail out any individual local projects in dispute with their local authorities'. Although the links with the Home Office and sponsoring research institutions tended to give some protection in the early and middle phases of the local CDPs, this protection was somewhat shallow, and the intention of the Home Office from 1974 on appeared to be to indicate to local authorities just how shallow it was. When projects came to a real confrontation with their sponsoring authority, what actally counted was the support they could muster in local project areas from sympathetic councillors, from the labour movement in general and, in some cases, from the research institutions. In this case, those project workers employed by councils were little different from community workers employed by a local authority. They were accountable for their actions to a committee of councillors which met frequently, were paid by the local authority and in frequent contact with councillors and officials. The projects were able to gain some freedom to act on occasions by playing upon the notion of an experiment, by underlying their parallel responsibilities to research institutions and to the Home Office, and by the use of inter-project work.

These ambiguities in the projects' mode of operation were not adequate by themselves to protect a local CDP from an authority bent on closure. This would only be possible in terms of political support derived locally for the programme which a project might want to carry through. In fact, following the 'reprieve' of October 1975, both Kirklees and Cumbria councils moved to close their projects. In the Cumbria case, the team had been the responsibility of a Tory-controlled council and it appears that, although reasons of economy were put forward for premature closure, it was largely the work of the leader of the Policy and Resources Committee, the politically most significant figure in the Tory Group. This man owned a factory in Cleator Moor and was becoming extremely concerned at the project's activity in the area over which he felt he had the hegemony. The Kirklees closure decision was the culmination of a long and well-publicised dispute. The authority had taken exception to the activities of a CDP-funded advice centre (ACT) in Batley, and some workers on the project had come out on strike and then resigned in protest at the decision of the council not to give a further grant to the Centre, which insisted on its right to promote squatting and criticise the council where necessary. A long and confused series of negotiations followed at the end of which, following the Centre's agreement to some conditions, it appeared that the council would give a significant grant to the Centre. However, the Labour group finally betrayed this understanding, whereupon the Labour councillor resigned in disgust (removing the Labour group's one-vote majority), and the remaining project workers, dismayed at the behaviour of the Labour Group, launched an attack on what they described as the politics of Labourism in the town. The decision to wind up the project and replace it with a number of workers closely tied to separate local authority departments followed shortly afterwards.

The Home Office, in neither dispute, was prepared to intervene until the closure was assured and then made token gestures, for example funding certain small elements of the work in both areas. In other project areas, notably Newham and North Tyneside, it seems likely that project closure was averted only because some significant political support had been obtained through the Labour Party or trade unions and tenants' associations, or through the political incompetence of the ruling Labour group. In Newham, the project decided to abandon the CDP experiment entirely and offered to close a year early, and the local authority later severely trimmed the proposal for a post-CDP Resource Centre. In North Tyneside, the Labour group took a soft line by setting up an investigating committee into the local CDP rather than deal with the political embarrassment of closure immediately prior to critical municipal elections. Some local councils indeed seemed unable or unwilling to grasp the fact that CDPs could, with determination, be closed almost immediately despite the fact that the activities promoted by local projects more often than not gave ample ammunition to their more vigorous opponents.

In their day-to-day work, most of the projects have concentrated on work which relates either to housing or employment issues, or to informational and legal questions. For reasons of space it is possible to describe only briefly the first two areas of work here.

Work on housing issues

Many of the local CDPs started work in a fairly typical 'community work' fashion, organising tenants' and residents' associations around specific issues such as repairs, environmental conditions, clearance and rehousing. While this form of organisation achieved short-term gains, its limitations as a strategy for broader change became apparent both to CDP workers and to the groups they were working with. For example, the Benwell Grove Residents' Association, which had been working with support from the Newcastle CDP team, had taken part in a GIA (General Improvement Area) environmental improvement 'participation' scheme organised by the local authority planning department. By 1975, in an article in *Community Action*,[32]   they were asking whether three years of 'participating' in street improvements was worth it.

> We don't think so because while this has been going on,
> — unemployment has been rising locally
> — Council house rents have gone up
> — the Council have bought lots of houses locally and are planning to modernise them
> — over 1,000 homes are still unimproved
> — housing action areas have been declared in the city so that GIAs are now second priority for improvement
> These are all much more important to local residents, yet we have not been invited to discuss them or take part in decisions about them. Participation in GIA work, we think, is irrelevant compared with these issues.

Elsewhere in Benwell, the tenants of Noble Street and Norwich Place were faced with the effects of life in a council ghetto created by a combination of cheap building in the 1950s and the grading system of local authority allocation policies which resulted in many homeless families with no bargaining power being 'dumped' there, and a male unemployment rate of 35 per cent, four times the average for Newcastle as a whole. This situation would not have been solved by forming a tenants' group to press for better amenities, although as an interim step playgrounds and youth work projects were initiated with tenant involvement. The tenants had to press for and have achieved a clear statement from the authority that all tenants would be rehoused within a short time and that the Noble Street blocks would not be used again for family accommodation.[33] But even this strategy would deal only with the immediate situation of those families housed in the blocks. It did not address itself to the question of overall housing allocation policy or to the financing of council-house building, which could be dealt with only on the basis of much wider struggles. These issues have been raised in subsequent discussions on the future of the flats, and links have been made at the same time with tenants' groups in other 'purpose-built slums' throughout the city.

In North Tyneside, the CDP was instrumental in establishing the North Tyneside Housing Campaign at a conference in North Shields in 1975 attended by tenants, trade unionists and Labour Party activists. Despite a council ban on organising the conference, CDP workers attended and subsequently supported the campaign committee, acting in an individual capacity. The objectives of the campaign have been to raise more general political demands for better housing, demands which attacked the collaboration of the Labour government with the ruling class in cutting public expenditure, and the council's passive acceptance of them. The campaign called for a return to earlier house-building targets, for the improvement of older housing by 1980, low rents, better repairs, and so on.

This strategy was developed with the campaign because the project had experienced the limitations of 'community work' at an area level, and decided that, rather than try to ameliorate conditions at a very local level in slum-clearance areas and old council estates, or try to make very local demands which often cut across or competed with the demands of other community action groups in the neighbourhoods, it was necessary to generalise the frustrations and the class position of local tenants and residents in order to build a wider political campaign. The importance of this development was to demonstrate that the appalling housing conditions in many working-class areas were a consequence of the forces of a private capital market acting against them, and not of inefficiencies in local government or the inadequacies of local people. It was also hoped that tenants would begin to see that they were all in a common situation in relation to the state.

The Housing Campaign during 1976 conducted street meetings in various housing areas raising demands on a wide basis alongside local demands. Local demands have to be met, since these are the immediate problems which make people angry, but at the same time the nature of the housing crisis, the financing of housing and the role of government (diverting housing funds to private industry, for example) is being explained. The campaign has been participating in a wider socialist struggle by means also of developing contacts with local trade unions such as UCATT and NUPE, who are also affected by cuts in house-building. This campaign has attempted to challenge the 'managers' of the local state and highlight the political realities of the area, rather than divert small local groups into what may become meaningless activities. As well as the difficulty of persuading local groups of the value of wider political action, the campaign has faced considerable hostility from the local council.

As a result of work such as this in both private and public

sector housing areas with residents' and tenants' groups, ever broader questions have been thrown up about improvement, financing, control, the role of local authorities and the government and of a variety of agencies such as building societies and housing associations. From 1972, several projects had begun to co-operate in inter-project work. Though little effective work was produced at this level initially, there was a growing volume of detailed work at a local level and an awareness that, behind the symptoms of the problems in a particular local project area, there lay perhaps causes which were common to all areas. This then gave rise to a useful period of collaboration between projects on various housing issues. The first Inter-Project Report, which followed closely on the implementation of the 1974 Housing Act, appeared in the summer of 1975 as *The Poverty of the Improvement Programme*,[34] and consisted of a critique of a succession of government improvement policies since the 1969 Housing Act. Its main conclusion was that the Improvement Programme, and particularly the notion of HAAs and GIAs, far from being a massive injection of resources into housing, actually represented a considerable potential cut in the housing standards of the working class. This was followed in early 1976 by a similar inter-project document on the public sector, 'Whatever Happened to Council Housing?', the result of two years' detailed work. The purpose of the Report, which was sufficiently controversial for the Home Office to attempt to censor it, was spelt out early on in the Introduction:

> Current media campaigns promote an image of council
> tenants as privileged and cosseted members of society. We are
> shown how enormous sums of tax and rate-payers' money are
> poured in to support incompetent local councils in providing
> high-quality subsidised housing at rents well below its 'econ-
> omic' costs. This approach is typified by recent articles which
> focus on the rising costs of council housing in terms of land,
> construction, loan debt and interest charges, and the demands
> made on central exchequer subsidies and the local authorities
> general rate fund.
>   Typically using the most extreme examples of subsidised
> costs and comparing them with tenants having high house-
> hold incomes, such articles either call for enormous increases
> in rent or for the almost total abolition of council housing in
> its present form.

Fortunately saner voices have demonstrated that the
current housing crisis has not been created by over-subsidised
council tenants. But this view rarely attracts publicity and is
not supported by an understanding of why council housing is
necessary and why it needs to be defended against the interests
who would seek to destroy it. To provide such a defence is
the major task of this report.

Both these reports illustrated the basic assumption which had
come to inform most CDP work by late 1974, namely that action
at a local level, though necessary in order to achieve small gains
and to give an insight into local issues, was not enough. It has to
be complemented by action at a wider, even a national, level and
that it should be action taken in conjunction with those institutions and agencies which were most likely to further the interests
of the working class. Thus the reports were written in defence of
the interests of the working class, were widely publicised and
provided material for trades councils and trade unions, tenants'
and residents' associations at a local level and for the labour movement generally at a national level. CDP was well placed to provide
this material with both national and local contacts, which had
been built up over several years, some national status, a variety of
local experience and the beginning of an analysis which indicated
that any particular local situation was not merely a local quirk but
a product of definite political and economic forces. The projects
have been able to use this combination of local experience and
analysis fruitfully in co-operation with other groups to publish
two further accounts of relevance to housing issues. In the first,
Cutting the Welfare State, written in collaboration with Counter
Information Services, CDP/CIS produced an account of the public
expenditure cuts in terms of a ruling-class attempt to prop up a
failing capitalist economy. This drew on material relating to the
cuts in several project areas, both in the public and private sectors.
The second,[35] written with members of the Conference of Socialist
Economists Housing Workshop, provided an exposition of housing
finance dealing in turn with land, production, consumption and
exchange and attempting to show the interrelationship of private
and public sectors and the ways in which housing development
tended to serve the interests of finance capital. Each of these
reports has contributed, with a mixture of local detail and broader
analysis, to debates which have been current, in the newspapers, in

Parliament and outside. The debate about public expenditure cuts was perhaps one of the major issues at the time of publication of *Cutting the Welfare State*. As a result, many trade unions gave the report wide coverage. The choice of subjects in this sense has been strategic at a national level though they relate to issues which are extremely important to the residents of local areas. It was not expected that the reports would produce significant changes of themselves but that they could provide ammunition for those organisations wanting to make use of such material. This has been achieved to a modest extent.

Work on employment issues

Not many 'community workers' have ventured into the field of employment issues. Those that have in the UK in recent years have generally confined themselves to issues such as the New Careers Movement, providing employment opportunities for unqualified working-class neighbourhood workers. These have tended to focus on widening the scope of community work to include employment possibilities for those who have traditionally been 'organised' by community workers. This has largely been an attempt to make community work more relevant to working-class people. It is, however, confusing several issues, for there is no particular reason why working-class people should not be used by the state, directly or otherwise, much as CDP workers were intended to be used, to control the activities of the working class. Thus those who have seen the New Careers Movement as offering wide opportunities for developing working-class action have largely been under an illusion.

Most local CDP teams have devoted a considerable proportion of their resources to employment work. The starting-point of most projects was often analysis of data concerning the industrial structure of an area (including general surveys of firms), employment trends, census data on unemployment, journey-to-work patterns and school-leavers, regional aid, and the like. It was not difficult to establish, in general terms, that many of the industrial issues resulted from decisions which were not located at a local level. Glamorgan, as we have said, reported in 1973 that the problems of Glyncorrwg derived from structural changes in the South Wales coalfield. Other projects reached similar conclusions. A consultant, hired by the Batley, Newham, Newcastle and North Tyneside teams to investigate large employers in their areas, reported[36] in 1974 that, despite massive government intervention, all of the areas had experienced a considerable decline of job opportunities. 'The role of the State has been piecemeal, lop-sided and inadequate. Meanwhile, industry remains unaccountable to the needs of the community, remains free to undermine the economic basis of whole localities and is in no sense required to take into account wider social needs when working out forward planning and investment decisions.'

Faced with this kind of evidence, projects came to the conclusion that, in general, the economic problems of project areas, and particularly unemployment, were a consequence of the withdrawal of private capital, often leading to redundancies and closures without any control by local workers or even by the state. In this kind of situation, a strategy for change is very difficult to devise. It was expected by government that policy changes from CDP experience would proceed by means of an 'up-across-down' type of mechanism. Reports from CDP would be channelled to the Home Office, passed across to the relevant department and down to the appropriate regional official, who would act on these findings. Nowhere more than in the field of industrial policy were the limitations of this strategy more clear. Several attempts at feeding information and recommendations to government departments concerned with industry and employment petered out because the bureaucrats lacked interest and were inefficient, and the politicians were unwilling to consider seriously the implications of such information. Project staff also became aware of the political dangers of channelling information 'from the grass roots' to civil service and political groupings with no control over how the material might be used. As a result of these early conclusions, and the failure to make much use of them, projects turned to the production of material for local audiences and the establishment of links with key groups locally. Most projects began to establish contact with trade councils, shop stewards, trade union branches, works convenors and the like and to provide material on local industrial issues relevant to their struggles. Members of North Tyneside and Newcastle CDPs have both been active in supporting the work of their local trades councils and, more recently, the establishment of a Tyneside Action Committee Against the Cuts and a Right to Work Committee.

Trades councils are well placed to develop this kind of work, being central forums for a wide range of trade union interests and generally composed of rank and file union members. Both projects have also developed close contact with shop stewards committees in local large manufacturing establishments. The aim, in general, has been to support the development of existing institutions of the working class, particularly those representing the interests of rank-and-file members. This is in contrast with housing work where, in general, CDPs, like most community projects, have had to build new organisations in areas where traditionally few organisations have existed, often in areas where political activity as a whole is at a very low ebb. (These factors, incidentally, have accounted in part for the failure of many housing campaigns to be sustained over a long period.)

The one exception to this type of approach in relation to trade union work has been the provision of information units locally for the trade union movement. The two Tyneside projects have collaborated in establishing the Tyneside Trade Union Studies Information Unit in Newcastle, which is staffed by three workers and which provides information, education courses, intelligence, data and newsletters to trade unionists. (The Birmingham project is also in the process of establishing a similar unit.) However, although the Tyneside Unit represents a new initiative, it is a servicing rather than an 'action' body and, though funded partly by two CDPs, is controlled by an elected group of trade unionists.

Work by CDP on employment has also focused on important current issues. For example, the wide-ranging debate on nationalisation and the National Enterprise Board which emerged after the election of the Labour government in 1974 has serious implications for those project areas (most of them, in practice) which have multinational firms operating in them (such as British Leyland, Vickers, Tate & Lyle, Tube Investments and Swan Hunters). The CDP-PEC document *Workers and the Industry Bill* outlined the course of legislation on nationalisation, the retreat of the Labour government from its manifesto and the implications for shop stewards. Individual projects produced their own documentation on the issue of multinationals and nationalisation.[37] The growth of combine committees as a response to the growth of multinationals has been taken up actively by shop stewards committees in some CDP areas and again this has been supported by CDP workers. The Tyne Shop Stewards Committee, representing shop stewards from many local multinationals, has organised a series of regional conferences on the formation of combine committees.

Another significant question taken up by projects has been the failure of regional policy. Several local projects, including both Tyneside projects, are in development areas which have been provided with regional aid through the Department of Trade and Industry for some years. The impact of regional aid on inner city areas has been, in general, negative, as much of the aid has had the effect of subsidising the movement of industry either out of the region's inner city areas or from outside the region into new town development and has thus accelerated the decline of older areas based on manufacturing industry. In fact, regional aid has been a direct subsidy to multinational companies which have generally used it for their existing programmes (including property speculation and overseas developments), while hiding behind the convenient political smokescreen of 'help to the regions'. This kind of issue is of relevance to a wide range of groups locally and nationally and, for this reason, projects have produced more general reports for local and national audiences to complement their detailed work with trade unionists. Apart from 'Jobs in Jeopardy', which had a limited circulation, five projects have published an interproject report on a range of employment issues in their project areas.[38] Individual projects, such as Newham[39] and Brimingham,[40] have separately published detailed accounts of the industrial decline of their areas, both of which are set within regions traditionally regarded as the more prosperous in the country. A joint analysis of the effects of regional aid is also to be published by the two Tyneside projects.[41] These reports have been used as a basis for discussion and action with a range of local working-class interests: the strategy underlying them all is a 'bottom-up' one, which contrasts sharply with the original mechanism described earlier in this section.

These strategies recognise that only the working class, through its collective action, is in a position to defend its class interests against the operations of capital, and that the role of CDP workers in a local area and other 'professionals' employed by the state should be to stimulate and support this action. Traditional forms of community work are dangerous in that they tend to socialise working-class areas into the existing economic system, and community workers who are developing such strategies must be challenged about their attempt to control and dispel working-class action and protest on behalf of the state.

Notes

1   Meyer Schwartz, ed. Henry L. Lurie, *Community Organisation,* National Association of Social Workers (America), 1965.
2   Ross and Lappin, *Community Organisation: Theory, Principles and Practice,* 2nd ed., Harper & Row, 1967.
3   *Community Problem-Solving: the Delinquency Example,* University of Chicago Press, 1969.
4   *The Professional Approach to Community Work,* Sands & Co., 1969.
5   *The Non-Directive Approach in Group and Community Work,* Oxford University Press, 1967.
6   *Communities and Their Development,* Oxford University Press, 1957.
7   Calouste Gulbenkian Foundation, *Community Work and Social Change: a Report on Training,* Longman, 1968.
8   Anne Lapping (ed.), *Community Action,* Fabian Tract no. 400, London, 1970.
9   R. Bryant, 'Community Action', *British Journal of Social Work,* 2 (2), 1972.
10 Community Work Group, Calouste Gulbenkian Foundation, *Current Issues in Community Work,* Routledge & Kegan Paul, 1973.
11 H. J. Griffiths, 'The Aims and Objectives of Community Development', *Community Development Journal,* 9 (2), April 1974.
12 T. Woolley, The Politics of Community Action, paper given to 'Press-ups' Conference, Edinburgh, December 1970.
13 Home Office, *The Community Development Project: a General Outline,* 1969.
14 For a discussion of this see, e.g., Barry Hindess, *The Decline of Working-Class Politics,* Paladin, 1971.
15 CDP will have cost a total of almost £5m by the time it ends—the Urban Programme, to date, has involved an annual average expenditure of about £6m.
16 A much fuller account of the development of CDP has been prepared by CDP workers: *Gilding the Ghetto,* IIU, March 1977.
17 Home Office, op. cit.
18 ibid.
19 Coventry CDP Report, August 1972.
20 Glamorgan CDP Report to the Minister, 1973.
21 National CDP Inter-Project Report, 1974, CDP IIU.
22 *The Costs of Industrial Change,* 1977, CDP IIU.
23 *Whatever Happened to Council Housing?,* April 1976, CDP IIU.
24 It was about this time that a Cabinet minute noted concern over the growing 'political' content of CDP and suggested that closer monitoring would be useful.
25 *Workers and the Industry Bill,* July 1975, CDP PEC; *Community Work or Class Politics?,* September 1975, CDP PEC.
26 CDP Forward Plan, 1975–6, May 1975, CDP IIU; *The Poverty of the Improvement Programme,* rev. ed., December 1977.
27 'How an Experiment in Social Help Went Wrong', *Sunday Times,* 19 October 1975.

28 November 1975, CDP/Counter Information Services.
29 Tory-controlled councils were instructed (or advised, depending on your view of that relationship) by Conservative Central Office in spring 1976 to have nothing to do with CDP. In the autumn of 1976, the Birmingham project narrowly survived an attempt by the Tory-controlled council to close it immediately.
30 See, for example, the following extract from the March 1976 *Gateshead News*, a municipal journal, for one of the authorities which announced the establishment of its CCP in that month. The rhetoric has a familiar ring about it, six years after CDP set off: 'The new strategy proposed by the Government will be known as Comprehensive Community Programmes (CCPs). The CCP will attempt to bring together the efforts of both local and central government in a concerted drive to explain and reduce urban deprivation . . . A council spokesman said that it would mean Gateshead would be in a position to look at all the problems of urban deprivation and co-ordinate the activities of many organisations and activities involved. "We shall know exactly what the needs are, who is involved, and what action is needed. From there we shall be in a much better position to take the necessary action." '
31 Newcastle and Tynemouth (then North Tyneside) became Labour-controlled in 1974.
32 No. 21, August 1975.
33 For further information on this campaign, see *Noble Street and Norwich Place*, 2nd ed. (available from Benwell CDP, 87 Adelaide Terrace, Newcastle 4). Various editions of the *Noble News*, a tenants' newsletter, and a further report, *End of the Road for Noble Street*, are obtainable from the same address.
34 CDP IIU.
35 *Profits against Houses,* September 1976, CDP IIU.
36 *Jobs in Jeopardy,* June 1974, CDP IIU.
37 See, for example, *Tate & Lyle*, a case study published for the Liverpool CDP in 1975 which shows how Tate & Lyle have been using their profits and government subsidies from refinery operations in Britain to buy into other more profitable areas of investment, with a total disregard for local workers who are made redundant.
38 *The Costs of Industrial Change.*
39 *Aims of Industry*, April 1975, Newham CDP
40 *Workers on the Scrapheap*, February 1975, Birmingham CDP.
41 *Regional Capitalism or Local Socialism?* (forthcoming 1978), Benwell and North Tyneside CDPs.

Following the premature closure of the CDP IIU, most CDP publications are available from Benwell CDP, address given above.

4 Ideology and practice

Harry Salmon

Community workers are increasingly concerned with ideology, with the view of society which informs their thinking and directs their actions. It is this which provides the drive and inspiration for their work. Some practitioners become very 'precious' about ideology, and in their presence you feel the silent questions: 'Where does he stand? On what analysis does he base his work?' There is an evangelical intensity about them which we do not wish to emulate.

In this chapter, however, we do want to examine some of the broad assumptions, convictions and prejudices which go to make up our ideological perspective and then to see to what extent this is reflected in what happens in the field. Part of the exercise is an enquiry into the relationship between faith and works, ideology and practice. We venture the suggestion that the enquiry will show that the more radical the ideology, the less correlation there is between it and practice.

Community workers—their values and ideologies

In the early literature on community work, very little was said about ideology. You scan the indexes in vain for references on the subject. Often the nearest you get to it is in short sections on 'values'. In the 'non-directive' period it seems vulgar to refer to the worker's own perspective. He was supposed to be 'value free', a neutral agent who enabled others to express their values and ideologies untainted by the intrusion of a worker. Of course, this was always misleading. A worker cannot operate without transmitting some of his own values and assumptions about the society in which we live.

Between 1973 and 1975, a working party drawn from the ranks

of the Association of Community Workers produced a pamphlet[1] in which there was a clear recognition of the importance of ideology. Four ideological trends were identified which were described as conservative, socialist, liberal and anarchist. The distinctions were rough but at least they indicated the range of perspectives likely to be found in community work.

Early in 1977 the Gulbenkian Foundation's Advisory Committee on Community Work convened a one-day national conference in Birmingham. All the people who attended were in some way concerned with community work and many of them would have claimed to be practitioners, and yet the spectrum of ideologies represented was immense. There were members of the Conservative Party and exponents of Marxism, with every other political stance in between represented.

We might wish it was otherwise. We might feel that community workers should have a clear, unequivocal commitment to a socialist position which kept all of them left of the centre of the Labour Party! But it is not like that. ACW—which has rightly refused to make 'professional' status a criteria for membership—is not likely to introduce an ideological confession of faith as a condition of joining the Association.

R. Perlman and A. Gurin[2] assume on the part of those for whom they are writing a 'broad value commitment to solve problems of inequality and social and cultural deprivation'. This also implies an involvement in the process of social change and an ideological perspective which does not see the problems in terms of individual pathology or malfunctioning. However, even this commitment leaves a lot of room for ideological diversity.

One attaches 'labels' to groups of community workers with some hestitation, because you know from your own experience that values and ideologies change over a period of time. Positions are modified in the light of experience, interaction with other people and personal reflection. Therefore, we intend just to distinguish between two broad categories of people.

The first consists of those who are more inclined to express themselves in terms of *values* than of ideology. In fact, when some of them use the word 'ideology' it is likely to be in a mildly pejorative sense. Their emphasis is upon creating a 'better' community, on enabling people to achieve their 'full potential' in co-operation with others, on improving the 'quality of life'. Process is important and takes precedence over the end product.

'Self-help' projects are encouraged and when groups engage in some form of community action there is little attempt to set this in a broader political context. Again the emphasis is upon the 'learning' experience of the group and the development of new skills by members of it.

Of course, there is an underlying ideology, but it is given a low profile and is not made explicit. It is a liberal, reformist, humanitarian approach with subdued political overtones.

In his contribution to *The Sociology of Community Action*,[3] Paul Corrigan suggests that community workers are currently drawn from three main backgrounds. These are social work, the church and the working class. (This is a slight over-simplification, for sometimes the backgrounds overlap. I come, for instance, from the working class and the church.) Some of those who enter community work from social work or the church have, as he says, already been 'radicalised' and are 'spoiling for a fight with the State'. Many more, however, fall—initially at least—into the category we have been describing.

The second category consists of those community workers who clearly see problems of deprivation in structural rather than individual terms. Their ideology is usually Marxist or neo-Marxist. Inequality is seen as the out-working of an oppressive capitalist system which has produced the class structure of society. The emphasis—at least, theoretically—is on changing the system, on revolution rather than reformation.

Workers in this group talk about 'raising people's level of consciousness', the process of 'politicisation', 'conscientisation', about helping the victims of the system to see the nature of their oppression. 'Class politics' and not 'community politics' are the focus of attention.

If the Marxist community worker pushes his analysis far enough, he becomes caught up in what Paul Corrigan describes as 'the contradictions' of his position. He begins to see himself as part of the problem, an instrument of the oppressive capitalist system. Does he look for a new job? Or re-define his role? Or allow his practice to fall well behind his ideology?

What happens in practice?

There is a high level of consistency between what our first group of workers set out to achieve and what happens in the field. They experience little tension between their values and ideology on the one hand and what they are actually able to do on the other. Their aims are modest, and their methods—though not always understood —do not present any serious threat to those who hold power and dispense resources. Let us take an example.

Coventry in 1972 adopted a policy of establishing community schools. They began with two new comprehensive schools and have since extended the scheme to take in two other schools. Each school has some members of staff who are regarded primarily as community workers. They are answerable to a head of community activities and most of them fall into our first category. (Two or three who did not have either left or been promoted!)

In terms of their own goals and the aims of those who decided to set up community schools they have had considerable success. Large numbers of people have become members of the School and Community Association. It has its own council and nominates people to a governing body which includes pupils, parents and users of the community facilities. The community workers service groups which have formed around the interests of the members. Some of these are not school based. One worker is currently operating with a group which wants an adventure playground. He sees his work very much in terms of adult education. The group should develop the capacity to produce business-like letters, discover sources of finance, learn and negotiate with various departments of the local authority.

If you are a worker wishing to enable people to meet together to build up their confidence and to function as a group, and if you are wanting to bring about some incremental changes in a large institution, then you are in on a success story.

Numerous other examples come to mind where community workers are using their skills successfully to achieve objectives which are compatible with their own values, beliefs and view of society.

When we turn to our second group, however, the picture is rather different. The workers are caught up in agonising over 'the contradictions' in their position to which we have already referred. In addition, they have to resolve the tension between the limitations of being locality-based and yet seeing the macro-implications of the issues they are tackling.

David Corkey and Gary Craig,[4] in their chapter in this book, illustrate this problem very clearly. They also describe two brave attempts, in the field of housing and employment, to deal with it in a constructive way. It is difficult to define and to measure success when operating at these different levels but we would hazard a guess that achievements have been modest. Even if they have been more than modest, then they are exceptional and they have come about because of an unusual experiment promoted by central government and which is not likely to be repeated in a similar form. In spite of all their imperfections, the Home Office Community Development Projects have provided small groups of intelligent and politically aware workers with opportunities which do not normally befall community workers who usually operate singly rather than in teams.

Harry Specht,[5] in writing about the CDPs, draws attention to some of the discrepancies between what was professed and what eventually happened. He distinguishes between those project directors who classified themselves as 'national strategists'—eight out of twelve—and those who regard themselves as 'local strategists'. The strategies were shaped as much by ideology as by the actual situation, and in both instances there was a lack of consistency between ideology, analysis and practice. (In fairness it should probably be pointed out that some of the apparent inconsistencies might have been because of changes in orientation which took place during the time of the projects. Pieces of work initiated in the early days had to be kept going even though the ideological justification for them had gone.)

However, it is not only in major projects like these that the gap appears between faith and what actually happens in practice. In the autumn of 1975, in the face of growing unemployment, in a Midlands city a small group of people—mainly community workers and all holding to a socialist ideology—met to discuss in a critical way local and central government's feeble responses to the problem. They went on to sponsor an Unemployed Workers' Centre. This was serviced by two community workers who had a sound structural analysis and who were committed to operating at the level of working-class politics. As a bonus, one of the workers had union experience and links with the trades council. The management of the Centre was very soon in the hands of the unemployed, but the numbers involved were always small—five to twelve people. After some nine months another full-time worker employed through Job Creation began to operate at the Centre. Again, he was someone with a carefully thought out left-wing philosophy and considerable experience of working-class politics. From the beginning, no worker wanted the Centre simply to be an information and advocacy service. They were all committed to forging links with other working-class groupings—shop stewards' committees, the trades council, union branches, the labour movement, the unemployed in other areas—and an immense amount of effort was put into doing this. Newsletters were produced, the workers and the unemployed spoke at meetings, the dole queues were leafleted, research was carried out, but after eighteen months the Centre closed. There were only three or four activists left and the modest trickle of donations from other working-class organisations had dried up.

Looking back, one has to accept that no progress at all was made in achieving the ideologically determined goal of collective action around the issue of employment. There was not even any significant collective action around welfare rights. A considerable number of unemployed people did get help in obtaining the benefits to which they were entitled and some received guidance about further training opportunities. A few, by means of teach-ins, became able to find their way through the jungle of means-tested benefits. These were not, however, the goals which followed directly from the ideology of the sponsors or workers.

Readers can draw upon their own experience for further examples where attempts to put into practice a carefully worked out socialist ideology have produced a mouse. Of course, we can explain our ineffectiveness by blaming it on to the 'capitalist system'. After all, the capitalists have most of the trump cards. But this is hardly a constructive response. Committed socialists who are community workers need to reflect critically upon their definition of the job and upon the techniques which they employ. We are inclined to agree with Perlman and Gurin when they say, 'effectiveness in achieving objectives must become the object of analysis and research, rather than a matter of faith and conviction'.[6]

Why the gap between ideology and practice?

Some of the reasons for the gap are easy to identify. Whether or not we have taken them seriously enough in the past is open to question. Let us look at three of them.

The first is that the employing or funding body is unlikely to share the worker's commitment. In the mad rush at the end of the

1960s by authorities and voluntary agencies to appoint community workers, there was probably some excuse for workers imagining that a new age had been born—an age in which a group of workers would be answerable in the first place to the consumers of their services, second to their 'professional' standards and only third to their employers. There is no excuse any longer for community workers cherishing that hope. Employers are not prepared to give them unlimited freedom, and central and local government are not going to fund indefinitely workers who are seen as agents of unrest.

People on experimental projects are likely to have a little more space in which to operate than workers in established departments. Even in these cases—as those employed on the Home Office projects discovered—the freedom is more fictional than real. The sanctions are always in the background. The project can be stopped, the flow of funds can be reduced, reports can be rejected, and the experiment can be contained by the larger system.

Central and local government have to preserve the myth that those who are employed as civil servants and local government officers are apolitical. They are there to service their political masters with technical information and to carry out policy, not to make political statements or to engage in political activity as part of their work. Of course, we know that class values and political beliefs do influence the way in which civil servants and local government officers operate. The sin is to make it explicit. And that is exactly what many left wing community workers do. Their ideological bias is made obvious. No statutory body will tolerate that for long—particularly if the people in question are effective.

Community workers in most voluntary agencies are likely to be only marginally less restricted. Management committees are generally composed of middle-class liberals with little sympathy for an ideology which leads to a structural analysis of problems. In addition, the voluntary agency will be anxious to protect its relationships with those who provide the funds for its activities.

In both central and local government and in voluntary agencies you will find considerable commitment to the need for social change, but change seen in terms of refinements and improvements to the existing system, and not in terms of a radical re-ordering of things. The community worker who is seeking much more fundamental change and who derives his inspiration from Marx rather than the reformers is bound to be viewed with suspicion. He is certainly not going to be given unbridled freedom to put his beliefs into practice.

This is one of the dilemmas for the worker who is committed to revolutionary changes in society. He has to have a base from which to operate, but the base is likely to be within the system which he wants to change.

Perlman and Gurin refer to the problem which practitioners face in this respect. To be effective, a worker needs an organisational base. Besides, he has to have a livelihood. He can eschew established agencies, but, as Perlman and Gurin say, he simply exchanges the constraints of one system for those of another. The only other possibility is to become a kind of community work entrepreneur. Coventry Workshop is an attempt on the part of a collective of five workers committed to a socialist ideology to remain free from agency constraints. They seek to work with and to make their services available to sections of the working class. Their policy is collectively determined. Though they have freed themselves from the inhibiting influence of an agency, their life-span is uncertain because of their precarious financial position. The hope is that the organised sections of the working class will deem that the services of the collective are worth paying for and that they will be prepared to make a substantial financial commitment. However, it seems unlikely that money required in order to finance several such groups will be forthcoming, and therefore one has to conclude that it is not a model which can be replicated.

The second reason for a gap between ideology and practice is that most of the people with whom we are working do not share our ideological perspective. Many of them reject it. Some people would argue, of course, that there is no justification for outside intervention; that those who intervene are usually middle-class professionals with an ideological axe to grind. They are not really part of the working-class struggle and are diversionary in their activities. Tom Woolley argues this very cogently in his paper, *The Politics of Community Action.*[7] Paul Corrigan, however, produces a Marxist justification for intervention, which he treats as a political rather than as a moral problem.[8]

In this chapter we are not arguing but are assuming a case for intervention. We refer to it as an issue only because it affects the relationship between the worker and the people with whom he is working. Apart from any barrier created by the consumers' perceptions of the worker's employing body, the fact remains that he is not of the area. Most practitioners can—given time—get over these problems. But our experience is that most of the people with whom we work are quite selective in what they take from us. They will make use of our technical knowledge and skills but often quietly reject our ideology and strategy. The danger of activists manipulating people is not as great as we sometimes imagine. People have their own way of dealing with the revolutionary-minded worker. Often they give the impression of going along with his analysis only to ignore it once he has gone!

We have had some striking examples of this in working with disadvantaged groups. In some cases, very competent left-wing students on community work placements have operated intensively with a group for up to nine months. They have felt that some progress was being made. People in the groups were sharing their experiences of oppression and were beginning to link these to the wider experience of the working class. When the next worker has gone into the situation, he has found no evidence of a developing political consciousness. In referring to the previous worker, a likely comment would be 'He was a bit left wing but he was nice', or 'She was too political for me but she helped us to get started.'

These instances cannot be dismissed on the basis of the inexperience of students. There are also very few positive ripples left behind in the wake of even the most competent and ideologically committed teams of community development workers from the Home Office projects. Nor is the position necessarily better where the practitioners have been drawn from the local working-class community.[9]

The failure of left-wing community workers to transmit their ideology to those with whom they are working can be attributed to a number of things—the ineptness of the workers, the apathy of the people, the cleverness of the system, the absence of issues crucial enough, and so on. It could, however, be because people have an intuitive assessment of the situation which is more realistic than ours. Their impression is that revolutionary changes are not going to happen; that they live in a society which is going to proceed by a process of adjustment and accommodation; and that there is no point in expending too much time on lost causes. If they belong to Laurie Freedman's 'underclass',[10] then as he points out, they have little political status. The Labour Party is more concerned with the broad spectrum of workers in the middle, and the extreme left is more interested in those who are located strategically at the heart of production. It is not surprising, therefore, that the unemployed and the low paid choose not to become involved in working-class politics.

Those on the receiving end of community work intervention also thwart the worker's pursuit of ideologically defined goals in other ways. They have a habit of choosing issues which have nothing to do with the class structure of society or with capitalist exploitation of labour. So, for instance, the members of the school or community association in a deprived area may be more interested in discussing the bar than the way in which the school reinforces middle-class values, or haggle over conditions of membership while ignoring the fact that many children live in homes where there are no facilities for doing homework. The residents of an inner-city district choose to campaign for a community centre rather than for better housing, and a group of one-parent families give more priority to planning an outing to Blackpool than to pursuing their campaign on welfare rights. Who are we to challenge their priorities?

Caroline Polmear, in her chapter in this book,[11] brings us face-to-face with some of the frustrating value-conflicts which arise within neighbourhoods. They cannot all be described in class terms. At any rate, whatever the explanation, they exist and they have to be coped with by the worker. A lot of a community worker's time is taken up in dealing with interactional problems— the relationship between the grass-roots organisation and their employees, the tension between 'elitist' working-class members of a committee and representatives of the 'underclass', the dominating chairman who blocks progress, the secretary who does not tell everyone about the next meeting, the caucus who make undemocratic decisions. These are the kinds of distractions which continually arise.

The worker who sees all problems in structural terms might feel that it is inappropriate to become involved in difficulties over values and relationships. He cannot, however, ignore the theoretical and ideological controversies of the extreme left. These, too, inhibit action.

And so we have a third reason why there is a gap between ideology and practice. *It is that we have to function in the world of reality rather than in the world of ideas and dreams.* In practice we are compelled to adjust to things as they really are. We have to lower our sights and go for that which is attainable. The real world is no world for the ideological purist.

Jack Jones and Len Murray are—according to many of their statements—committed to greater equality and the protection of the interests of the low paid and those on pensions. But they have shop stewards on their backs who are worried about the erosion of differentials, and Clive Jenkins with his cohorts fighting for the working-class elite. Hugh Scanlon has to distinguish between the society he would like to see and the one in which he has to function. All are operating within a capitalist system, and the ideologists who think they know what should be done are usually very marginal to the system.

Community workers with a strong socialist ideology have to struggle with the frustrating, time-consuming difficulties which we have mentioned. They have to work with the material which is available and be prepared to face up to the problems which arise. Our impression is that quite a lot of workers spend a number of years fleeing from reality in search of an ideal base and a responsive constituency. Usually they find neither.

In writing about the constraints upon the community worker arising from his local milieu, we should probably go on to make a few comments about the macro-setting. None of us can dissociate ourselves from the influences and pressures emanating from the wider society in which we are operating.

The emphasis on finding the middle ground in politics has not helped those of us who are concerned with sharpening up the contrasts in society. The vast majority of citizens in this country are suspicious of those who talk about ideology, who refer to class differences and basic inequalities. Political fervour is no longer popular. Trevor Smith, in his contribution to *Direct Action and Democratic Politics*,[12] attributes the growth of protest to the diminution of political activity and the movement towards consensus planning. Of course, to say that this trend has been reinforced by the media is no doubt true, but it does not change the climate in which we operate.

In the mid-1970s there has been a resurgence of interest in political ideology, but it has been slight, considering the economic crisis through which we are living. The disturbing feature about this is that it has been more to do with the ideology of the right than of the left. Anyone who has been out canvassing for the Labour Party knows that it is the racialist ideology of the National Front which has captured some members of the working class. Again it is too simple to explain this as a capitalist plot to divide and rule.

This means that the left-wing community worker is operating in an unfavourable climate. The vast majority of the working class are more alienated than ever from traditional politics. They are understandably suspicious of anyone who seems to be using a situation to convey a political message. Many of them have been down blind alleys before.

Another factor which has made the community worker's task more difficult has been the drastic cuts in public expenditure which have been a feature of the mid- and late-1970s. Good Marxist theory would say that the cuts are a glorious opportunity to politicise the working class by showing that again they are the victims. In practice, however, it is not as simple as that. The effects of the cuts only gradually became apparent, and the unemployed and people on social security have been protected to some extent by the index-linking of benefits. It is the skilled working class and the middle class who feel that they are carrying the main burden of the economic crisis.

In addition, it is now harder for community workers to justify their intervening in some situations because they know that, in the short term, people have no chance of achieving quite proper and reasonable objectives. Many of the people living in blighted inner-city areas and on bleak estates sense this themselves and are little inclined to invest energy in what is, to them, obviously a fruitless exercise. If a community worker intervenes simply in the hope of making a political point, is this justifiable?

An accommodation between ideology and practice

In this final section, the question we want to tackle is whether or not it is possible to hold a socialist ideology and retain a commitment to community work.

Some would say it is not. Marjaleena Ropo[13] was employed by the City of Toronto as a community worker to operate in an urban renewal area. After six months she resigned. She continued to work in the same locality with the help of a grant from the Company of Young Canadians. Not only did she change employers but she changed her role. She ceased to operate as a community worker and instead became engaged in political education. Her critique of the 'liberal radical' approach is quite trenchant and her comments about the way in which middle-class interests dominate in localities which are not homogeneous in class terms are perceptive. Both experience and analysis led her to move outside community work.

In September 1975, *Case Con*[14] devoted itself to a very critical look at community work. The editorial posed the question whether there is such a thing as radical community work. On the whole, the issue conveyed the strong impression that there is not. Community work is seen as being diversionary, as distracting people's attention from the 'class struggle' and directing it towards the myth of 'participation'.

David Corkey and Gary Craig take the same line in chapter 3. They regard the activities of community workers as being a hindrance to the development of collective action by the working class.

We believe that these views are based upon an exaggerated notion of the positive and negative effects of intervention, a too rigid adherence to ideology and a failure to come to terms with the complexity of the real world. To argue that community work is inhibiting the development of working-class politics is to dart down a side road which leads nowhere. Community work is comparatively new. Who was diverting the working class from the real struggle before the community worker came along?

Before the practitioner feels that he has become part of the repressive capitalist system and abandons his role as a community worker, he needs to consider very carefully the direction in which he should move. It is easy to wander into another dead end or to be trapped in another capitalist snare or take the soft option and engage in endless research. He also needs to look critically at his ideology and at what he sees as constituting community work practice.

We would maintain that it is possible to hold a socialist ideology and to retain a commitment to community work. It is necessary to remember, however, that reality is always more complex than an ideology suggests. Daniel Bell's comment is pertinent: 'ideologists are terrible simplifiers. Ideology makes it unnecessary for people to confront individual issues in individual situations. One simply turns to the ideological vending machine, and out comes the prepared formula.'[15]

It is also important that we accept a number of facts.

In the first place, *we have to recognise the limitations of community work*. Some of us have never been too depressed by our modest achievements because we had never imagined that community work was going to change society. In the early days of community work and Community Development Projects, many workers saw themselves in almost a messianic role. They quickly became disillusioned. Juliet Cheetham and Michael Hill make the same point in a paper they contributed to the *British Journal of Social Work*. 'It is possible that the problems of living with the gap between his personal ideology and his working principles leads the community worker to hope for more from his activities than is realistic'.[16]

Harry Specht, in his address to the annual meeting of the Association of Community Workers in 1974,[17] drew a distinction between a social movement and a profession. He makes the point that community work has more in common with a profession than a social movement. To some of us this is an unpalatable proposition but one which we have to accept. Employers do not engage people to take part in either a social movement or political action. A community worker can participate in both, but primarily as a private individual. Obviously his involvement, his convictions, values and ideology will influence what he does as a community worker and, if he is a shrewd operator, then he will probably be able to create some space for himself within his employing agency. Community work on its own, however, can never promote revolutionary changes or capture the crusading spirit which pervades a social movement.

Second, *community work is not restricted to key political issues*. The ideology of the left is most clearly expressed in the issues which are taken up in the strategies which are adopted. Housing and employment, for instance, are clearly crucial both in personal and political terms: but they are not the only things which are of concern to working-class people. And even if you are dealing with housing and employment, sometimes long-term strategic aims have to be subordinated to short-term objectives. The political activist can focus exclusively upon those aspects of the economy where the inequalities resulting from the operation of market forces are most apparent and he can pursue a purely political strategy. The community worker cannot restrict himself in this way.

Sometimes he will be working with people around an issue where he is able to establish links between their own experience and that of other working-class people. He might even be able to link their residential experience of inequality with problems of insecurity within their workplace. But on other occasions he will be servicing people engaged in activities which have little to do with the more fundamental structural problems of our society. And there will be times when he will work with people on a basic issue like housing, but they will not move beyond the local problem of getting repairs done to the houses in their own street. To work with users of a community school to improve provision, or with one-parent families around nursery facilities, is not incompatible with a social-ist position and it is difficult to see how such work is likely to divert people from engagement in working-class politics.

This leads to a third fact. *The community worker operates with many different constituencies.* Some are more likely to respond to a political interpretation of their situation than others. A good community worker takes cognisance of the structural position of the groups with whom he is operating. He will recognise that a group of working-class women is less likely to take a strong polit-ical line than a residents' group containing men and women with trade union experience. A group of immigrants will have less con-fidence in pursuing the implications of a class analysis than a group of shop stewards.

A skilled practitioner is also alive to the interests, inclinations and potential of individuals. Some people are never going to be-come active in a political sense. Others are simply waiting for an opportunity to share in reflections on society and to become involved in collective action. A few are already active in working-class politics and only need to be supplied with information.

We remain unconvinced by the argument that community workers tend to defuse working-class action and to seduce working-class people into accepting the existing economic system. On the one hand, it exaggerates the impact a worker makes on an area, and, on the other, it assumes that the people who become involved in a whole range of community groups would otherwise become engaged in working-class politics. A few of them might, but many others would not. Some—not many—use the experience gained in one arena and apply it in another.

In addition, a community worker—particularly if he has a strong socialist commitment—is likely to have created a situation for him-self in which he is able to relate some of his work to wider political processes. He will be better able to justify this part of his work to his employers if he can show that he is working with a variety of groups and is not simply using his position to work out his own ideology.

Finally, *we need to accept that it is necessary to work in different contexts and at different levels.* Structural changes in our society will not come about as a result of the activities of any particular group. They will be achieved through complex processes which we will not be able fully to understand. Political activists, workers on the shop floor, radicals in the professions, community workers, writers and propagandists—all will make their contribution. There will have to be people operating at every level and in many different settings. Some of the factors which will precipitate the changes will probably be quite unforeseen.

The community worker has a part to play but it is a modest part. Most of his work will be at the micro-level and not all of it will contribute to the process of change. He will, however, have some opportunities of relating private ills to public issues, of linking locally experienced problems to national policies. Those practitioners who are wise will see the importance of creating links between people at different levels. The grass-roots worker has a job to do in keeping the visionary and the political activist earthed in reality. We need the contribution of Carole Polmear as well as that of David Corkey and Gary Craig. The socialist cause is not served by idealising the working class.

Any community worker—in fact, any professional—who professes a socialist ideology should be expressing his personal commitment through involvement outside his employment. It is a luxury to be able to use our job as a vehicle for our beliefs. Like other politically motivated people, we should be using our own time to work through either the trade union movement or a political pressure group. A job as a community worker is not a substitute for direct involvement as a private individual in the complex and confused task of striving for a more egalitarian and just society.

Conclusion

Let us summarise the drift of the argument.

It seems inevitable that a community worker with a strong commitment to a Marxist position will experience tension between what he believes and what he does. There is bound to be a gap between ideology and practice. His study of Marx will have informed him that people's lives are shaped by the economic system and the prevailing mode of production. In the field, however, he will be diverted into activities such as promoting participation in the local community school, helping residents to get marginal improvements in the environment, setting up a playscheme or an information centre. Agency, consumers and the total context in which he operates impose constraints and influence the kinds of projects in which he becomes involved.

The persistence of the gap between ideology and practice, rhetoric and action should prompt workers to examine carefully their ideological assumptions and also their expectations of community work. Ideology should not become absolute. It should be capable of re-formulation in response to current understanding and experience. It is equally important to have a realistic appreciation of the limitations both of yourself and of community work. In this way we avoid becoming emotionally drained and depressed by the constant contrast between high expectations and low achievement.

There is a tendency for Marxist community workers to underestimate the complexity of society in which they operate. Ideological bias means that experience in the real world is interpreted so that it will fit into the overall analysis. Reality is made manageable in terms of personal beliefs by oversimplification. Almost everyone who is ideologically committed does this. This means that the difficulties of putting our ideology into practice are not faced up to fully.

We agree, for instance, with Paul Corrigan, that it is important to relate people's own experiences of oppression to a wider class analysis. But community workers are short on the skills and techniques which would enable them to do this. He stresses the achievements of communist activists in other parts of the world. We have to ask why their achievements here have been so modest. Are there facts which we are either ignoring or interpreting in such a way that they fit into our preconceived scheme of things? Marx himself appeared to have been aware of the dilemma. The conditions seemed to be right, but the revolution did not come. In many working-class areas the quickest way for a community worker to alienate himself from his constituency is to refer positively to communists or communism. A National Front candidate is likely to poll more votes than a Communist! It does not solve the problem to say that it is because of the influence of the media which remains the mouthpiece of the dominant class.

The community worker cannot become purely a political activist. If he wants to be this, then he must ultimately seek alternative employment. He has, however, an opportunity to make some contribution to the task of establishing a socialist society. Even when his work is not directly related to key political issues, he is helping people to gain some experience of the potential of collective action. A large part of his work is likely to be in connection with working-class people's relationships to unhelpful institutions and large bureaucracies. If people become aware of the nature of such systems and acquire some confidence through collective action in confronting them, then that is a modest but useful step in working towards a society which is both socialist and more humane. In short, our assessment of the place of community work in relation to broader economic and political processes coincides in many respects with that of Jim Radford in chapter 6.

References

1 Association of Community Workers, *Knowledge and Skills for Community Work*, 1975, pp. 5—7.
2 *Community Organisation and Social Planning*, Wiley, New York, 1972, p. 271.
3 *The Sociology of Community Action*, Peter Leonard (printed by J. H. Brookes (Printers) Ltd, Hanley, Stoke-on-Trent, 1975), pp. 62—5.
4 See chapter 3.
5 *The Community Development Project: National and Local Strategies for the Delivery of Services*, National Institute for Social Work, 1976, pp. 19, 23, 31.
6 op. cit., p. 273.
7 *The Politics of Community Action*, 1972 (available from author at 8 Almond Place, Holytown-by-Motherwell, Lanarkshire).
8 op. cit., pp. 67—71.
9 T. Scoggins, 'An Experience in Neighbourhood Community Work', *Community Development Journal*, 11 (1), 1976, p. 36.
10 *The Politics of Radical Community Action*, ACW, 1974.
11 See chapter 7.
12 *Direct Action and Democratic Politics*, ed. Robert Benewick and Trevor Smith, Allen & Unwin, 1973, p. 307.
13 'The Fallacy of "Community Control" ', *Transformation*.
14 no. 20.
15 *The End of Ideology*, Collier Books, new rev. ed., 1962.
16 'Community Work: Social Realities and Ethical Dilemmas', *British Journal of Social Work*, 3 (3), 1973, p. 13.
17 *Community Development in the U.K.*, ACW, 1975, p. 4.

5 **Criticism and containment**

Martin Loney

This paper stems in part from a larger work on the role of the
Canadian state in financing the voluntary sector and indirectly
determining the paradigm within which the voluntary sector
operates.[1]

My purpose here is both to summarise some of the Canadian
findings, and to raise some questions about the autonomy of the
voluntary sector in Britain. My argument is properly situated
within the much larger debate about the nature and origins of the
Welfare State and the growth of corporatism in Western capitalist
societies. We are concerned with the questions which emerge as
the state seeks to resolve the underlying contradictions of capitalist
society through the involvement of previously independent organisations in the state system. We are also concerned with the significance of the state's role in providing employment to those who are
surplus to the needs of an economy which is unable to escape
'stagflation'.

The political dimensions of the Welfare State are now well
established. Titmuss, for example, argued[2] against the

> assumption that the establishment of social welfare neces-
> sarily and inevitably contributes to the spread of humanism
> and the resolution of social injustice. The reverse can be true.
> Welfare, as an institutional means, can serve different masters.
> A multitude of sins may be committed in its appealing name.
> Welfare can be used simply as an instrument of economic
> growth which, by benefiting a minority, indirectly promotes
> greater inequality.

In this paper we are concerned with a number of related questions.
The larger canvas is the growing role of the modern state in all
areas of social and economic activity. The paper explores some of
the implications of the increasing interdependency, both political

and financial, of the voluntary sector and the state apparatus. It examines the implications of state funding of the voluntary sector and the political and organisational paradigms this relationship may produce. The paper takes issue with the political assumptions on which many pressure-groups base their activities. In 1971 Michael Barratt Brown, reviewing the welfare state in Britain, wrote: 'Child Poverty Action, Housing Associations, Shelter, Care, and other groups have shifted *fundamentally* the grounds at least of the argument and increasingly of the policies pursued.'[3]

This paper argues in contrast that the new pressure-groups, like the old, operate firmly within a pluralist social democratic framework which does not challenge the dominant assumptions of the political debate.

The paper also explores some of the implications of the rapid increase in local voluntary organisations, officially sponsored participation strategies, and the use of community workers.

The area covered is both controversial and extensive. My objective is not to seek to establish a theoretical paradigm within which these events can be understood, nor to demonstrate definitively that financial and political reins hold the voluntary sector firmly and immutably in check. The object is altogether more modest: to raise a series of critical questions for those working in the social action field, which may lead to some fruitful debate, which in turn might contribute to a more effective and genuinely subversive radical practice.

Citizen participation in Canada

Historically the Canadian state was not particularly active in the social field. Leo Panitch in his analysis of the development of the Canadian state argued 'in terms of legitimation the State's role has *not* been comparatively active, imaginative or large . . . In terms of concrete State activities . . . directed at the integration of the subordinate classes in capitalist society either through the introduction of reforms which promote social harmony or through the co-option of working-class leaders'.[4]

In the 1960s the Canadian public sector underwent a relatively dramatic shift, influenced by a number of factors. Federal revenue rose from $7,323,000,000 in 1963 to $15,528,000,000 in 1970. In the same period the accession of Pierre Trudeau to the leadership of the ruling Liberal Party, with his much publicised commitment to the 'Just Society', increased the influence of reform elements in the Federal government. The radicalisation of some elements of the population stimulated by the war in Vietnam and the rediscovery of domestic poverty and racism—directed predominantly against the indigenous native population—produced a cadre of organisers and a growing discontent amongst some of the poor and ethnic minorities. This increased the number of demands on the Federal government which the reform Liberals were ready to meet. There were also a growing number of civil servants, themselves occasionally on the periphery of the radical movement, who sought to make the system more democratic and egalitarian. These civil servants, who might usefully be called the 'go-betweens', made a conscious effort to bring government resources to the aid of radical youth and other disaffected groups and to involve some of the leadership of these groups in government programmes.

There were also others in government whose strategy was more Machiavellian. For them government largesse was a weapon to be used to aid their friends and debilitate or attack their enemies. A clear example of this was the decision to fund the Black United Front (BUF) of Nova Scotia which brought together some of the different groups in a black population, largely ignored and overwhelmingly disadvantaged, which have been in that province for over 200 years. Support for the group, which was to amount to over half a million dollars, was urged in a memorandum to the cabinet of 16 June 1969. The memorandum, signed by the Secretary of State and the Minister of Health and Welfare, urged financial support for BUF *inter alia* because 'agitation which began last fall injected the potential for racial unrest and perhaps violence such as had been seen in similar situations in the United States'. BUF was seen as representing 'a constructive and moderate element within the black community of Nova Scotia', while 'the failure of this organisation will result in the discrediting of these elements and the shift of power to more extreme elements'.

The effect of granting funds to the BUF was to entrench the position of the conservative black leadership and to provide them with both the patronage and the credibility to undercut the militant element. BUF not only ensured that mainstream black politics was directed away from broader political and social questions, but also provided a useful buffer, since black militants were now compelled to confront first BUF and only then the Provincial and

Federal governments. The first year after the grant was received, BUF's exclusive offices were occupied by black youth protesting, among other things, about the £10,000 salary paid to BUF's first director.

Such Machiavellianism was the exception. More generally the availability of funds, the commitment to the 'Just Society', and the decision to involve previously excluded groups in decision-making combined with growing activity at the grass roots to produce a rapid acceleration of government activity. The scale of the change is indicated by two sets of figures. A study undertaken for the Canadian Council on Social Development of 304 non-government agencies in thirteen Canadian cities found that government funding rose from $9,578,115 in 1962 to $51,467,044 in 1972. In 1962 government funding accounted for 45 per cent of these agencies' budgets and in 1972, 64 per cent.[5] The two departments most centrally involved in the new thrust—the Department of the Secretary of State and the Department of National Health and Welfare—underwent dramatic expansion. Between 1968 and 1972, the number of employees in the Department of the Secretary of State increased by 100 per cent; in the same period the increase in the staff of the Department of National Health and Welfare was 350 per cent.[6]

Job creation schemes initiated by the Department of Manpower and Immigration supplemented other government funds available for the amelioration of social problems. The ease with which well-informed low-income groups could obtain government funds led to the situation in Montreal where the local employment exchange was referring people to the Greater Montreal Anti-Poverty Movement for jobs. Indeed, the added factor of separatism made Quebec a particularly favoured recipient of government funds. One consequence of this has been the subsequent decision by some low-income organisations in that province to reject any further federal funding in order to avoid co-option.

At the local level, government funds have a mixed effect on recipient organisations. On the one hand, the funds facilitate group activity and effectiveness. On the other, the source of the funding may reduce the autonomy of the group. Groups which receive government funds may find their original goals both re-formed and displaced, as they seek to accommodate their programme to funding categories. Funded groups become increasingly dependent on the sponsoring agency to the detriment of

internal democracy and control. Low-income groups are particularly vulnerable to this displacement. A grass-roots anti-poverty
organisation which seeks government funding might proceed
through five phases:

(1) the group comes into existence with a generalised commitment to improve the lot of the poor;

(2) in order to obtain government funding, this commitment
must be programmatic, for example the group will seek funds to
open an office and run a Welfare Rights Information Service;

(3) the receipt of funding produces a division in the organisation
between those who now become full-time workers and other
members who retire to a peripheral position, reinforced by the
idea that 'they're getting paid to do it; why should we work for
free?';

(4) the core group ceases to be dependent on grass roots involvement, since the future programme, as it is now defined, depends
on satisfying the funding agency;

(5) the group becomes an adjunct of the existing Social Services.
Grass roots involvement is minimal.

Not all groups necessarily pass through these stages, but the broad
outline should be familiar to anyone who has observed the process.

Loss of autonomy and a subtle shift in direction is not inevitable.
Some groups use government funds to build combative grass roots
organisations, but these tend to be the exception. In Canada the
fate of such groups has frequently been the denial of government
funds. In Hamilton, Ontario, the Welfare Rights Group used Health
and Welfare funding to create a militant opposition to the inadequacies and injustices of the welfare system, much to the anger of
municipal and provincial politicians. In terminating their funding
in 1971, John Munroe, the Hamilton MP and Health and Welfare
Minister, advised them:[7]

> continuing alienation of the larger Hamilton population by
> the use of militant tactics and radical rhetoric will only cause
> the city's low income residents to lose public support for the
> progressive reforms . . . which they require, and for which
> they have called on urgently . . . Confrontation tactics by
> people on Welfare do not work, they alienate Canadians who
> are asked to support those less fortunate than themselves.

The Company of Young Canadians (CYC) established in 1965

as a government-financed social change agency provided perhaps the most dramatic example of the limits of government tolerance. 'You will be asked', the Canadian Parliament was told, 'to approve the establishment of a Company of Young Canadians, through which the energies and talents of youth can be elicited in projects for economic and social development . . . in Canada.'[8] The Company of Young Canadians was to be based on the recruitment of 'volunteers' who were to be paid a subsistence salary plus $50 per month honorarium paid out at the end of a two-year contract. At the peak of the Company's activities in 1968, there were 225 volunteers, mainly engaged in community-organising activities with groups which included tenants, ethnic minorities, welfare recipients and unorganised workers. The aims and principles adopted by the first CYC council included 'a society in which people are in charge of their own destinies' and a commitment to 'support projects which will, hopefully, help to alleviate causes of problems and will not simply "bandage" a symptom.'[9]

It is now part of the historical record that to the extent that CYC volunteers actually sought to place people 'in charge of their own destinies', they encountered intense hostility, and that in Quebec, the most politically sensitive Canadian province, the Company was accused by the chairman of the City of Montreal's Executive Committee, of terrorism and subversion. This accusation led to a parliamentary enquiry and the removal of political power from the hands of the Company's volunteer employees into the hands of government appointees. In 1976 the Company was finally closed down.

Generally, the process of government funding is not characterised by dramatic controversy, but it is important to remember, that, as one researcher put it:[10]

> the grant is provided because it fits into the general social scheme of the grantor . . . if the government's policies are to encourage innovations within the social services, grants will reflect this; if the policies are to suppress change or merely to maintain stable norms, grants will similarly be reflective of these policies.

A grant officer in the Canadian Department of Health and Welfare summarised the effect on the recipient organisations thus:[11]

> the objectives of programmes change as soon as they get money—they tend to shift in accordance with the outlines

laid down in the funding process. They have to start making compromises when they get government money. They just can't cope. This is a condition of being funded.

The politics of pressure groups

The Canadian government also provides funds to a number of national pressure groups. The Canadian Council on Social Development, which portrays itself as an independent grouping, received only 10 per cent of its $1,000,000 1971 income from individuals and groups, the bulk of the remainder coming from different levels of government. The Council frequently appears as a critic of government policies, but its criticism falls within a very narrow range. Noticeably excluded from any of the Council's publications are theories of society which suggest an underlying structural critique. Miliband has argued: 'it is the capitalist context of generalised inequality in which the state operates which basically determines its policies and actions . . . the state in these class societies is primarily and inevitably guardian and protector of the economic interests which are dominant in them.'[12] More specifically, Miliband has argued:[13]

> the fact that governments accept as beyond question the capitalist context in which they operate is of absolutely fundamental importance in shaping their attitudes, policies, and actions in regard to the specific issues and problems with which they are confronted. The general commitment deeply colours the specific response, and affects not only the solution envisaged for the particular problem perceived, but the mode of perception itself; indeed, ideological commitment may and often does prevent perception at all, and makes impossible not only prescription for the disease, but its location.

This description could equally be applied to the Canadian Council on Social Development. The objective of the Council is not confrontation with government, but collaboration; not a root-and-branch critique of the class inequalities and injustices which characterise Canadian society but a piecemeal description of some particular facets of poverty. As two critics of the Council note: 'one reason we may assume the Council has done well, therefore, from a financial perspective, is that its research and criticism of government has dealt with administrative details rather than fundamental issues.'[14]

This attention to administrative detail and to particular programmes, rather than to a fundamental study of the roots of inequality and poverty, strives to appear non-partisan and value free,
but such 'pragmatism' remains essentially conservative. The
Council and other similar institutions serve to maintain the dominant social democratic paradigm, and confine the debate within
its boundaries.

When debate threatens to overstep those boundaries, the Council
stands ready to step in to restore the paradigm. Faced with the
minor uproar which greeted its Green Paper on Immigration, the
Canadian Department of Manpower and Immigration turned to
the Council with offers to finance the sounding of views on the
Paper from across the country. In announcing the project, Council
director Reuben Baetz said: 'we have heard the most emotional
and most radical views on the immigration and population policy
. . . we must ensure that the loudest voices are not the only voices
heard.'[15] In short, it was time to hear from that old stand-by, the
silent majority.

The British experience

British government involvement in promoting and aiding the
voluntary sector would not appear to be as far advanced as in
Canada. To some extent this must reflect the relatively more
stringent economic circumstances of Britain, and also the fact that
the traditional political structure, particularly the Labour Party
and trade union movement, are, in spite of the relatively moribund
state of the former, able to provide the cohesive and integrative
channels which are needed for effective government. At the local
level, English-speaking Canada has no equivalent to the Labour
Party and the trades councils. The trade union movement has, by
British standards, a relatively narrow focus, while the social democratic New Democratic Party has never had the strength of its
British equivalent.

None the less the decline of the British Labour Party[16] and the
accelerating inner city crisis have increased grass roots discontent
and the need for the state to create new devices for securing consent, and strengthen existing ones. The Houghton Committee has
proposed that the major political parties might be funded in part
from tax revenue. The Labour Party is thus able to continue to
ignore the demands of its own rank and file, secure in the know-

ledge that tax revenue will more than compensate for the loss of disillusioned individual members. This move will further strengthen the position of the Party leadership and is paralleled by the sizeable EEC grant which will be made available to the major parties to contest elections to the European Parliament. The state has also assumed a far more active role in relation to the voluntary sector. By 1977 there were few national voluntary organisations which were neither candidates for, nor recipients of, government funding. Even the National Council for Civil Liberties, watchdog for the individual's rights, has broken a forty-year tradition and accepted government financing through the Equal Opportunities Commission. The independence of other pressure groups from the state has become questionable.

The British pressure groups: struggling for consensus

The Child Poverty Action Group was established in 1966 by concerned academics and welfare workers, backed by money from the Rowntree Trust, to promote 'action for the relief, directly or indirectly, of poverty among children or families with children'. The group now receives a significant part of its finance from the Home Office Voluntary Services Unit, which in 1977 provided £4,600,000 in funds to the voluntary sector.

CPAG's relationship with the state and the elite is not one that would be expected of an organisation which puts itself forward as a hard-hitting champion of the poor. In the early 1970s CPAG anticipated future financial problems. Rowntree prefer to support the establishment of new groups rather than tie their resources up in sustaining existing groups. This maximises the impact that the Rowntree Trusts have in the voluntary sector. Rowntree money gets things going, and other trusts, individuals or the government sustain the project. This policy has however created considerable difficulties for some groups. CPAG appears to have sought a solution to their funding problems by deliberately courting government support at the highest political level. At the time the Conservative Party were in office, and CPAG director Frank Field was able not only to secure a commitment at the *political level* to back CPAG through the Voluntary Service Unit but, when the Tories were forced into a surprise election, to obtain a letter from Lord Windlesham, Minister of State at the Home Office, confirming the intention to support CPAG and thereby effectively committing a successive government to implement the promise. A three-year Voluntary Service Unit grant was awarded in 1974 by a Labour Home Secretary.

CPAG then started a search for more permanent funding. CPAG treasurer, millionaire Gary Runciman, who combines an academic career at Cambridge with an active involvement in his family's shipping interests, set about establishing an endowment trust with a quarter-million-pound target. The objective of the trust was to raise a sizeable sum privately through individual or corporate donations before going public. In fact, the initial returns were disappointing but the appeal became public in 1976.

What is of interest about the appeal is that an organisation directed to the elimination of poverty should be willing and able to seek its funds from the rich and powerful. This is indicative both of the organisation's view of society and its public image. No doubt the proclaimed commitment of its director to a 'thriving private sector',[17] and his controversial support for the sale of council houses, has helped to maintain a suitably moderate image for CPAG.

CPAG's involvement with government is not limited to funding. Brian Abel-Smith, one of the key figures in founding CPAG, is now senior political advisor to the Secretary of State for Health and the Social Services. Tony Lynes, first CPAG director, is also a DHSS political adviser. David Piachaud, an LSE academic who collaborated closely with Frank Field, served in the Cabinet office. Yet despite these links and the generally acknowledged sophistication of CPAG's research and campaigning, poverty is, according to CPAG, getting worse. Even its director has talked of the group's 'failure'.

In fact, of course, there are a number of factors involved in the persistence and intensification of poverty, but CPAG's failure to have a significant impact must raise doubts as to the viability of its incremental change model. In documenting, analysing and proposing reforms to tackle particular aspects of poverty, CPAG eschewed any attempt to come to grips with any particular theory of society which might account for poverty.

Jane Streather, who was its deputy director from 1972 to 1975, comments: CPAG has always resisted a holistic critique of poverty in favour of a series of piecemeal approaches'.[18] In part this was no doubt a function of its middle-class membership, as Bill Jordan has argued that the kinds of reforms sought by CPAG would not be the kinds which claimants themselves would put forward: 'they would tend to press for some form of guaranteed income . . . that would not have to be crawled and grovelled for at the feet of a bureaucratic overlord'.[19] Equally, there is no doubt that its leadership is committed to a pluralist view of society in which incremental reform can be precipitated by well-researched documentation and sustained lobbying. This activity is congenial to the government, providing to some extent a relatively cheap source of outside research and comment, and acceptable to funding trusts, who are themselves commited to consensual politics facilitated by more effective 'communication'.[20]

National pressure groups which concentrate on feeding criticism into the existing political and bureaucratic system may deflect attention from the need for grass roots organising. One academic investigator commented on CPAG: 'the danger is such that academic debate becomes a substitute for organising the poor'.[21]

The Campaign Against Racial Discrimination (CARD) rejected grass roots organising in the immigrant communities in favour of respectability and influence in the corridors of power: 'the promotional route was seen as incompatible with the organisation of immigrant communities', yet in the end, the corridors of power proved meaningless since the illusion of power was not the same as power itself. There was no base in the immigrant communities from which C.A.R.D. could either try to speak or try to bargain.'[22] As Britain tightened immigration controls, CARD was powerless to resist or to take action to achieve effective anti-discrimination legislation. If there is a basic consonance of interest between government and the lobby group, no doubt reform and agreement are possible; if not, lobbying is a dubious tactic and a questionable substitute for the grass roots organising which could bring political muscle to support demands.

Our purpose here is not to enter into an extensive debate about the effectiveness of CPAG or other national pressure-groups but rather to raise questions about the funding patterns of such groups and the political paradigms within which they operate.

The constraints of outside financing are not restricted to government funding. Pressure-groups which deal with the problems faced by the poor or disadvantaged sectors, but rely on more privileged sectors for financial support, will reflect the ideology of the latter rather than the former. The activities of charitable trusts controlled by the corporate elite is of key importance in shaping the voluntary sector. The decisions of Rowntree, Gulbenkian or Cadbury which, like all the decisions of private capital, have no public accountability, are a matter of life and death for many voluntary organisations. The organisations and individuals they sponsor prosper; those they reject may die out. Given the source of their wealth, the nature of the ideological commitment of the trust's executors hardly requires spelling out.

Shelter, for example, which is not financed by government, has found its political activities conditioned by its financial base. Reliant upon affluent middle-class home-owners for much of its income, Shelter is deterred from a radical critique of the existing system of housing provision by the commitment of many of its donors to individual home-ownership, tax relief on mortgages and their belief in the benefits of a healthy private sector. This is not to argue that Shelter has therefore allowed its policies to be narrowly determined by middle-class interests and prejudices, but rather to point out that these must remain an important factor in Shelter's strategy. Patrick Seyd in his analysis noted that in emphasising 'public rather than private housing Shelter has come into conflict with many of its individual supporters who happen to be owner-occupiers and mortgagees'.[23]

One issue which demonstrated the sensitivity of Shelter and the much more explicit strings which may be attached to some funding is the minor uproar which followed the publication in 1976 of *The Great Sales Robbery* by the independent Shelter Community Action Team (SCAT). The pamphlet was sponsored by a number of local community groups, trades councils and local constituency Labour Parties. The pamphlet, an attack on the sale of council housing, suggested among other things that council workers involved in the sale of council houses might go slow, or black, sales. The pamphlet also talked of the 'struggle for a socialist society' and the need to 'demand the nationalisation of all land, and effective public control of the banks and financial institutions together with the construction and building industry'.

When the pamphlet came to the attention of Horace Cutler, the then leader of the Tory Opposition on the GLC, he immediately wrote to the sponsoring organisations asking them to dissociate themselves from what he first called the 'illegal' and subsequently the 'subversive' proposal to black or go slow on council-house sales. He argued that this was an attack on the democratic process.[24] The sponsors, including the North Southwark Community Development Group, refused to repudiate the pamphlet. North South-wark wrote back: 'there is nothing in the report which we wish to repudiate; on the contrary, we publicly affirm our support for the contents of the report and the wider campaign to protect and extend council housing'.[25] Cutler replied threatening, implicitly, to oppose further public funding of the group: 'Since you will not repudiate this suggestion I take it (and I will make it publicly known) that you favour erosions of our democratic traditions. What is more you will receive support after next May neither from the GLC nor from any other organisation which I am able to influence'.[26] Such a threat carried little weight with the North Southwark Group, which is an effective and firmly based com-munity group with a sophisticated understanding of local politics, and more particularly the planning industry. In any case, the group receives no GLC support.

Cutler's threat did, however, cause more concern at the Associ-ation of London Housing Estates (ALHE) which is heavily depend-ent upon financial support from the GLC. While the ALHE refused to recant publicly, a great deal of internal controversy and conflict followed Cutler's letters.

Cutler was not the only one to attack the pamphlet. The *Daily Telegraph* called editorially for an investigation by the Charity Commissioners, who in fact did request information from Shelter, which provides part of SCAT's funds.[27] Lord Soper, Chairman of Shelter's trustees, used Shelter's 10th anniversary rally to warn SCAT:[28]

> we cannot permit the use of money raised with such dedica-
> tion by our supporters for the promotion of a particular
> ideology. Shelter must inevitably be involved in the political
> debate on housing policy but must not be seen to be associ-
> ated with any one party . . . we have had to ask SCAT for a
> written assurance that no further documents of this kind will
> be produced . . . if such an assurance is not forthcoming then
> Shelter projects committee will have to reconsider whether
> the grant promised to SCAT this year can be paid.

Strangely, these same strictures on the need to remain political but not partisan did not apply to Shelter's subsequent request, early in 1977, to the Liberal Party to keep Labour in office, in order to save Stephen Ross's Bill on the homeless. Others in Shelter privately advised SCAT staff that their argument could be made equally by talking of 'the fight for social justice' rather than 'the fight for socialism'. A point which is rather disingenuous, since, while the latter calls for the structural transformation of society, the former would appear to be more of a state of mind, or at least an opinion.

None of this is to suggest that all national groups with elite or state funding are inevitably hopelessly constrained. Some of the local projects funded by Shelter engage in effective grass roots organising to compel structural change, and the crack of the financial whip is not always heeded. Some individuals within the larger pressure-groups attempted to propagate more radical critiques. But it is important at least to analyse critically the world within which the pressure-groups operate and the role they play. Gouldner wrote[29] of liberal sociology as

> the new ombudsman sociology, whose very criticism of
> middle level welfare authorities and establishments serves as a
> kind of lightning rod for social discontent, strengthening the
> centralized control of the higher authorities, and provides
> new instruments of social control for the master institutions.

It is at least an open question as to whether that might not be an apt description of many of our national pressure groups which deal with social issues.

Those groups which have decisively rejected the dominant value assumptions from the outset, such as Radical Alternatives to Prison, or have shifted drastically to the left, like the Institute of Race Relations, have found difficulty not only in raising funds but in getting anything other than unfavourable attention from the media and decision-makers.[30]

Thomas Mathiesen, a Scandinavian criminologist who has been actively involved in the prison movement, has attempted to provide an avenue out of this impasse in *The Politics of Abolition*, which develops the concept of the unfinished.[31] He defines the task of those seeking fundamental and genuine social change as the explication of an idea which will both compete with and contradict existing practice. The revolutionaries who demand from the outset the destruction of bourgeois society can be dismissed as irrelevant to the debate about a particular social policy issue since, it will be argued, they are really concerned with other issues. But the revolutionary who concentrates on the detailed critique of the failure of bourgeois society to attain bourgeois values—equality of opportunity, equality before the law, the abolition of poverty, the rule of reason—and demands the abolition of repressive measures inconsistent with those values, cannot be so easily dismissed, yet the realisation of those values would, in itself, be revolutionary. The debate must be entered into and conducted in a manner which simultaneously challenges the domain assumptions of the ruling decision-makers and the media without allowing them to exclude the critic from the debate. In addressing any particular issues the key step is to pose the question in such a way as to point to the inter-relationship between that issue and the larger society, and, in so doing, raise basic questions about the organisation of that larger society.

Controlling the grass roots

Grass roots organisations, often lacking either the sophistication or the diversification of funding which characterise the national pressure-groups, are potentially subject to much greater financial control. Often such control is institutionalised, as in the case of Urban Aid. Anxious to avoid the conflict between nationally-funded groups and local government which had characterised the American War on Poverty, the architects of the British Urban Programme determined that all applications for Urban Aid should be funded through the local authority which would establish priorities. This not only gives the local authority the key role in sponsoring local projects but also permits subsequent reconsideration. The Home Office provides 75 per cent of the funds, often for up to five years; the remaining 25 per cent comes from the local authority which may review the expenditure as part of its annual review.[32]

Law centres, settlement projects, community relations councils, advice centres and tenants' associations have all run into conflicts over funding. In Liverpool the Vauxhall Law Centre's support for housing cases taken against the local authority resulted in an announcement by Liverpool Council that the centre would be closed. Only a prolonged campaign which diverted work from other issues kept it open.[33]

There have been numerous conflicts around local community relations councils which reflect the deep divisions created by racial conflict over scarce resources and the willingness of local politicians to use racism for electoral advantage. Renewal of local CRC grants is often controversial. In Lewisham the 1977 grant was not opposed by the Tory Opposition, but the Conservative Deputy Leader wanted to 'sound some warning bells'. Another Tory councillor accused the CRC of giving 'only the views of life seen from the West Indian point of view'. This and a subsequent funding issue were sufficiently heated to cause a 30-minute adjournment on a Labour motion to protest against the 'filth' which the Tories had spoken.[34]

Frequently local CRCs have come under attack from black organisations which have accused them of being more concerned with 'the absorption and negation of black discontent' than with fighting racism.[35] In most areas the Indian Workers' Association has refused to co-operate with the CRCs. As race has become an increasingly important and controversial political issue, the mediating role envisaged for the CRC became a difficult one to fulfil. To retain any credibility with ethnic minorities, CRCs frequently had to pursue policies which brought them into conflict with the more neanderthal local councillors.

While funding constraints are frequently implicit, Westminster Council have made theirs explicit. The Pimlico Neighbourhood Aid Centre and the 510 Centre were required to give written undertakings to the Council before grants could be made. These undertakings committed the funded staff not to support or assist squatting activities or engage in party political activities. The staff were also obliged to agree 'that the workers and Committee at the Centre will not, whilst acting in their official capacity, take sides in contentious political issues and will do their best to ensure that clients and client groups do not use the premises or facilities for one-sided political activity.' The Westminster Council, which provides only a minority of the Centre's funds, thus seeks to use them to determine the acceptable parameters for the whole Centre and explicitly to use employees to control voluntary groups who may step into what the Council calls 'contentious issues'. Since it is difficult to find a more avid defender of the interests of rich residents and property developers than Westminster Council, the Council view of 'contentious' can be imagined. Indeed, the restrictions on the Centre's activities were reportedly introduced after the local Conservative agent had seen a poster in the Pimlico Centre window calling for more nursery provision. On detailed examination it turned out that this subversive demand was being propagated by the Communist Party, who had issued the poster.

At one level, the results of the Council's restrictions are simply ridiculous. A poster in one of the Centres advertising: 'A . . . Festival of Music' turns out on closer inspection to have the word 'Socialist' blanked out. The Centre workers are aware of the need to be more cautious in the issues that they and the Centres publicly support. They also recognise the danger, not only that tactical considerations may lead to them using a different address, or sponsoring committee for a particular campaign, but also that slowly the thrust of the Centres can be blunted and distorted, as a consequence of their caution over funding.

It could be argued that in fact Westminster's requirement is quite legitimate, and that Council funds should not finance partisan politics. The major flaw in this argument is simply that the status quo is never seen as political or contentious—only change is controversial. Hence activities which sustain the existing social order are approved; those which challenge it are excluded. Beneath an apparently impartial principle lies a considerable political bias.

The pressure on council-funded organisations does not always come from Conservative councillors. In Islington, where the ruling Labour Party are proud of their support for voluntary organisations (even those in conflict with the council), Islington People's Rights had an economic rent imposed on the building they were using after Councillor Baylis had attacked them for harbouring *Gutter Press* (a local militant community paper), and giving advice to squatters.

This is not to argue that local groups can survive only by becoming council lackeys. Clearly, councils prefer local groups which concentrate on service provision or activities which support council policy, but councils ultimately have to secure electoral consent. Just as the development of the Welfare State can be seen both as a means to socialise and control an emerging working class, and as a victory of the working-class struggle for reforms, so growing citizen participation is both a necessity for the governing institutions and a victory for local militancy. Concretely, coucil funding may be granted as a result of local pressure and may be retained, after a controversy, as a result of a successful fight against the council.

Cynthia Cockburn has put the argument succinctly:[36]

> by the 1970s . . . those caught in the poverty of the inner cities became more disorderly and even more militant. The state was forced to extend outwards its management concerns. To the preoccupation with budgets and plans was

added another: managing people and their relation to authority. Offers of 'participation' were made to render more
acceptable the actions of the state. Community work was
interposed to meet and manage the spontaneous expressions
of popular unrest. But these very measures also made the local
state vulnerable to working-class militancy.

It is not possible to explore all the dynamics of funding which
occur and the attendant organisational and political paradigms
which happen at a local level. Our concern is rather to focus attention on the question, to suggest that the consequences run very deep,
and to urge community workers to a more sophisticated awareness.
The annals of history are already well stocked with accounts of
those who have been led from the political wilderness to the
centres of power by the carrot of state largesse, without achieving
any significant social changes—except in their own life-styles.

Two final questions are worth raising. The first is the way in
which funding sources might influence not simply the content of
the programmes offered but, more subtly, their type. The provision
of money for neighbourhood work, but generally speaking not for
issue organising, may serve, for example, to direct settlement work
into channels which are intrinsically more conservative in terms of
the demands raised and the levels of consciousness attained.
Organising around issues leads more readily to macro-criticisms of
the socio-economic system than does geographically-based organising. Second, no matter how combative local groups may be, the
British political system has been remarkably immune at the local
level to the emergence of 'independent reform slates' aiming to
take over local government. There are many reasons for this, but
the growing dependency of local groups on council financing must
be a strong deterrent to action which directly challenges the existing party political structure. In Lambeth, the local council established neighbourhood councils with their own community work
resources, and Urban Aid has funded many citizens' groups. The
level of discontent with the council is, justifiably, high. The Conservative opposition and the controlling Labour group offer little
choice. Yet the question of forming a new political force to run
for council does not seem to have been seriously considered. To
ask how much this may have to do with the old prescription against
biting the hand that feeds is not to impugn the integrity of those
involved, but rather to suggest that pressures are both pervasive
and subtle.

Conclusion

As the state increasingly moves to corporatism in an attempt to manage society, it requires greater and greater citizen participation. The choice which the state faces is between more sophisticated strategies to secure consent or more overt and comprehensive coercion. The growth of community work, the encouragement of local voluntary activity and the establishment of discreet mediating institutions such as the local CRCs are a part of this larger development, as is the increasing incorporation of the trade unions into the governing structure. But, as the social contract fails to contain the real contradictions between capital and labour, so participation remains a two-edged sword.

The conclusion of this paper is not that the power of capital is all-pervasive, that outside funding is invariably corrosive, or that participation strategies are inherently co-optive. The argument is rather that in being aware of these tendencies we can more effectively counteract them. Elite money can, at least in the short term, be used against the elite, government funding can be fought for and retained for an effective radical programme, and participation can be used to unmask the present system and accelerate the pace of action against it.

Notes

1 'Political Economy of Citizen Participation', in L. Panitch, ed., *The Canadian State, Political Economy and Political Power*, University of Toronto Press, 1977.
2 R. Titmuss, 'The Limits of the Welfare State', *New Left Review*, 27, September–October, 1976, p.33.
3 'The Welfare State in Britain', in R. Miliband and J. Saville, eds, *Socialist Register 1971*, Merlin, 1972, p. 25 (my emphasis).
4 'The Role and Nature of the Canadian State', in L. Panitch, ed., op. cit.
5 N. Carter, *Trends in Voluntary Support for Non-Government Social Service Agencies*, The Canadian Council on Social Development, Ottawa, 1974, p. 9.
6 D. Rosenbluth, 'The Effects of Government Funding on Community Associations', unpublished MA thesis, Carleton University, Ottawa, 1973, p. 33.
7 *Globe and Mail*, Toronto, 9 December 1971.
8 Speech from the Throne, 5 April 1965.
9 I. Hamilton, *The Children's Crusade*, Peter Martin Associates, Toronto, 1970, pp. 8–9.
10 D. Rosenbluth, op. cit., p. 24.
11 ibid., p. 50.

12 R. Miliband, *The State in Capitalist Society*, Weidenfeld & Nicolson, 1969, p. 265.

13 ibid., p. 72.

14 G. Drover and L. Ouaknine, 'Social Policy in the Making: the Function of the Canadian Council on Social Development', unpublished paper, p. 21.

15 Canadian Council on Social Development, press release, 23 June 1975.

16 B. Hindess, *The Decline of Working-Class Politics*, Paladin, 1971.

17 Letters, *Guardian,* 16 March 1977.

18 Interview, 27 April 1977.

19 B. Jordan, *Paupers: The Making of the New Claiming Class*, Routledge & Kegan Paul, 1973, pp. 72–3.

20 To a great extent the consensual basis of pressure group policies is institutionalised by the charity laws. One director of a major charitable pressure group believes that 'anything that achieves charitable status is unlikely to rate in real terms, if one is concerned about serious social or political change, at best they serve to broaden the area of acceptable debate' (off-the-record interview, 4 May 1977).

21 P. Seyd, 'The Child Poverty Action Group', *Political Quarterly,* 24 (2), April–June 1976, p. 200.

22 M. Glean, 'Whatever Happened to C.A.R.D.?', *Race Today*, January 1973, p. 15.

23 'Shelter: the National Campaign for the Homeless', *Political Quarterly*, 46 (4), 1975, p. 425.

24 Letter to North Southwark Community Development Group, dated 2 December 1976. His concept of the democratic process is, to say the least, peculiar. In any case he is hardly in a position to advocate an exclusive focus on the ballot-box. On 7 January 1968 the *Sunday People* carried an article concerning the refusal of Cutler's company to observe Hillingdon Council's orders to make 21 Mount Pleasant fit for human habitation. The article suggested that Cutler was refusing to make repairs in protest against the Rent Acts. The victim of Cutler's protest was a seventy-two-year-old pensioner suffering from pneumoconiosis.

25 Letter dated 14 December 1976.

26 Letter dated 15 December 1976.

27 *Daily Telegraph*, 30 October 1976.

28 *Sunday Telegraph*, 5 December 1976.

29 A. Gouldner, *The Coming Crisis of Western Sociology*, Heinemann, 1971, p. 501.

30 M. Ryan, 'Radical Alternatives to Prison', *Political Quarterly,* 47 (1), January–March 1976; A. Sivanandan, *Race and Resistance: the IRR Story*, Race Today Publications, 1974.

31 Martin Robertson, 1974.

32 This is not to accept the more conspiratorial critique provided by some critics; see, for example, L. Bridges, 'The Ministry of Internal Security', *Race and Class*, 16 (4), 1975.

33 John Linden, Law Centres, Block V, Social Work, Community Work and Society, Open University, forthcoming.

34 *South London Press,* 22 April 1977.
35 A. Sivanandan, 'Race, Class and the State: the Black Experience in Britain', *Race and Class,* 17 (4), 1976, p. 364.
36 'The Local State: Management of Cities and People', *Race and Class,* 18 (4), 1977, p. 364.

6 Don't agonise — organise

Jim Radford

Fifteen years ago the term 'community work' would have meant very little to most people. Those of us who were doing it did talk about community action, but we answered to different names and we were called a variety of others. Anarchist and troublemaker were among the more common descriptions. Nevertheless, we produced results, some of them dramatic. And it was those results which produced the prestigious reports which led to the government decision to co-opt us, nine or ten years ago.

The professionalisation of community work that has taken place since then has brought with it some advantages and opened up some new possibilities, but it has serious drawbacks. One of these is the attraction it has given community work for the academics and sociologists who have swarmed among us: evaluating and analysing, converting simple truths into complicated concepts, devising their incomprehensible definitions and generally creating a complex intellectual theory that leaves many of the new recruits confused and guilt-ridden, and that raises precisely the kind of elitist barrier that community workers are supposed to be breaking down.

Of course we need to think carefully about what we are doing and how, not to mention why. And no doubt the army of researchers and theorists serve a useful purpose by helping us to do that. But their influence has produced a flow of newly trained youth and community workers who have been taught how to communicate with other professionals to such an extent that they have almost forgotten how to be relaxed and explicit with ordinary people. I have yet to meet a course tutor who takes students out on the knocker, and yet the ability to communicate freely and spontaneously with people in the community is the basic skill that every field worker needs in order to be effective.

I regret the neglect of basic communication skills and the need for professional status that has developed. I firmly believe that the tenets of community work are simple enough and that a community worker must be able to explain his position in terms that most people can understand. Research and evaluation are obviously necessary, but community work is about doing more than measuring, and the leaflet and the broadsheet are therefore more important and relevant to it than the PhD thesis or sociological survey.

I may fall into the jargon trap myself, since one can hardly avoid knowing the words after long exposure, but I will not be quoting from books and reports, because that is not my style. This chapter contains my opinions on community work, some of its problems and its political significance. If you disagree with any of them, you can be sure you are disagreeing with me, not with something I have read.

As far as I am concerned, community work is a particular way of working in the community for the benefit of that community. It almost always has practical objectives to do with the needs of people in that community, but since those objectives will vary from time to time and place to place, and may be shared by people who work in quite a different way, it is the way in which we seek to achieve those objectives that makes community work different.

The way of working that most community workers prefer is to promote group organisation, group development and group action to try to bring people with common problems or interests together, and to encourage them to make decisions and to take action to solve those problems or to further those interests. Most community workers would agree that they are concerned to help people to do things for themselves. In practice this often means helping them to acquire the confidence and the ability that will enable them to exert influence or pressure on other agencies with power over resources.

The importance of this approach is not only that it can often get results where other methods have failed, but that the experience can change the people who take part by increasing their understanding and ability. It teaches them how to create and use power. Community work is therefore an educational process.

Because some people are likely to continue using the knowledge and skills they have gained to make or to influence other decisions, successful community work changes the balance of power in that community, if only slightly. Community work is therefore a political process.

It can be regarded as political with a small p, because community work usually starts with local groups and with the issues that immediately concern those groups. However, the combined effect of many small changes in the balance of power can lead to major changes, and every now and again a local initiative can develop into a national campaign with mushrooming effects. By either route, national decisions can be influenced and the small p can become a large P. I would cite the spread of local welfare rights activities as an example of the cumulative effect, and the early growth of the squatting movement as an illustration of the mushroom effect.

The political significance of community work is still plainly obvious even after eight years of professionalisation in which training has been controlled by social workers, sociologists and administrators, while employment has been largely funded by government and local authority grants. It was even more obvious ten years ago when effective local activists neither knew nor cared about professional etiquette and, without salaries or grants to consider, made few bones about the political nature of their challenge to authority and the accepted processes. It is not surprising that the government should have decided to harness and co-opt this dynamic source of energy and influence by creating a new profession and setting up training courses all over the country.

Looking back on the spread of the free-lance political campaigning and direct action that took place in the 1960s, we can regard this development either as a cynical attempt to buy off trouble or as a genuine conversion to new ideas about democracy and participation. Since the Establishment consists of a good many people, I think it was probably both, but in either case it was quite a sensible response to the situation. It gave the authorities a considerable amount of control over future developments in this field, in return for funding and supporting a widespread promotion of the basic idea of organised participation. It made it much easier for party politicians to identify themselves with some of the useful and popular things that were being done, which helped to obscure the fact that what most of the free-lance agitators had in common was their rejection of the hitherto preferred formula for political involvement—i.e. membership—and faith in the leadership.

It was a classic example of 'if you can't beat them, co-opt them', and those whose activities had helped to bring it about had no real grounds for complaint, because if we didn't want to apply for the new courses or to take the new jobs, no one was making us. I was not inclined to complain, partly because I had long taken the view that victory for the campaigner begins to come into sight only when those you have been campaigning against say that they agree with you, and partly because of the attractive possibility that the spread and acceptance of our ideas about involvement, and group action, even with new constraints, might lead more quickly to a general demand for democratisation and participation at all levels.

I was worried about the adverse effects of professionalisation, and I fully expected the new youth and community work courses to have a non-political bias. But it seemed to me that infiltration could be just as effective a tactic as co-option, and having witnessed at first hand the accelerated learning process that occurs during struggle, I was hopeful, even if gentler strategies became the norm, that new community workers would develop their own political consciousness in the field, no matter what they were told during their training.

The growth of community work in the early 1970s did not always support this optimistic view. The number of full-time paid workers increased, but because of the deliberate and unnecessary bracketing of youth work with community work, many of them were going into uncontentious youth work jobs. Others seemed to be turning into group social workers, as a result of being success-fully indoctrinated with the belief that a good community worker must, at all costs and in all situations, be non-directive. This was sending workers into the community with an absolute determin-ation *not* to provide leadership, even where that was clearly what was needed and missing. It also provided a simple formula for elitism and manipulation!

Elitism, because a worker who sees it as his job to encourage local people to do that which he must not do himself is auto-matically setting himself apart as someone special: to be judged by different standards. Manipulation, because a group worker who had no views about what the group could and should be doing, or who genuinely made no attempt to influence the group's thinking, would be of little value in most situations; and the only alternative to being an open influence is to be a subtle or hidden influence, i.e.—a manipulator.

At the time, it seemed to me that this particular fault could be traced to the many social workers who had moved over into community work. Some of them became trainers, even when they themselves lacked any practical experience. Non-directiveness may be essential in counselling and personal support. It can be a gross betrayal in certain group situations.

My views on this were coloured by long experience of conflict situations where determined morale-building leadership had often been vital. And, to be fair, perhaps the cult of non-directiveness could equally well be traced back to those well-publicised action groups, since we had often strongly denied that we had leaders. What we meant was that we had no appointed or permanent leaders, not that we had no leadership. Within those groups there were always people equally prepared to give or to follow a lead when that was necessary.

I had hoped that community work, as the broader discipline, would become a radical influence on social work. I became increasingly worried by the extent to which the reverse was happening and at the number of newly trained workers who were going straight into narrowly defined social-support-type jobs under the supervision of social workers. This is not to knock social work—which I happen to think is important and necessary—but simply to say that community work is different and in the long run more important. In the same way, public health measures are more important than remedial medicine.

At one point I began to think that perhaps the Establishment had got much the best deal after all, and that the expansion of community work was being achieved at the cost of its political virility. The youth and community work courses seemed to be turning out a large number of workers with enlarged vocabularies and good intentions, but in many cases with little understanding of, or commitment to, the basic educational and political task that has always faced the community activist. This task is effectively to challenge authoritarian solutions and to change or replace authoritarian structures.

The problems caused by dual standards and academic castration are still in evidence, and too many of us have substituted the skills of report-writing and grant-getting for those of community organising. But the situation has changed! In some respects for the better, because it is clear that the educational process has been doing its work and that more and more workers, as they gain experience, are developing an overall political outlook that enables them to see the connection between different issues and between the problems of the neighbourhood and those of society. Where this goes hand in hand with the development of practical skills and the setting of realisable goals, the result is likely to be an effective worker who is concerned to link issues and to press for closer collaboration between groups and agencies.

However, one trend follows another, and while I am glad that non-directiveness is now being put in its place as simply one technique to be used where appropriate, I am increasingly worried that the pendulum may be swinging too far in the other direction. This is because one drawback to the educational effect of community work is that it politicises some people more quickly than others. If that makes them more effective, it is good, but the danger exists that it can make them *less* effective. Some workers, highly motivated to bring about social change and frustrated by the slowness of the process or the failure of their strategies, now appear to be moving full circle. Having re-discovered (almost to their surprise it would seem) that every local issue of injustice, powerlessness and deprivation is invariably linked to wider issues and policies, and above all to the economic structure of society, they are turning again to overall political formulas. This is more likely to happen with those whose commitment to the community work process in the first place was theoretical rather than based on their own experience and personal disillusionment with traditional politics.

Since I too am politically motivated, in that I believe the long-term objective of community work must be to encourage ordinary people to increase their awareness and competence to the point where they will use their experience to tackle the wider issues and needs of society, I have no quarrel with the view that an overall political theory is necessary to bring about fundamental structural changes. But if, by definition, community workers are committed to the development of anti-authoritarian solutions, we must equally be committed to the development of an anti-authoritarian political theory.

We may hope that certain ideas will ultimately prevail and we may believe that the implications of community work are radical enough to be called revolutionary, but if we want to think of ourselves as revolutionaries we must accept that ours is a piecemeal revolution that must be built step by step, and that must convert and carry people with it at each stage.

Many community workers are professed socialists. I don't think they have to be, any more than I think that a belief in the jury system necessarily indicates a commitment to one verdict more than another. But since the general objectives of both community work and socialism can be expressed in the same terms—e.g. to create a caring, sharing society in which power, responsibility and resources are more evenly distributed—the two positions are perfectly compatible.

Some community workers have reacted to frustration and disappointment by openly proclaiming their loss of faith in community work and by announcing their conversion to a Marxist programme, which is honest enough. They say that their experience has shown them that action at local level is not enough, which is perfectly true, since action at all levels is obviously needed. From my observation, however, this kind of disillusionment usually stems from a failure to generate the mushrooming process, or to achieve any significant results at local level. For this failure, I make no criticism of the workers I have in mind, since I do not know the local situations they worked in; but I reject their conclusions. There can be no more guarantee of success in community work than in any other field in which the human factor predominates, except possibly an absolute determination not to accept defeat and to continue working and struggling until you do succeed. But my own experience has shown me over and over again that a few people, with planning, determination and organising skills, can mobilise a local community around the issues that affect them to achieve real results that benefit not only the community concerned but people with similar needs throughout the country.

Most of the campaigns and movements that come to mind owe their beginnings to a few people who decided to do something, usually at local level. Think of pre-school playgroups and adventure playgrounds, claimants' unions, the women's aid groups and battered wives' centres, and literacy and the right to fuel campaigns. Think of Ringway, Stansted, Foulness and the growing environmental lobby. In each case organisation and action produced results and created platforms which made it easier for something else to happen. The causal connection between the action is frequently as plain as that between the issues. The homeless hostel campaign, the squatting movement and the campaign against empty office blocks and property speculation all grew out of each other in logical succession. These and other initiatives have not only benefited tens of thousands directly; they have also led to changes of policy, priority and legislation at national level, and they have opened the eyes and ears of millions to an increased awareness of the causes of the social problems that triggered them.

I fully agree that none of these developments has fundamentally altered the capitalist structure of society, but that objective would seem a rather ambitious one for a community group to tackle. And looking back on the measurable results of the campaigns that I have personal knowledge of, I find it very hard to believe that the handful of people who embarked on them would have been more usefully occupied in making those vague calls for concerted working-class struggle that never seem to specify the administrative solutions and structures that the struggle can be expected to achieve, nor how these will resolve the practical problems that ordinary people are facing.

There is this essential difference between the community campaigns that I have experienced and the wider political struggle that the new Marxists call for. We have started with the needs and concerns that people themselves feel, and the issues have therefore been smaller. They have been real and important enough to the people we sought to mobilise and demanding enough in relation to the resources we could expect to deploy, but at least we have been quite sure about our objectives and of our ability to explain them, and to justify our methods. For this reason, we have usually been able to involve the people most affected by the issue in making decisions and taking action at each stage. We undoubtedly led people into conflict from time to time, but only with their full understanding and approval after other methods had been tried and failed, and only when we collectively believed that this was a necessary strategy—and that we could win. We did not put people's freedom and future at risk simply to expose the inadequacies of the system or to give them political insights, although some of us welcomed these side-effects. We encouraged people to join us in direct action and to put themselves on the line because we honestly believed that it was in their best interests, as they defined them, to do so. I would accept that in certain circumstances it may be necessary to enter into conflict, even when it is not possible to foresee a successful outcome, but such a decision should always be taken after the fullest consideration by the people who would suffer the consequences of defeat, and not by political activists who can move on to another location or issue and put their failure down to experience. In one or two conflict situations that have attracted some attention in recent years, there has been some reason to suspect that the tactics and principles at stake were clear only to a few individuals who seemed bent on leading local people to certain defeat and discouragement, when the objectives and principles that really mattered to the group would have been better served by compromise and conciliation.

Community workers employed by local authorities need to exercise particularly sound judgment and diplomacy, since they are open to suspicion from both sides of the fence—from community groups who, for whatever reason, distrust the authority and suspect that the worker's loyalty will be to his employer, and from councillors who resent his advocacy or support for groups that openly criticise their decisions.

Such a worker is obviously not free to choose from the whole range of options because aggressive pressure towards the authority would either lose him his job if he openly identified with it, or—if he supported it secretly—would place him in the manipulative position of leading from behind. However, since most community work does not call for conflict, local authority workers can be enormously valuable to developing groups who need both support from and to liase with the council.

One would not expect a conflict-orientated community worker to take a job with a local authority, yet oddly enough a few have done so, apparently in the belief that the community worker's mystical accountability to the community would protect them from the need to be accountable to the employer. It doesn't, of course, and such workers should not be too surprised when they get the sack.

Some workers in the CDP projects appear to have made the same mistake. Certainly there has been conflict, and while I would hesitate to criticise any particular tactics at long range, it is clear that the overall experiment has not been a tremendous success. Since that experiment was important in that it might have moved community work into a new and more overtly political dimension, we should be concerned to understand why.

Reams have been written, with more to come, and perhaps that is one of the mistakes. I know that some very good reports and analyses have been produced, but we are beginning to drown in paper these days and I wonder how many people will read them and how many of those who read them will make use of the information.

My general impression has been of a number of workers who appear to have expected far too much from small- or medium-sized opportunities and who therefore failed to devise a strategy that might have produced medium-sized results on which they could build. I know that some workers have been intensely frustrated, possibly because they tend to see each issue and local problem as a microcosm of wider problems and to believe that if only fully correct, socialist solutions could be implemented, they would be able to fulfil their high expectations and to show the way for everyone else.

I sympathise with the frustration and with the dislike of compromise that has led such workers into advocating a more general struggle, but I think that that conclusion is wrong and that they are now simply choosing the easier option. That is not to say that implementing the revolution is easier than organising the community, but that advocating the revolution is easier than organising an old folks' outing.

Of course those who now reject the community work approach are absolutely right when they claim that the kinds of minor reforms that community work can bring about are helping to postpone fundamental changes by making the present system more acceptable.

What are the alternatives? to leave it as it is, or to make it worse? Improvement is precisely what community work should be about, because one improvement can and does lead to another and enough of them add up to major change. I do not see each problem as a microcosm, though some of them may be. I do see each improvement, each reform, as part of an interlocking jigsaw which makes it reasonable to believe that, ultimately, especially if we can speed up the rate of improvement, we will create a totally different picture of society.

People are rightly sceptical of elaborate and complex political programmes that have not been tested, because history and our own experience of life have taught us that too many things can, and usually do, go wrong. For example, I can see very little evidence that fundamental changes in our society right now would not take us in the opposite direction to the one that I would prefer, since I am aware that the majority of people do not share either my vision of the ideal society or that of the Marxists.

'Progressives' may appear to be more active and organised in Britain at the moment, just as the Catholics appeared to be in Northern Ireland at the peak of the civil rights campaign. But if fundamental political issues were forced at this time I have little doubt that reactionaries would emerge as the majority, just as the Unionists did in Ireland.

I put the word 'progressives' in quotes because I take the view that the way in which we treat one another is more important than the labels we give ourselves. From that standpoint, the world-wide swing is towards authoritarianism rather than socialism.

If we use the term 'reactionary' to describe those who claim the right to impose their views and theories on others, it is clear that the threat to individual rights and freedom and to genuine participation is just as likely to come from the extreme left as it is from the right. A community worker who really believes in the principles he has been trying to apply, as opposed to an opportunist who will use any means, must be concerned to help people resist either brand of authoritarianism.

Some workers are trying to resolve the contradiction between a rigid political overview and community work. I do not see how they can succeed. If the personal politicisation of community workers leads them into trying to sell an overall programme to people who have had no hand in compiling or testing it, they are stepping back into the traditional political arena where policies are sold or imposed from above, instead of being created and passed up from the people. If belief in the need for a correct and comprehensive political line is used to justify leading people into struggles they are unlikely to win, for objectives they do not fully understand, when those they do understand might more easily be achieved by compromise and persuasion, then we are again talking about manipulation instead of leadership. If community workers turn to polemic and diatribe first, instead of last; if they neglect the basic tasks of organisation, group development and shared decision-making, and rely instead on appeals for working-class solidarity; and if the shortcomings of the economic and political system become the ready-made excuse for every failure at local level, then we are right back where many of us started.

The parties and programmes may change, but the formula is depressingly familiar: membership (solidarity) and faith in the leadership (programme). The overall critique may be sharp and accurate; the major conclusions sound. It is the method that we have rejected, because it is far from new and it hasn't worked yet. I am reminded of the Socialist Party of Great Britain whose arguments and objectives have been impeccable in the eyes of many socialists for more than sixty years, but whose effectiveness has been minimal for the same length of time because they argue convincingly that socialist principles cannot be implemented on anything less than a world-wide scale, and it logically follows that any activity other than the task of preaching this truth is pointless.

I have indicated that, to some extent, I share the view that the acceptance and support of community work by the establishment is evidence of a desire to use it to maintain social control. That was expected and inevitable, and it seems to me pointless and naive to wax indignant about it. Community work can still succeed as a cumulative political process, but only if it succeeds practically at a local level, and this means achievement, acceptance and consolidation at each stage. Those who have developed a more ambitious and far-reaching political theory as a result of their experience must recognise that the people they are now attempting to speak for, instead of with, also need to gain experience in order to reach their own conclusions. I am sure they are genuinely concerned to encourage working-class groups to raise their political sights, but I would argue that the task of helping this process may require them frequently to lower their own.

Community workers and community groups can, and do, learn from failure. But success usually has more educational effect and is always more encouraging, even if it is limited. It is part of the community worker's job to help to set realistic and achievable targets: to build platforms from which people can see further and from which they can start on the next and higher one. Sometimes it is necessary to stop and re-assess your chances of success: to adopt a different strategy or even to settle for a lower platform. You don't opt for glorious failure if you can possibly avoid it (a) because you are working with people that you have taken a commitment to and to whom half a house, or whatever, will usually be better than none, and (b) because failure can mean the disintegration of the group or base you are working from and from which you could try again.

If you deliberately set out to interfere or intervene in other people's lives and problems, whether for pay or politics or however you choose to describe it, you take on a moral responsibility to those people. That responsibility should be made explicit in the agreement between the worker and the group. It rarely is. The obligation, put simply, is that you do not use or con them, and all the rules of conduct we need can be derived from that basic duty and common sense.

There is room and need for different kinds of workers and it would be an absurd contradiction to try to impose a uniform approach or priorities. But if we want to restore the confidence that appears to be flagging, I think we do need to establish an agreed commitment to the basic objective of community work that can be easily explained and understood. This sums it up for me:

> The purpose of community work is to encourage and enable people to move towards a caring, sharing society; to bring about the maximum involvement of the group, neighbourhood or community in solving the problems that concern them, in participating in the decisions that affect them, and in running their own affairs.

This shows that the objective and the process cannot be separated, and that the worker is committed to that process more than to particular tasks or strategies. If we look at all the areas in which power is exercised and where decisions are taken by a few people that affect many, we can see that we have a long way to go.

Representative democracy is insensitive to the needs and views of many people and it is fashionable to be cynical about it. Nevertheless, it is still the best decision-making principle we have, and an essential safeguard against the cruder forms of oppression. If community work continues to develop, I believe that it can be the tool that will revitalise democracy at local level, and that it can make a vital contribution to the general movement towards greater participation and power-sharing at all levels.

Community work has developed so far because it offers people the opportunity to do something themselves instead of simply supporting activities outside their own control. It has produced results because it has concentrated on achievable goals. It has involved new people because it has taken as its starting-point where they are, and what they feel concerned or angry about.

If it can avoid the trap of creating its own brand of alienating dogmatism, it can hope to change the relationship between the governors and the governed and no doubt it will change itself in the process. But that is in the future, and it will not continue to develop and fulfil its potential if those who should be most committed to it are uncertain and confused about what they are doing and why.

In spite of these critical warnings, I am not unduly pessimistic. An understanding of community work practice and principles is spreading. There are more community workers now than ever before. The overall political and economic situation may depress us generally, but it also opens up opportunities to re-think, to organise and to demonstrate that people can work together in new ways. The lessons of the past two decades need to be learnt and applied on a much wider scale. We have demonstrated that ordinary people can come together to help themselves and to create power. There is much that we can build upon including a greater awareness of the drawbacks of centralised control and a growing interest in the possibilities of power sharing at all levels. The potential for a new movement of people exists in the tens of thousands now working voluntarily in and for their communities. Community workers have a great deal to contribute if they can keep in mind that theirs is the practical side of politics, and if they can resist the temptation to opt out of responsibility, compromise and hard work, for the easier option of becoming professional and political gurus. My message is simple and not new: Dont agonise—organise.

Part II Local Politics and Community Work

7 Brown rice or rice pudding: some dilemmas in community work

Caroline Polmear

It is not unusual to hear community workers complaining of exhaustion, and feeling that at the end of a three-year stint they deserve a break. When we look at the nature of the work, it is hardly surprising that it is so exacting. There are seldom any routine tasks to retreat into; every situation may be looked at afresh, the elements in it assessed, the growth points found, moves planned and consequences and implications of actions speculated on. The dynamics of a community are seldom repeated elsewhere, or two days running in the same area, making community work a continuously creative exercise.

Since there can be no set pattern of recommended moves, we have to be sure of the principles guiding our actions and the beliefs, values and techniques guiding our choices. Community work theory is remarkably unhelpful. Statements such as Murray Ross's on community organisation:[1]

> In the process of identifying and dealing with a common
> problem, sub-groups and their leaders will become disposed
> to co-operate with other sub-groups in common endeavours,
> and will develop skills in overcoming the inevitable conflicts
> and difficulties which emerge in such collaborative tasks

are, we hope, true. Such statements serve to inspire us to action, to take up our community work banners and march, but leave us unaided when we get our first blister.

How do we decide which leaders to support in an internal struggle in a community association, which group to work directly with in an area torn by strife and conflict? The passive words of community work theory, 'enabling' and 'non-directive', are deceptive when the work itself is so active.

This chapter is about the minutiae of community work: the daily decisions we make, the value-judgments we are never quite sure about, the complex series of chess moves which make up an ordinary day in the life of a community worker. What follows is an account of three incidents in three different areas where community workers made some difficult decisions. They are examples rather than 'true stories', but are derived from work in Inner London. From the details, I hope to ask some questions based on those which students commonly ask, and perhaps suggest some guidelines.

'The good, the bad and the ugly': Station Road Community Association

The area

An inner London area dominated by a main line railway station bringing people into the city from all over the country. An area of mixed housing: 1950s Council blocks, substandard, privately-rented blocks dating from the early 1900s and owner-occupied flats of a similar period; small specialist shops, a few local food stores and a laundrette.

Blue- and white-collar workers are mixed with actors and musicians who needed a home near the West End and liked the anonymity of inner city life. Residents had developed a degree of toughness through their struggle to survive their own and other people's problems. The traffic was a constant worry to parents, and playspace—a scruffy public square and the common parts of the blocks of flats—was shared with prostitutes and 'winos' making a living from the flow of people brought in by the station.

But the other side of this inner city struggle was the energy, the constant bubbling up of new ideas and plans which characterised the area. There was no shortage of leadership, in fact there were constant leadership struggles within the Community Association. A pattern had developed in which a leader would be favoured and put in a key position which he would hold shakily for a month or so before a coup would be declared.

Committee procedures, constitutions and precedents were agreed and adopted at long and heated meetings and the following morning one or two individuals would rush off and act unilaterally, undermining all joint decisions. Nervous breakdowns and mysterious illnesses were a feature of this vicious cycle, as the discarded leaders out of favour retired to lick their wounds.

Community work involvement

The local Council of Social Service in discussion with their contacts in the area convened the Station Road Forum (SRF), a group of about twenty-five first-level leaders. The purpose of the group was to take the heat off the Community Association where the 'assassinations' were in full crescendo, and to get local leaders working together on neutral ground, thus harnessing the mass of creative energy which was being used to split the area rather than unite it in common achievement. Meeting as necessary, usually every three weeks, the members discussed the major problems facing the area, and planned actions involving the whole community to tackle them. At subsequent meetings individuals reported back on their progress and planned further tasks.

The SRF developed well. Campaigns and projects burgeoned; the excesses of jungle behaviour were contained and breakdowns were held at bay. A playspace and traffic campaign rolled into action, an environmental planning and action group formed; summer playschemes and outrageous and dramatic neighbourhood festivals occurred; a directory of local contacts and facilities were compiled, tenants' groups began negotiations with the Borough Council and a pioneering community care scheme was launched.

After 18 months a discussion of the future of the Forum and the Community Association was initiated by the community workers and a small subgroup of the Forum met to consider the matter and report back to the whole group. They proposed that, because of its unstable history, the Community Association should be allowed to lie fallow and several small groups dealing with issues in the area should be formed. At a later date, when the groups had developed (meanwhile continuing under the guiding hand of the SRF), the Community Association might be re-formed as an umbrella group with a more stable basis of organisation, achievement and leadership to build on. The proposals were accepted.

The following morning brought a flurry of heated phone calls and a further coup. New leaders had been 'appointed', the Community Association would not die. The leaders appeared in the office armed with their manifesto and looking as if they expected resistance. They could stand on their own feet, local people were behind them and the Community Association would go forward from now on. The community workers, keeping a cool countenance (they hoped), agreed to close the Forum, and offered any help and support to the Community Association that it should feel it wanted.

What had been achieved? The Association was still characterised by a good deal of highly explosive energy, and there was still a few casualties, though these were fewer. The major elements of the subgroup's proposals to the Forum were intact. Six or seven interest groups actively involving some 200 local residents and workers were to be developed, but instead of the Forum being the co-ordinating body, it would be co-ordinated by the Community Association.

The essential style of the area has not changed, but the SRF had provided a neutral ground and authority long enough to establish a new pattern of achievement.

'The bad and the beautiful': Boroughs End Redevelopment Area

The area

A triangle of streets bordering two other boroughs, far from the pulse of its own borough and poorly served with public transport. A self-contained area served by basic shops, a laundrette and a small library.

The same families had lived there for many generations, hard-working 'respectable working-class' people.

Things began to change after the Borough Council decided to re-develop that triangle. The area was compulsorily purchased. Local people did not want this, but their messages never got through, and they were not at that time well enough organised to make a fuss. As the years passed and planning blight took a hold, morale in the area fell and anger rose. Empty houses were let in haphazard fashion to homeless families, to organised squatting groups and fringe religions and voluntary organisations, while some were left empty long enough to be squatted by individuals or groups of young people.

Dates for demolition came and went until newcomers felt they had a permanent home and long-term residents became more cynical and angry. This small seething triangle contained groups of people with strongly conflicting values. Older residents were hard working, many had achieved white-collar status, their standards were publicly maintained. Of the newcomers, some did not believe in the value of work, preferring peace and love and brown rice at home, but others were struggling to change their position, to find work and make a home for their children.

Community work involvement

The Council of Social Service agreed, at short notice, to a request from the Town Clerk's department to open a Neighbourhood Centre at Boroughs End. The aim was to facilitate a two-way flow of communication between residents and Borough Council, to bring people together about issues concerning them and to work towards reviving community life in the new Boroughs End, which would house those long-term residents who wished to stay and some new residents from the Council's housing waiting list.

Early developments included the formation of a Tenants' Association to support and assist those moving out in the first phase of redevelopment and a Tenants' Association of those remaining. The leader of the latter Tenants' Association was the strong and active Ms Fixit, who held extreme and violent attitudes against squatters. She had many successful campaigns on behalf of residents to her name, which gave her standing locally, and meant that her leadership went unchallenged.

The issue of lack of facilities for children and young people was expressed at an early stage. Long-term residents complained of the unruly behaviour of the newcomers' children (variously known as the squatters, the hippies, the welfare families and the problem families). The newcomers complained that there was nowhere for their children to play without getting into trouble.

The community workers saw it as essential to work with the children and young people and through them with their parents. They felt that unless they could create small pockets of constructive activity in this cauldron of destruction, the ever-increasing rift between old and new would probably lead to organised violence.

With a Youth Service grant, they employed a worker who was attached to the Centre, but worked on the streets with the young people. His tasks were to make contact with the young and to work with them towards establishing temporary play facilities. Through this he hoped to involve adults and young people in managing the facilities and negotiating with the authorities involved for permanent provision in the building plan.

His work with the children was scrutinised by long-term residents who complained that he was encouraging the youngsters and condoning their behaviour. When any child got into trouble, or even had some noisy fun, he was blamed.

Work in the Neighbourhood Centre was similarly watched over by the Tenants' Association and it became the cry of their leader that the Centre was yet another prop for the scrounging hippies and problem families and should be closed.

Council elections came into sight and Ms Fixit, the Tenants' Association leader, a staunch Labour Party member who could rouse the tenants into voting, or keep them away, became an important person in this marginal ward. A meeting of the Association was called to discuss the work of the Centre and the youth worker, and all local councillors and prospective councillors turned out in force.

It was alleged that none of the tenants used the Centre or found it of any value. The community workers watched the silent rows of tenants whom they knew well and had helped many times, and who now avoided their eyes.

In a series of soul-searching discussions, the Council of Social Service decided to close the Centre. Without the support of the leadership of the long-term residents, the work in its current form could not flourish. The workers knew that most residents were involved in the community work and saw it as the way forward, but would not publicly stand up against Ms Fixit.

The story continues many years after this incident. The next task for the workers, after asking themselves what they had learned and what the growth points were in this new situation, was to find forms of community work which were more acceptable to the local leadership and more in keeping with their style.

These forms included moving to more structured youth work and from a Neighbourhood Centre to a Citizens' Advice Bureau with direct services from the Borough Council's Housing and Social Services Departments attached, and through community organisation, co-ordinating local views and various authorities on the re-development question.

'The middle man': Penzance Park

The area

In some ways the Penzance Park story is like that of Boroughs End. Another redevelopment area, but this time with earlier community work involvement and several different ingredients in the mix, produces a very different pudding.

The area is hard to define in terms of community.[2] Streets and individual blocks had unity, but long-standing traffic schemes had fragmented Penzance Park itself. Housing was a mixture of Council-owned streets awaiting redevelopment.

Just as the area was physically separated into small pockets, so the character of each pocket was recognisably separate. But the few streets in this example were those scheduled for redevelopment. Here there was a mixture of elderly people, many of them single women, and a few families with school-age children. The rest of the houses, about a quarter, were beginning to be squatted and more were becoming vacant each week. There was a corner shop which was the natural centre of gossip and a main High Street just out of the area. The pub had recently closed. A few small industries squeezed a living in some of the untidy corners and added life to the dying streets.

As in Boroughs End, anger and bewilderment were present but seemed to be modified by contact with the outside world as the boundaries were crossed daily for work or shopping. However, morale was low and houses which had been structurally sound when the decision to redevelop was taken were falling into bad disrepair; conditions for many inhabitants were becoming intolerable.

Community work involvement

Neighbourhood community work began as a result of work done by a group of local leaders and professional workers convened by the Council of Social Service. The group had defined certain problems felt by the residents, of which the redevelopment had been one. When the community workers began talking to local people, this issue did indeed figure strongly.

The workers were anxious about the possibility of conflicts increasing between long-term and new residents which might deflect energies from trying to affect the redevelopment. They also feared that if squatters figured too strongly in the leadership of the group it might be discredited in the eyes of the Borough Council with whom there were bound to be long and detailed negotiations.

They met a group of squatters to discuss their fears, and received a very sympathetic response. The squatters, employed as teachers, youth workers and manual workers who had found it impossible to get housing in the ever-decreasing private rented sector, agreed to do all they could to help other residents achieve their ends, even if this meant staying in the background themselves. They agreed to help to select out potential squatters who might not empathise with their neighbours and might too stridently oppose their way of life. Their house had become an unofficial estate agency for those looking for squats, and it was at this point that the selection could take place. As a result of this intervention, houses filled up with a mixture of families with children and single employed people.

At early meetings to discuss feelings about and problems created by redevelopment, the participants were a mixture of old and new, reflecting the population mix of the area. As the group hammered out its plans and decided on its aim to change the redevelopment scheme to a rehabilitation programme, they were able to call on the skills of many of the newcomers. The group had valuable resources which without the squatters it might have lacked, and residents met as individuals first and squatters or others second— in fact the polarisation never occurred. The work that the squatters had done on their own houses to arrest the decay was appreciated too and several offered their help in halting the worst decay of the elderly residents' homes.

The group was successful not only in changing the Borough Council's policy on the plans, but also in rebuilding morale in the area.

Questions

When there are conflicts of values or interests in an area, whom do you work with?

The community worker aims to work with a whole community; different groups and individuals, professional and other workers serving it. And in one sense this simple base line is always true. The worker sees the composition of the area as it really is and not as he'd like it to be and recognises this mixture as the raw materials of his work. A community worker's presence in an area will affect every group or individual in it, whether or not he or she is actively working with them.

But in a situation such as Boroughs End, what is the workers' role where there is open conflict of values? Should they work with long-term residents, their leaders, the newcomers or all of them? Here they were trying to act as a bridge between the groups, to help those with entrenched views of each other to gain insight into the real nature of their problems so that they could do something constructive about them: in this case to focus their energies on changing, adapting or trying to live through the redevelopment.

And when the leaders of the Tenants' Association said they would keep members away from the Centre if it offered help to the squatters, what then? The workers knew that they had the support of most tenants who would quickly come back again, and although the leadership was very powerful, largely through its special links with the Council, it was not very representative. However, they decided that in this area, given the special power of Ms Fixit and the interest of the Councillors, from their present community work base they could not act as a bridge between the value systems as they felt they should. To battle on would have been a waste of time. Perhaps what they learned most clearly was that they had misread the structure of the area. The leaders had struggled hard for their respected status in the community and the wider society, their standards and values were too hard won for them to be flexible and to remain unthreatened by opposing principles.

And they learned, too, to follow the culture in the way they made contact with people. A neighbourhood centre and detached youth work, however restrained, smacked too much of trendy community work to be regarded favourably by some locals, and the later forms of entry into the community proved far more successful.

In Penzance Park, the workers were able to help bridge the gulf which might have widened and stopped any further work. Attitudes here were not so rigid. Their early intervention to select squatters who would hold the interests of the neighbourhood at heart was a bold and successful move and made further work possible. Not only was it important to gauge the attitudes of the people living in the area, and their level of tolerance of different values, but also the perceptions of the Council were important. The workers ensured that spokespeople were 'from the area' and not 'outsiders', and made a point of describing the full composition of the neighbourhood group on any documents.

In the work with SRF, the workers were constantly aware of the whole community they were working with. The leadership at any time would change, and those out of favour today might be in favour tomorrow. It was for this reason that a neutral forum, meeting on neutral ground, out of the immediate area, was chosen rather than neighbourhood-based work. It could span the interests and keep constant membership while power in the area was tossed from one to the other. It was neutral ground on which to make some of the conflicts open at the same time as driving on to plan actions and achievements.

In summary, then, the worker aims to work with the whole community and tries to read the culture and politics of the area to find ways of doing this. It probably means working in different ways with different groups of people, and in some cases it will mean not having any contact with some, but realising that this can be as much a positive form of work as daily discussion. Thus if a small group of winos are a problem in an area, and by spending time with them the worker loses credibility with residents, then a community organisation approach might be adopted. A mixed group of local leaders, organisations and departments who are or should be doing something for them, would be convened to work on solutions, while face-to-face community development continues in the neighbourhood.

Where do our own values fit in?

Social workers talk endlessly about their feelings, analysing their transferences and counter-transferences; community workers prefer to talk about their values. But there may be areas of overlap between feelings and values which we would also do well to be aware of.

We all base our work on a more or less well worked out set of values about the kind of society we want to live in. We decide which agency we will work for in the full knowledge that each agency, be it trade union, social services department, voluntary organisation, educational establishment or church, imposes its limitations and expectations on the type of work we will do. In our three examples the work was sponsored by a voluntary organisation. We could perhaps characterise the underlying values and beliefs as a desire to help individuals to realise their full potential and feel committed to, and able to bring about, changes in aspects of their lives; perhaps an unstated value belief was that while coming to recognise their own power by working together to achieve their ends, people would also grow more caring and understanding of each other. Thus in Boroughs End the workers could not support the Tenants' Association when they threatened to burn the squatters out of their houses in order to get the Council to take notice of them.

In other agencies the emphasis might be more directly on different aspects of the above values. Although for students and many community workers this appears to be a problem, it seems to me to be not only a useful guard against our own sometimes confused values or feelings running riot and clouding the decisions we take which may affect people's lives, but also an opportunity to make a commitment, to say, 'Here I stand. For the time being, these are the values which guide my work.' An overdose of value confusion, of constant reappraisal of the 'right' course of action, leads to paralysis, which is far more dangerous for the communities for whom one works than a fairly clear and humble statement to them of one's aims and beliefs.

It is the 'feeling-based' beliefs which I think we must be suspicious of—our fears about chaos or our dislike of conflict and, linked, our assumptions that unity is always best and right; our feelings about authority; either deep dislike or too ready acceptance; our need to be liked and fears of rejection and our preference for certain kinds of people.

The Station Road example illustrates some of these pitfalls avoided. The jungle-like behaviour of people to each other was often hard to take, and feelings of rejection when the Community Association got up and walked out could have clouded the community workers' view that the time had come to let them go, while offering support, if ever they wanted it, in the background.

Our natural tendencies towards conservatism, our dislike of 'death' which may spell failure, and our unwillingness to kill any project which offers us some kind of status or leadership opportunity are particularly dangerous traits when doing community work.

In Boroughs End, a young community worker's preference for some of the young squatting population rather than the more conservative leadership of the Tenants' Association could have clouded the original purposes of the work at a time when the squatters were saying—'Don't leave now, stay here and fight with us.'

Is this a recipe for change or conservatism? How much change can we expect?

If we are stressing the importance of reading the cultures of a neighbourhood, working through it and often acting as a bridge between value systems, are we eliminating any possibilities of bringing about a change? This type of community work is not so much a recipe for conservatism; it is based on a belief that change is organic in nature, that to be successful it recognises an existing culture which itself grows and develops rather than is swept away. Japan's successful industrialisation seems to be to some extent due to the new forms of social organisation being grafted onto, rather than breaking down, existing forms. And the very different forms of communism which nations have adopted seem to owe more to internal characteristics and existing culture than to any detailed blueprint.

An analogy comes to mind of a village greengrocer living in the community and dependent on local people for his livelihood. When he goes to market he finds various exotic new vegetables being introduced. He must supply his customers with the things they know and like, otherwise they will go elsewhere, but he introduces some of the exotica as well, recommending them and offering tips for cooking. In many cases they gradually become accepted as people overcome their prejudices against foreign food—anything too way out will be rejected and he won't buy any more for the time being. He's not going to change their basic diet, but he is developing and extending it.

How shall I know when to let go?

Surely the answer to this should not be as undignified as 'when you fall off', but on the surface it may look like that and momentarily it may well feel like it, too. In two examples, Station Road and Boroughs End, the workers were asked to go. In both cases they could say 'yes' or 'no'. In Station Road they said 'yes', in Boroughs End they in effect said 'no'. The difference was that in the first case when the workers asked themselves, 'Have we done what we set out to do?', the answer was, 'As far as it is possible to tell, we have', and in the second, 'We have not.' The special characteristics of an area are again important when making assessments of when to leave or loosen hold of group or a project. An area with a historical association with the agency and respect for it may have to be pushed into getting up and walking without it, while another, such as Station Road with a history of kicking its leaders or leader figures out, may not necessarily be as ready as it thinks. The only thing community workers have to hang on to is their job description, the aims of the work they are there to do.

Every day brings a reshuffle of the cards—new leaders in a coup, a fresh crisis, a new date for demolition, a shift in power of councillors with 'our' councillor ending up on the bottom of the heap, a midnight party on the squatters' side of the road which have frayed nerves even further, or a letter demanding the end of the community work contract with the Association or neighbourhood. The community work task is to look creatively for the growth points in this new array of material; to assess how much nearer to, or further from, the overall stated aims it brings them. This, clearly, is when it is important to distinguish between those stated values and feelings-based ones.

Leaving an area or a group must be looked at with the same cool eye. Are we nearer or further? What do we know about the style or culture of the area which might help us understand the meaning of this latest reshuffle? And what do we know about our own propensity to hang on, which might be clouding our judgment? It is as important a part of the community work task to look for the signs which tell us we should now leave, as it is to look for the signs which help us to clarify needs in an area.

References

1 Murray G. Ross and B. W. Lappin, *Community Organisation: Theory, Principles and Practice*, New York, Harper, 1955.
2 McIver and Page define 'community' as 'an area of social living marked by some degree of social coherence', quoted in R. Frankenburg, *Communities in Britain*, Penguin Books, 1969, p. 15.

8 Politics and participation: a case study

Florence Rossetti

Community work is about helping groups of people who feel themselves to be without influence and power, and who are often seen to be so by the rest of society, to take action collectively to solve some of the problems which they believe importantly detract from the quality of their daily lives. Such a statement carries with it value assumptions which may to some degree veer from the position of other people involved in one part or another of the wide spectrum of activity covered by the umbrella term 'community work'.[1] However, probably most of them would agree that the problems confronted in community work, of whatever aspect, are ultimately concerned with social policies whether major or, as so often in practice, minor ones. It is therefore not necessary to enter into the debate about whether the nature of the help provided to such groups should be conflict or consensus oriented, directive or non-directive, to agree that community work operates in a political context. This is so whether the particular issue of the moment is a relatively uncontentious one such as playspace or a more controversial matter like housing and planning. If community work is about social policies and the capacity of relatively deprived people to influence them, community work operates in the world of politics and, because of its localised base for collective action, it operates primarily in the world of local government politics.

Thus community workers must inevitably expect to be called upon to help local groups influence local government and must be capable of suggesting strategies to do so effectively. The intricacies of local power and politics are therefore central to the task and the fluctuating political currents must be continuously studied and properly interpreted if those strategies are to be successful. Some idea of the complexity and size of the problem can be gauged from two studies of London boroughs in recent years. Dearlove described in detail a council which, in a borough well known for its pressure group activity, has none the less been able to go on for many years with 'non-policies' which added up to a clear policy to contain change to the minimum.[2] His study is a reminder to those in community work that the 'non-decisions' of government can affect people's lives as significantly as its decisions.[3] Baine studied another borough which appears to be considerably more receptive to change but which nevertheless reveals complexities and ambiguities which defy simplistic assumptions about what, in practice, can be expected from 'left' and 'right' political labels.[4]

Relatively few such studies have been published and it is probably true to say that, popularly, local government is seen as an administration or a political body speaking and acting with one voice, the voice of the political party in power. Behind corporate policy decisions, however, lies a network of interacting interest groups which can be party political, administrative or professional, or a combination of all three, and which may also consist of single, powerful individuals.[5] Any policy proposal, however modest, can be a potential ally or threat to their differing priorities of interest, though what those priorities are may not always be immediately clear to the outsider. Any cause can become a pawn in political activity centred upon a totally different issue, and while to be so used unconsciously may prove disastrous for a community group it can be turned to advantage if used strategically by a politically astute one.[6] It can be assumed that those social policies which do emerge at local government level, especially in fields where central government chooses to be relatively non-directive, may be as much the result of bargains between powerful factions inside the local authority as the effect of pressure for them applied from outside. Similarly, how far such policies become implemented and sustained may also depend on the relative power of different internal interest groups and on how far they perceive those policies to reflect, to be against or to be irrelevant to their own priorities.

This is not to deny the importance of external factors in influencing policy decisions or non-decisions. The role of central government has already been mentioned and its legislative and economic power ensures an important generality of conformity in local government policy across the country. Within the local responsibility for national policies, however, there is often room for some degree of autonomy and it is the particular, very localised policy area in which community work is in fact engaged for the most part. (Similarly, there will tend to be a measure of local autonomy attached to the policies laid down by the major political parties.) There are also the unpredictable external factors which can enormously influence local policies such as, for example, the child-battering revelations of recent years which have affected priorities in social services departments towards vigilance against child abuse and thus attention and resources in that direction. Community work itself, of course, represents a belief in the efficacy of external pressure in promoting local policy changes.

It is the interaction of external factors and pressures with the internal political dynamics which determines policy making and implementation. As Baine suggests, the US policy-decision-making model of Bachrach and Baratz would seem equally applicable to local government in this country.[7] Their model posits a series of gates or barriers in the policy making process, operated by those in authority and which control attempts to introduce change by weeding out many proposals put forward. Among such barriers they suggest 'community values' or the way in which local government interprets common feelings and values about certain issues to justify decisions or non-decisions; 'procedures' is another, where the need to follow the 'normal channels' may be invoked on some occasions but not on others. These gates or barriers are capable of wide interpretation and may therefore afford the opportunity for authorities to do so to suit their own purposes. However, it is suggested here that those purposes are not necessarily mutually agreed ones for all factions making up a local authority, and the interpretation of the particular moment is likely to reflect the view of the currently dominant factions. In order to exert pressure from outside effectively to influence policy change it is therefore important to be able to identify the various sectional interests and to understand their relative power and influence over each other. In community work with socially deprived people whose political influence is by definition minimal, it seems clear that strategies and tactics will crucially need to exploit the internal politics of these large and powerful organisations. It is as important therefore for community workers to try to understand them as it is for them to be familiar with the social networks of the neighbourhood in which they are working.[8] Until very recently, however, there has been little theoretical perspective to guide them. The micro politics of policy making and implementation at local government level does not appear to have received much attention from British academics.[9] This is perhaps not surprising, because any study of internal political dynamics, whether of local government or any other institution, is difficult to carry out from an external or independent base and infinite permutations in patterns are, in any case, to be expected. Individual case studies are to that extent likely to be of limited use in practice, but they do have value in bringing to wider awareness a too little discussed aspect of democratic local government. They may also serve as a reminder in community work that, once people have been stimulated to express their needs, the major problem lies in devising strategies to achieve their self-determined objectives.

The following case study is therefore offered only as an illustration of the complexity of local government internal politics and their significance in community work. As such, it relates to but one particular place at one period of time, from a view which is necessarily subjective and restricted. It therefore relies a great deal on interpretation, as community workers have to do in practice, knowing that the success or failure of the resulting action will prove its accuracy or otherwise. The interpretation here is that of the author, who was the team leader of the community project involved in the case during the period discussed.

Background to the case

An inner London local authority, the London Borough of Southwark, is analysed on the basis of the experience of workers attached to a community project which, in the early 1970s, tried to help residents in a locality covering approximately one ward, Newington, to become involved in its redevelopment and thereby to respond to the Council's decision to introduce an experiment in participation in planning there.[10] The project was assigned to that particular neighbourhood by the local authority which had agreed to employ it as part of the government-sponsored national Community Development Project. The project staff were responsible both to the local authority and the government.

The ward had several years earlier been scheduled for redevelopment. The physical blight and mental stress now commonly associated with the long-drawn-out urban renewal process were already manifest in the area. A variety of circumstances arising since the original planning decisions had led to the probability that revised plans would have to be drawn up. The borough planners now saw that a measure of choice existed in determining new ones and were keen to have some feedback from local residents to assist in making new and appropriate decisions for the ward. The project's recent arrival in the neighbourhood, the crucial significance of future development plans to all the residents and the recent publication of the Skeffington Report's recommendations for greater public participation in planning all pointed to the desirability of trying out in the ward an exercise in participation in planning.[11] At a time when it was thought likely that the Skeffington proposals would be incorporated into new legislation requiring public participation in planning and with the Council committed to substantial redevelopment all over the borough, such an experiment made sense. As well as benefiting the ward residents, its findings could help the Council to assess the administrative and financial implications of any future legislation on participation for the borough as a whole. In due course, the Council approved, without any apparent internal dispute or dissent, a ward experiment in public participation in planning and invited residents to take part. It also made known its intentions to the media.

It was agreed that the exercise was to be under the co-ordination and responsibility of the Planning Department. A revised draft plan for the area was drawn up, as a basis for consultation with residents, and exhibited for three weeks in the local premises of the community project, with officers from relevant Council departments on hand to explain and discuss it. The participation process itself was programmed to take place over the ensuing months through a system of informal discussions in the first instance between street groups of residents and Council departmental officers, after such groups had been helped into existence by the community workers. In due course, when ideas had been clarified, it was agreed that groups would meet with committee chairmen and ward councillors. Then, at the end of the participation process, modified and final plans would be decided by the Council and exhibited in the ward again before being put into effect.

Within a fortnight, the public participation exercise as planned was at an end before it had barely begun. After the first informal meeting between a street group and officers, the Council banned any further meetings and no explanation was offered to residents. The Planning and Development Committee chairman, who was also a ward councillor, had turned up unexpectedly at that meeting and had met with a somewhat aggressive reception by the residents, and this was then assumed by them to be the cause of the volte-face. It generated considerable anger in the ward and stimulated the rapid development of street groups fired to take on the Council in a battle to regain the right to the participation originally offered them. The community project decided that its own priority was also to regain that policy and, indeed, any other would have totally forfeited its credibility with the local people. However, as a direct employee of the Borough Council but indirectly responsible also to the Home Office, the Inner London Education Authority (ILEA) and the Greater London Council (GLC), as well as professionally responsible to the project area residents, its position was ambiguous. This ambiguity was exploited over the ensuing months by dividing roles and tasks within the project team so that some were more closely involved in negotiation with authority and with information retrieval, while others concentrated on direct assistance to local groups.[12] Efforts over the following year to achieve the goal set by residents and workers drew them into the complex interaction of local influence and power and forced them to think and act in terms of strategies and tactics relevant to that situation.

Several official meetings with the Council were eventually achieved by groups, although the proceedings were fairly hostile and the outcome not entirely productive. After a year, the Council offered what was generally interpreted as an apology to all the groups, and reinstated a conditional participation. The conditions were for departmental autonomy, rather than the original combined operation co-ordinated by the Planning Department, and for the exclusion of the community project from the issue altogether. The latter was difficult for the Council to implement in view of the close working relationship already established with residents; and an internal enquiry had already been initiated by the Chief Executive to investigate ways of improving inter-departmental co-ordination in the urban renewal process. Residents and workers therefore considered that their immediate goal, at least, had been largely achieved.

History and analysis of the local politics

It has been pointed out that the policy decision to have a participation in planning exercise had positive advantages for the Council in terms of both research and public relations. While enabling it to collect data for future commitment planning and budgeting, it also fostered an image of a progressive Council. Why then, after announcing the policy to residents and to the press, should it have foreclosed its implementation so suddenly and without explanation? Was the Council as a whole really prepared to have its credibility so easily put into question and its public image damaged because one elected member, the Planning and Development Committee chairman, had been upset by angry constituents? The action taken by the Council was, at first sight, out of all proportion to the incident. In order to be able to conceive strategies to help residents get back the implementation of the participation policy, the community workers had to try to make sense of what appeared to be irrational and politically stupid Council action. A rational organisation view of the Council as a political unity was clearly inappropriate. Gradually the following historical picture of the Council and the ruling Labour group as a number of interacting interest groups or factions emerged, which seemed to offer a more coherent explanation of its action in this particular case.

The Labour group exhibited various rifts and divisions, but one in particular seemed to be commonly accepted as significant. This was the boundary between the three old metropolitan boroughs (Bermondsey, Camberwell and Southwark), which had amalgamated to form the present one in London government reorganisation six years before. Although also the subject of jokes in public, the old rivalries still seemed to have political significance. The metropolitan borough origins of both members and senior officers were frequently put forward in at least partial explanation of political stances and on more than one occasion Council members spoke of 'take-over bids' by one of the three sub-groups over the others. Some senior officers complained of difficulty in communicating with certain committee chairmen because they had different metropolitan borough origins. Several of those officers remained active in the old constituency Labour Party cells. However, middle and lower management, probably because of their relative lack of political influence and perhaps also because of their more recent arrival on the scene, did not appear to be so affected.

The formal administrative divisions within the Council were also strong, however. Service committees, with their corresponding departments, appeared to enjoy considerable autonomy: there was no specific policy co-ordinating committee although the Finance

Committee had the strongest membership and by definition was more powerful than the rest. Although a chief officers co-ordinating committee met, staff at all levels within the administration seemed to see their primary accountability along the vertical department/ committee line and, ultimately, to the committee chairman. Where a chairman's wishes were at variance with, for example, the Town Clerk's or, later, the Chief Executive's, the chairman was quite likely to be obeyed, despite the fact that staff were officially answerable to the chief officer. However, there was always the possibility of the old metropolitan borough loyalties cutting across the otherwise tight department/committee accountability.

Inside the Council, then, was a tangle of lines of communication resulting from the various formal and informal ties of authority, loyalty and accountability (Figure 1). Interwoven with this net- work was the similar web of the wider London government system. In inner London, with its tripartite system, the close political ties between the members of the three administrations cut across the functional differences of interest between them. At officer level, among senior planners, there were strong ties between the borough and the GLC, the officers being ex-GLC staff transferred to the borough with the new planning powers under London government reorganisation. There was also, in this case, strong kith and kinship ties between senior members of the borough Labour caucus and the local MPs. Given the strong interdependence of local, regional and central government, both administratively and politically, all these links were of potential significance and entered into the situation in some way and at some point in this case.

Since amalgamation, the Council had pursued a strong municipal housing policy which reflected the power balance within it. By the time of amalgamation Bermondsey, in contrast to Camberwell and Southwark, had cleared away much of its unfit housing, built up a large municipal stock and achieved, for inner London, a relatively short waiting-list. In the new, enlarged Council former Bermondsey members were dominant, providing leader, chief whip, finance chairman and other key positions. Thus Bermondsey's traditional policy priority became that of the new Council; the Housing Com- mittee chairman and Housing Manager were both Bermondsey men and the department itself was located there. A direct building depart- ment was established and, in 1964, when the new Labour govern- ment introduced high increases in central funding for redevelopment with a priority for municipal housing, the Council moved rapidly

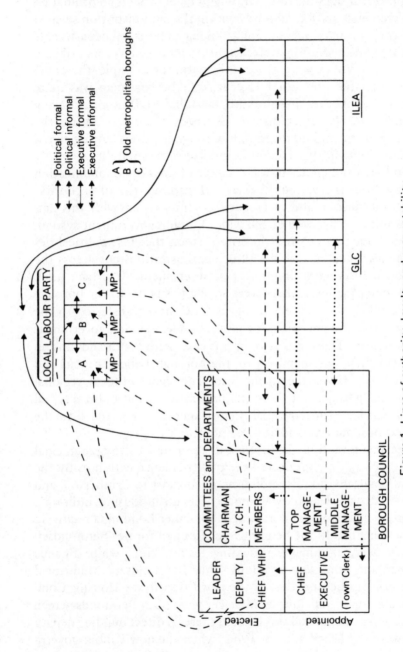

Figure 1 Lines of authority, loyalty and accountability

Note: *There were originally four MPs (later reduced to three), so constituency boundaries were not coterminous with metropolitan borough boundaries.

to prepare the redevelopment of large areas of old Southwark (in which Newington ward was situated) and Camberwell. It needed to move rapidly in order to claim the grant aid, for the government allowed only a limited period within which applications could be submitted. Draft plans were drawn up in great haste: legend speaks of them being devised in a single weekend with a taxi ride round the borough, a large map and a red pencil! Certainly they were ill conceived and they condemned, along with unfit housing, large amounts that were structurally sound. Central government's urgency in this matter may prove to have been an important factor in the widespread planning blight which followed the national upsurge in urban renewal in the 1960s and which led to the public outcry against indiscriminate redevelopment a few years later.[13] But this criticism developed only gradually and for several years it seemed that the Borough Council enjoyed a reputation for urban renewal which responded to the needs and interests of the majority of its residents.

The security and confidence of the ruling caucus was somewhat shaken in the late 1960s by two events which appeared to lead to some structural and power changes. One event was the 1968 local election when the traditional comfortable Labour majority was reduced to a handful: some of old Southwark and most of Camberwell became Conservative. The other was the discovery of serious financial mismanagement in the Council's direct building programme. As in other traditional Labour areas which lost power altogether in the 1968 election, the close result in the borough brought into question within the local Labour group the validity of its existing power distribution. Combined with the need for the Council also to be seen to be making a clean sweep after the direct building crisis and removing those held to be responsible, it enabled several less traditional members to take more powerful positions. It also therefore weakened the grip of Bermondsey members and, although a Bermondsey member was appointed as the new leader, important positions such as deputy leader and chairman of Planning and Development went to old Southwark men. A series of innovatory policies seem to derive from this period, supported and in some cases initiated by senior officers not generally thought to be close to the Bermondsey caucus. With the power change towards the left in the membership a parallel change in the administration appeared evident.

Certain policies initiated at this time are described as innovatory in the sense that their implementation involved changes in the existing organisational structure and its modes of operation. First, with the resignation of the Town Clerk it was decided to appoint a Chief Executive. A major effect to be expected from such a structural change would be the loss of autonomy of the committee/department dyads, a move which could be argued as politically necessary for the Labour group in view of the new strength of official opposition on the Council and the publicity over the building department mismanagement. Second, but far less significantly it seemed at the time for many councillors and officers, the Council welcomed community development into the borough. The National Institute for Social Work negotiated and won in 1968 Council agreement for it to set up a community project aimed both at stimulating neighbourhood community action and at improvements in service delivery which would enable resources more effectively to match needs. It started work in 1969, at about the same time that central government in turn obtained the Council's agreement to joint sponsorship of the community development project figuring in this case. It was conceived with broadly the same dual aims of the independent project.[14] A further commitment of the Council to community work was evident at this period in its plan to employ community workers within the new, reorganised social services department as recommended by the Seebohm Committee.[15] Thus, by the end of the 1960s, an outside observer might have assumed that the Council was fairly radically minded, interested in new ideas, in taking a critical look at its traditional modes of operation and in encouraging the active involvement of the general public in dealing with important issues confronting them. It would not have seemed surprising for such a Council to initiate an experiment in participation in planning, particularly in view of the growing national lobby against massive redevelopment and its associated planning blight and also the increasing local pressure for the Council to reconsider its existing urban renewal plans.[16] Furthermore, the incoming Conservative government quickly redirected central funding away from large-scale slum clearance and redevelopment and towards rehabilitation and small-scale improvement areas, thus creating powerful incentives to local government to change their policies in the same direction. And, as already mentioned, imminent participation in planning legislation seemed very likely.

The problems of the participation experiment could be seen in retrospect to be closely linked with attitudes in the Council to the community project itself. There was a lapse of almost two years between accepting the government's invitation to set it up and in actually doing so. The decision to accept had come in the post-1968 radical wave with particular support from the Chairman of Welfare, the Chief Welfare Officer, the Children's Officer and the Town Clerk. None of these officers had traditional Bermondsey ties and, during the period between acceptance and implementation of the project, two of them resigned to take posts elsewhere. However, another chief officer, the Medical Officer of Health, had also supported its acceptance and had pressed and at first succeeded in having it assigned to the same part of the borough, undoubtedly one of the most deprived, as the independent project. But both the government and the independent project had objected and forced a change in location, after which the MOH, a Bermondsey man in origin, had dissociated himself from the project altogether. Newington ward in old Southwark, whose councillors were respectively chairmen of Planning and Development, Welfare and Health committees, had been chosen from a shortlist drawn up by the Planning Department.

There was evidence to suggest that elements in the Council may have interpreted the relevance of the much advocated community work approach along the lines of the Seebohm Committee and may have seen a second project as an opportunity to try out a pilot exercise, possibly linked to the work of the independent project, in area-based, integrated personal social services provision.[17] However, by the time the project was in operation and the participation experiment agreed upon, the Council had already begun to feel pressure from tenants' associations in the other project's area who lived in some of the worst housing in the borough. Squatters on empty Council property had also recently become active and these kinds of pressures on the Council began to be equated for many of the members with the effects of community work.[18]

Although the chairman of Welfare was not perturbed by such pressures and, on the contrary, openly welcomed what he interpreted as healthy democratic activity, his view was perhaps unusual among the ruling members. A Scot, though he had lived for many years in the borough, he was to some extent an outsider in the traditional Labour group both in origin and in his more radical ideas. When the project finally started up, attitudes expressed among councillors suggested that most of them would have preferred not to have a community project in their constituencies, and the other two representatives of the project ward were no exception. There was already by that time something of a rift between the Newington ward councillors. The chairman of Health had followed her chief officer in dissociating herself from the community project, and the chairman of Welfare had announced his intention not to stand again at the forthcoming local elections. He expressed disillusionment with his less radical colleagues and bowed to the numerical strength of the traditionalists who appeared to have regained their sense of solidarity in the two years since the 1968 set-backs. The slim Labour majority on the Council would have been a powerful incentive to do so, requiring old boundary rivalries to be temporarily shelved in the common interest. The most radical voices in the local Labour Party, as elsewhere in the country, were coming from the wards which had been defeated in the last elections. The Welfare Chairman's ideological support now in fact existed, if at all, only outside the elected body. His announcement was soon followed by the departure of the one remaining promoter of the community project among the chief officers, the Children's Officer. Widely respected professionally, he had been generally expected to become the borough's chief officer of the reorganised personal social services department. Instead, he was given to understand that he would not be appointed, and resigned to take the same new post elsewhere. The Deputy Chief Welfare Office was appointed instead.

By the time it actually started, therefore, the project lacked support from its own employers and was viewed by some with suspicion. This might have been because of not only the growing belief that community action produced uncomfortable effects for those in authority but also the project's second aim of improved service delivery. The independent research arm of the project was already studying some departments where agreement had been given, but it would not have been unusual for officers to resent enquiry into their operations from outside.[19]

With such a situation, the Council's decision to have a participation in planning experiment in the community project area could also be interpreted as offering a means of keeping some control over the project. An internal memorandum referred to the desirability of 'containment', which could be assured through having the exercise firmly within the control of the Planning and Development Committee and Department. However, considerable reservations about the participation exercise were later found to have been expressed by the Housing Manager with support from his chairman. Their chief concern was to maintain as far as possible the original redevelopment programme for the borough so as to ensure that the several massive estates already under construction had enough people from other clearance areas to fill them when completed. Public participation in the project area involving possible changes from redevelopment to rehabilitation could upset this urban renewal rhythm, apart from creating administrative inconvenience through allowing people a greater degree of negotiation over their future housing. However, the events already described meant that they were not, by 1970, on strong ground to oppose the exercise when it could help the Council's faltering reputation in the politically sensitive area of urban renewal and provide valuable data.

The position of the chairman of Planning and Development was of some significance. During the radical wave he had been seen by others in the Council to be a supporter of that movement, in close alliance with the chairman of Welfare. However, his subsequent behaviour suggested that he was closer to the traditionalists in political ideology. By the time of the other's withdrawal from local government, a rift was already evident between them. Given that the participation in planning exercise had some political importance it could, if kept under his control, help the Planning chairman to consolidate his position in a now more strongly Bermondsey-dominated caucus. Similarly, it could also give him some control over the community project which might not only directly benefit him and the other local councillor, the chairman of Health, but also indirectly help their situation in the Labour group. In addition, it could offer a progressive image externally for his committee and department and, not without importance, go some way to still the growing criticism of urban renewal in his own constituency and home base.

The decision to have the participation exercise was also of some interest to another party, the newly appointed Chief Executive who arrived just after the start of the project. He filled a totally new post and was faced with the problem of establishing effective central executive control in a situation where departmental autonomy could be expected to have hardened during the considerable time-lag since the departure of the town clerk. As the exercise actively involved several departments, it could be expected to provide him with information which might assist him in his task, and he had particularly strong potential control over it. Its co-ordinating department, planning, was temporarily answerable directly to him as long as its chief officer post remained vacant (which it did throughout this period); and the community project itself had been administratively placed in his own department.

The decision to have a participation in planning experiment can thus be viewed not only in terms of its obvious political and research advantage to the Council as a whole, but also in terms of its usefulness to particular elements within it. But its containment and control by them was a crucial condition.

Participation and people

Had those elements in the Council been more aware of the real feelings of residents at the time they offered participation in planning, their methods of operating the containment and control terms might have been more sophisticated and possibly more successful. The Labour group's unbroken period in office may have dulled members' political sensitivity to their working-class supporters towards whom the traditionalists tended to be highly paternalistic. Working class themselves, 'we know what people want' was their frequent claim. However, the common reactions of disbelief on the part of ward residents when first told of the invitation to participate in planning, as well as the regularly low local election poll (31 per cent in 1971 for the ward), suggested that they considered themselves effectively disenfranchised despite the fact that their elected members came from the area and still lived there, and also held senior positions in the Council. However, that very seniority was likely to distance these members even further than less influential ones from their constituents. Responsible since London local government reorganisation for a huge area and population, and for ever-increasing legislation, most councillors spent six nights a week on Council or group affairs, as well as holding full-time jobs. Though they clung to the myth of being local representatives, in fact it was their duty to take decisions in the wider borough interests which might at times conflict with the particular interests of their own wards. The time they could devote to explaining this reality of local government representation to their constituents or to listening to their views, assuming they wished to, was minimal.

The Council, both members and officers, were out of touch with the people to whom they were offering participation. Senior officers were just as likely to make generalised assumptions about the public they served. Other studies have pointed out this tendency of local authority officials to assume they know what is best, for working-class neighbourhoods especially, whose people they take for granted as incapable of understanding issues which crucially affect them.[20] Members and officers misjudged the mood of the people and were not prepared to cope with the immediate reactions to their invitation to the participation experiment.

Initial hostility from residents to the Council's overtures was not exceptional or unpredictable in the light of their situation. The opening up of a real communication system with the authority gave them means to express frustration built up over years of ineffectual individual attempts to negotiate with a system which was having a major effect on their future lives but which had until then seemed intractable. Only a few months earlier, while revised draft plans and the participation arrangements were actually being worked out in the Council, a local meeting had been called to request information on the future plans, and councillors had firmly reiterated that the old redevelopment plans were still official policy. In fact, the planning officers had brought the new plans to the meeting on the assumption that members would be making some mention of the new developments, but both plans and officers had been quickly sent away by the members. When that deception was revealed by the participation offer, some hostile reaction was hardly surprising.

Anger was also to be expected given the fact that plan revision was taking place because large parts of the neighbourhood could now be improved rather than pulled down as originally planned a decade earlier. Residents quickly realised that the blight they had been suffering ever since had been unnecessary. Apart from making them angry it also raised doubts for them about the Council's competence, especially as some of them had voiced individual complaints in the past about pulling down structurally sound buildings.

An initial aggressive response to the Council was therefore predictable. It is a common enough experience in community work to find that when people, long forced into a passive acceptance role in local affairs which control their lives, are given the opportunity to be active, their immediate reaction is often disbelief, followed by hostility. However, it is also possible to find, where the offer is genuine, that aggression is soon followed by a positive response which allows constructive work to be developed on the basis of equal partnership.[21] The fact that within a few weeks of the Council's invitation several small area groups were beginning to form from among people who had not previously been publicly involved or organised suggests that a positive response was likely in this case.

However, as already pointed out, the powerful elements in the Council were not seeking participation as an 'act of sharing in the formulation of policies and proposals' but for reasons of political expediency and on terms of containment and control.[22] Their subsequent responses were a reflection of their different priorities of interest and power positions.

Politics and participation

The year-long struggle to reactivate the participation exercise was essentially a political one for all concerned. The position of the residents was unambiguous: they wanted the participation which had been offered to them and been immediately withdrawn. To preserve any credibility with the people they had been employed to help, the community project workers were also clear in their minds that they had to support the resident groups against the Council's sudden policy change. Community workers employed by local authorities are in the position of all 'semi-professionals', facing potential conflict between their responsibilities towards those employing them and towards those they are employed to help professionally.[23] In this case two additional factors were relevant: in the first place, as professional members of its staff they could justifiably, and did, point out to the Council the likely adverse effect on its public relations image of its 'go-stop' policy. In the second, they were also directly responsible to central government, which had an interest in seeing the project work along the principles laid down for it, and were further related, though less clearly, to the GLC and the ILEA. With the strong interdependence of local, regional and central government illustrated earlier, the position of the community project workers therefore offered rather more scope than is perhaps usual for either independent or council employed community workers.

The position of the different elements in the Council was

obviously less clear and was never completely understood. From the effectiveness with which the community project was isolated from the rest of the Council immediately after the abrupt halt to the participation exercise, it was evident that most elements agreed that the containment and control objective could best be secured by removing the project from that sphere of operations into less controversial social welfare concerns. The fact that the project workers would not agree to do so, and that they were in a good strategic position to resist, produced a more untidy and complex situation.

Informal channels of communication were quickly made available to the project from several of the departments, chiefly via middle and lower management levels, some of whom seemed genuinely interested in the participation exercise. They were not as close to the elected membership as their seniors, had no ties of accountability other than the vertical departmental ones and were willing to help unofficially. As mentioned earlier, senior officers of the department involved, other than planning, had always feared the administrative problems likely to arise from the participation experiment and wanted neither them nor interference in their ways of working from either the project or a 'co-ordinating' planning department. Senior planning officers were, on the one hand, naturally interested in implementing an experiment they had initiated, while on the other they needed to keep good working relationships with both the Chief Executive and their chairman. However, the Planning chairman was effectively attempting to take on the chief officer role; he had issued the original instructions to stop the participation exercise. Such a situation could not be acceptable, however, to the Chief Executive to whom, in the absence of a chief officer, the planning officers were directly responsible. His major need was to be seen to be effective in establishing authority in his newly created position of central executive control, by influential people outside the Council as well as his subordinates and employers in it. He had therefore some interest in supporting the participation policy and the project.

At first the political leadership appeared to support the chairman of Planning and the main body of senior officers involved. However, that leadership also needed to be seen to be supporting the efforts of its new chief executive in the corporate management task they had assigned him. They were pulled in one direction by the need to change and in the other by their own strong reluctance to do so. They wanted the principle but not the practice.

During the course of the year almost the whole wider political network (see Figure 1) was at some time or another brought into the conflict, including, after the local elections had returned a Labour Camberwell, the new, more radical element in the Labour group who, though still relatively powerless, tended to support the policies that the earlier radical breeze blowing through the Council had brought in. They were, naturally, interested in strengthening their position in the group and this kind of political 'gaffe' on the part of the traditionalists served their cause.

However, in the end, it was probably the pressure from the residents' group themselves that achieved the promised reinstatement of the participation in planning exercise. At first the opposition asserted that the hostility was promoted by the community project; then that the residents' groups, when their existence could not be denied, were not representative of the people in those streets. After a year of hard work by those groups, including a detailed survey of housing conditions, study of the redevelopment and rehousing processes and their effect on residents, work on traffic problems, securing safe play areas, etc., as well as widespread lobbying to regain the promised participation, it was no longer possible for local councillors or senior officers to claim that they knew what people wanted and at the same time to oppose their demands.

The reinstatement of the participation in planning exercise was offered to the combined residents' groups called to a meeting in the Council chamber. But how far, if at all, did this indicate any real political change in the Council? The conditions laid down by the Council for departmental autonomy (i.e. participation would not be co-ordinated by planning department), and the exclusion of the project, indicated that there might be none. Although, as earlier pointed out, the project was by this time well established in the ward and working closely with more than a dozen residents' groups, and the Chief Executive had already set in motion an inter-departmental working group to improve co-ordination in the urban renewal process, thus making the conditions look rather weak, the traditionalists among members and officers still had strong enough voices at least to have those conditions laid down. The question still remained as to how far those conditions—that new shred of policy—would be implemented in the future. Again, this depended on the relative strength of the different factions inside the Council, their priorities, and the way in which they perceived external pressures to relate to them.

At the point of the reinstatement of the participation in planning exercise, the principal objective of the residents' groups and the community project since its abrupt suspension, the author resigned from her job and another phase of work was begun with a new project team leader. Although the subsequent development of participation cannot therefore be described here,[24] the implications are that the need would have remained for the groups and those helping them to go on studying and interpreting the political dynamics of the local power system in order to be able to act effectively.

But the question should perhaps be asked: Is the situation described here typical? It gives a picture of a traditional Labour-controlled Council, composed to a large extent of working-class members, the majority of them beyond middle age and having spent a large part of their lives in this form of public service. Not a few of them openly scorned young, university-educated professionals; they took the view that their life-long experience of the local 'grass-roots' was as good, and probably a better basis from which to form judgments about priorities and policies for government. A number of such traditional Labour strongholds in the country fell to the Conservatives in the 1968 local elections and made it thus possible for younger, more radically-postured elements in local Labour Parties legitimately to claim the right to lead the next attempt to regain power. Where they did so and won, has a reduction in the complexity of the political dynamics followed? Baine's account of one such borough suggests that the internal political tangle does not necessarily become any simpler with attempts at more open government and greater participation.[25] Has the now fairly widespread introduction of corporate management techniques had any effect in this respect, or has it merely served to polarise the division between the administrative, professional and party political clusters of systems within local government, whereas in this case they were less sharply defined?

It is extremely difficult for an external enquirer to sift the myth from the reality of the internal politics of local government organisations. On the one hand, there is the problem of the divergence between the traditionally accepted roles and functions of councillors, administrators and professionals and the ones they now perform in practice. Dearlove appears to have found the officers quite unwilling to admit they were anything but advisers implementing the policy decisions of elected members.[26] But the scale and technical complexity of local government today affords considerable potential and actual power to such 'advisers', effectively presenting them with political functions and roles. Assuming that, like the Kensington officers, local government servants generally reject the political image, the researcher is left to probe other sources to assess when, where and to what extent officers may be acting politically.

On the other hand, internal politics in large organisations, be they local government, industry, university, etc., are often associated with the personal and group fantasies of those who work in them about who really wields power and influence, about how much of it they have and about who is in league with whom. The size and breadth of interests of such organisations limit direct interaction and communication between the majority of their members to a few departments or sections. Insofar as they are affected by decisions taken elsewhere in the organisation, knowledge about the rest of it will rely on indirect experience in which, it is suggested, rumour or fantasy play a considerable part. To the extent that it does, the reliability of information proffered to the researcher about internal politics is in doubt.

However, a great many more case studies and accounts are necessary, whether emanating from inevitably partisan insiders or relatively handicapped outsiders, in order to assess the normality or otherwise of the situation described in this one. In the meantime it does indicate that community workers cannot simply assume that because a certain social policy is officially adopted, it will be carried out, and it suggests that by seeking to find out *why* it has been adopted, they may more effectively work towards assuring that it is. There is a whole hidden world between policy-making and policy-implementation.

Notes

1 See the Study by the Community Work Group of the Calouste Gulbenkian Foundation, *Current Issues in Community Work*, Routledge & Kegan Paul, 1973, chapter 2, for a discussion of the range of activities covered by this term.

2 John Dearlove, *The Politics of Policy in Local Government*, Cambridge University Press, 1973.

3 The importance of non-decisions is discussed in Peter Bachrach and Morton S. Baratz, *Power and Poverty—Theory and Practice*, New York, Oxford University Press, 1970, chapter 3.

4 Sean Baine, *Community Action and Local Government*, Occasional Papers on Social Administration, no. 59, G. Bell, 1975.

5 See, for example, Jon Gower Davies, *The Evangelistic Bureaucrat*, Tavistock, 1972, on planners as a professional interest group.

6 The late Saul D. Alinsky was a past master of such strategy. See various films on his work listed by Concord Films Council Limited, Ipswich, and also his books, *Rules for Radicals*, New York, Random House, 1971, and *Reveille for Radicals*, New York, Random House, 1946.

7 Baine, op. cit., p. 84; Bachrach and Baratz, op. cit., p. 52.

8 Mention has already been made of the late Saul Alinsky's work which rather colourfully illustrates the tactical exploitation of large organisations' internal politics to help deprived community groups. A British example might be the original squatting movement begun in the Greater London area in the 1960s; see Ron Bailey, *The Squatters*, Penguin Books, 1973.

9 American sociologists have given it attention within the field of community studies in particular. In social policy in this country a start has now been made, with reference to central government, by Phoebe Hall, Hilary Land, Roy Parker and Adrian Webb, *Change, Choice and Conflict in Social Policy*, Heinemann, 1975.

10 It does not take into account changes which may have taken place since that time.

11 *People and Planning*, Report of the Committee on Public Participation in Planning (Skeffington Report), HMSO, 1969.

12 The use of different roles and tasks within a community project team is also discussed in David N. Thomas, *Organising for Social Change*, Allen & Unwin, 1976, p. 52.

13 See, for example, the cases studied in Norman Dennis, *People and Planning*, Faber, 1970; Davies, op. cit.

14 For an account of the National Institute's project see Thomas, op. cit; the aims of the National Community Development Project are reproduced in R. Lees and G. Smith (eds), *Action—Research in Community Development*, Routledge & Kegan Paul, 1975.

15 Report of the Committee on Local Authority and Allied Personal Social Services (Seebohm Report), Cmnd 3703, HMSO, 1968, paras 501—7.

16 Combined local voluntary associations organised a well-publicised and reported conference on planning blight in the borough and its social costs in early 1970: *From Rumour to Removal*, Southwark Council of Social Service Redevelopment Link Group.

17 Seebohm Report, paras 501—7.

18 Bailey, op. cit.

19 Members of the research team have produced an account of their work in Southwark, in Stephen Hatch, Enid Fox and Charles Legg, *Research and Reform: Southwark CPD 1969—72*, Home Office Urban Deprivation Unit, 1977.

20 See, for example, Davies, op. cit.; Norman Dennis, *Public Participation and Planners' Blight*, Faber, 1972; Richard Batley, 'An Explanation of Non-Participation in Planning', *Policy and Politics*, 1 (2), 1973.

21 There are one or two examples, for instance, in Sidney Jacobs, *The Right to a Decent House*, Routledge & Kegan Paul, 1976, as well as examples of non-genuine overtures from a local authority.

22 Skeffington Report, p. 1.

23 A. Etzioni, *The Semi-Professions and their Organizations: Teachers, Nurses, Social Workers*, New York, Free Press, 1969.

24 For the final report of the Project see A. Davis, N. McIntosh and J. Williams, *The Management of Deprivation*, Final Report of Southwark Community Project, Polytechnic of the South Bank, London, 1977.

25 op. cit.

26 op. cit.

9 The Community Development section of Liverpool City Council, 1972—5

Peter Clyne

The appointment of a Community Development Officer by the City Council in 1972 had been preceded by a long history of community action and change in Liverpool. The Liverpool Council of Social Service had been concerned with and directly involved in community work and community development since the early 1960s—in 1961 it was partly responsible for the creation of the first Community Council in Liverpool in Toxteth. Later, full-time staff and honorary officers joined with members of the City Council on the Joint Community Development Committee of the Education Committee. In 1968 the report of a working party set up by the Youth and Community Services Sub-Committee and the Joint Community Development Committee attempted to define community development, and this report was subsequently quoted in a report of the Chief Executive of the City Council on Community Development Policy in 1971: 'Amongst other things, community development emerged as the deliberate encouragement of people to become more competent in solving problems of city life . . . the deliberate approach to a community'. The clear view at this time was that voluntary organisations and those few people employed as community workers within the City Council were in the business of developing communities and not improving services. This was the time, 1968 and on, when Liverpool enjoyed a rapid growth in the number and variety of community groups, when an Educational Priority Area (EPA), Community Development Project (CDP) and the Shelter Neighbourhood Action Project (SNAP) all existed within two miles of each other in the inner city and when the City Council itself was considering and partially implementing recommendations on structures and services emanating from a major management services study. Everything was happening at the same time, but there was general agreement among all concerned with community work in Liverpool that:

1 A Community Development Officer (CDO) should be appointed to the Chief Executive's office.
2 The City Council should identify a positive community development policy.
3 The City Council should make funds available to support and encourage voluntary organisations.

The City Council finally agreed to the appointment of a Community Development Officer at the end of 1971 when accepting a report which stated, inter alia:

> community development is of an evolutionary nature, much of it is experimental and the Council's policy should be aimed to achieve community development which complements the work of the Authority within the democratic process. Liverpool is and has for some time been in a dynamic situation and, as in many other social matters, has been well ahead of its time. Actions taken by the Council should not inhibit but should take full advantage of the initiatives which exist in the City for the good of the community as a whole. There is certainly no single right solution to the problem of selecting a community development policy . . .

Implicit in the decision of the City Council was a clear belief that there can be a partnership between the local authority and voluntary organisations in the field of community development.

I took up my post as CDO in October 1972, working to the Chief Executive and with the following basic duties:

1 To assess the present position of community work in the City; indicating the roles played by the local authority and by voluntary organisations;
2 To exercise a co-ordinating role for community work as between different departments of the local authority;
3 To examine the possible need for redeployment of existing resources applied to community work and make suggestions for any such redeployment;
4 To make suggestions for new lines of development of community work with an indication of the likely financial implications;
5 To act as a point of reference within the local authority for all requests from community organisations for information about, or action upon, services rendered by any local authority Department.

In many ways the job to which I had been appointed was unusual and possibly unique in local authority work. Although concerned with the extent, nature and quality of community work I was quite deliberately located in the Chief Executive's office and thus removed from direct involvement in any spending department. The work was seen to be relevant to the newly established corporate management structure. This was evident in two ways. First, I was entitled to information from all departments as if I were indeed a member of all departments and, second, the post of CDO was considered to be an essential expression of public contact, involvement and influence for voluntary organisations in the corporate management process. Unusually for a local government post, the CDO was recognised at the outset as an officer required to serve both the local authority and voluntary organisations, even if the two were to be at loggerheads. At the time of my appointment, the Housing Finance Act was a live issue.

My aims and priorities during the early months were inevitably connected with establishing credibility for the position in the eyes and attitudes of voluntary organisations and members and officers of the City Council. Something had to be done and done quickly, and I endeavoured to be constructively critical of the practices of the Council and of the existing consultative and advisory machinery while making it apparent that the active efforts of the CDO could lead to an increase in the allocation of resources from central and local government to voluntary organisations. It was important for the establishment of the post that I was seen to be working not only with the committees of the City Council in the Municipal Buildings but also with voluntary organisations in different neighbourhoods throughout Liverpool.

The City Council established a Joint Advisory Committee on Community Development 'to review progress made on a community development policy for the City'. A measure of the importance attached to the community development commitment was the fact that the Joint Advisory Committee comprised the Leader of the Council (Labour) and the leading spokesmen on the Social Services, Housing, Policy and Finance, Environmental Health and Protection and Education Committees. Included in the membership were the Leaders of the Conservative and Liberal Groups.

This Committee met five times between November 1972 and August 1973. During this period it considered various papers on aspects of provision and policy, recommendations for community development, staffing and resource allocation. Partly in response to the dynamic and multi-faceted voluntary organisation scene and partly as a way of relating the statutory services more appropriately to the needs of the local neighbourhoods, various departments of the City Council had established posts in the field of community work. In September 1965 three Area Community Wardens were appointed to the Further Education Section of the Education Department 'to co-ordinate and to develop fully the various services in a given area of the City, in co-operation with Principals of Evening Institutes, Superintendents of Play and Recreation Centres'. Four Community Work Organisers had been appointed within the Children's Department. After the reorganisation of the Children's and Welfare Departments into the Social Services Department, the posts were redesignated Social Work Liaison Officers. In 1971 the Housing Department, with an Urban Aid grant, had created a Community Development Officer post within the Housing Improvement Division. Subsequently three Neighbourhood Worker posts were established to operate in General Improvement Areas. The City Planning Office, through its Area Planners, was endeavouring to carry through the Skeffington Report ('People and Planning') recommendations and were, consequently, in close contact with the community organisations of the city.

In addition to the variety of full-time staff in post in City Council Departments, the Liverpool Council of Social Service employed a small team of full-time workers spanning youth, welfare and community work. At this time, late 1960s to the early 1970s, there were also in Liverpool a CDP in the Vauxhall area, a Department of the Environment Inner Area Study, a major Home Office initiative in the South City Centre area. The EPA project ended in April 1972 and there were some important community work consequences deriving from that work. Also in April 1972 the SNAP ended in Granby, leaving a Housing Aid Centre which had social and communal significance far wider than its title suggested.

The Joint Advisory Committee on Community Development was thus considering many initiatives and arrangements which needed to be co-ordinated in some way. However, the co-ordinating exercise should not stamp out the richness derived from variety.

One of the crucial issues during the first few months of 1973 was the political sensitivity of community development work.

Elections took place in April and May 1973 for the new Liverpool District and Merseyside County Councils. As CDO, I had been actively pursuing ways of increasing public involvement in decision-making, public access to information and City Council support for voluntary organisations. In January 1973 the Committee discussed a report which touched specifically upon these issues. I was anxious, for reasons of self-preservation as well as guidance for the future, to ensure that the implications of accepting a positive community development policy were understood. Feelings of remoteness, isolation and weakness on the part of individuals, in the face of large and often complex local authority structures, breed resentment, apathy, mistrust and hostility. This is hardly conducive to community development work. While elected representatives rely on information and advice from officers appointed to specific tasks, it was important to ensure that officers did not come between members and the community. The objectives of a community worker and his position within the community differ fundamentally from the objectives and position of elected members. In a clearly understood, but none the less dynamic situation, there should be no danger of an 'alternative democracy' emerging as a result of the actions of community workers whose prime task must be to aid local people without being personally involved in polarising political attitudes. Elected members are concerned with policy formulation, financial control and dealing with issues raised by electors individually or in groups. Community workers are concerned with advising, encouraging and supporting the community towards the achievement of their own defined objectives. It is neither wrong nor damaging that community groups will at times conflict with councillors. In social situations conflict can often be a valuable process towards progress and change. As the elections of spring 1973 approached, the policy of grant aid with 'no strings attached' became questioned. In one instance a full-time worker with a community group, whose salary was grant-aided by the City Council, stood as a candidate against the sitting Labour member. In another instance the Liberal Party objected to the display of Labour Party election material in the office of a community group which was receiving a grant for office running costs. The debate around these examples and the broader questions was resolved by an acceptance by the City Council at the time of the policy that no conditions could or should be attached to grant-aid to limit political involvement and action. Such conditions would inevitably nullify the overt expression of commitment to community development processes by the City Council and within Liverpool as a whole.

Towards the end of March 1973 the Chief Executive of the City Council submitted a report to the Joint Advisory Committee on future arrangements. This report was accepted by the City Council and then, because of the intervening local elections which brought into existence a 'shadow' Liberal District Council, was passed to that District Council for consideration. The report made a number of specific points. It first recommended the creation of a Community Development Section within the Chief Executive's Office. The Section would comprise myself and my secretary plus two Assistant Community Development Officers, four Area Community Development Officers and an administrative assistant. These last seven posts would be newly created and filled. It was recommended that the following statement be included in the terms of reference applying to the Section:

> The Community Development Section shall be led by a Community Development Officer who shall be a member of the staff of the Chief Executive. The Section shall have a co-ordinating, creative, experimental and monitoring role in the field of community work. The co-ordinating role implies consultation with and advice to the Departments of the Local Authority engaged in community work, to ensure the maximum impact from such work by the co-ordination and concentration of effort, the avoidance of overlapping, and the full use of resources. It implies, too, consultation with voluntary agencies directed to these ends. The creative and experimental roles imply the suggestion of lines of development for community work within any Department of the Local Authority, or collectively between Departments, or through voluntary agencies; including suggestions for the redeployment of resources provided for community work within a Department or between Departments. The monitoring role implies the duty to keep under review the community work undertaken separately or jointly by Departments of the Local Authority and to seek to assess the impact of such work for the guidance of the Local Authority and its Departments in determining future action.

This important report recommended, second, that the Joint

Committee should continue in existence and that it would not be appropriate to establish a separate standing committee of the City Council for community development matters. Third, the report recommended that the Community Development Section should provide elected members with up-to-date information on community work and organisations and likely future developments, and assist members in clarifying their own roles in relation to voluntary organisations.

It was soon apparent that the newly elected Liberal Liverpool District Council had a different view of community development work from its predecessor. The 1973 election was fought at a time of rising fortunes for the Liberal Party nationally and locally, the national President and Chairman of the Party were Liverpool councillors and the 'community politics' platform was largely erected in Liverpool. One of the foremost objectives of the Liberal Group on the Council was to bring the processes of local government closer to the electorate and, wherever possible, to involve the electorate in various aspects of decision-making. In this context the work of the CDO was considered to be central to political debate and action in Liverpool. Thus, it was not surprising to find that the Liberal Group decided to establish a Community Development Committee (CDC) as a standing committee of the Council, equal in status with the committees concerned with Social Services, Education, Housing, etc.

Having determined to create the CDC, it was inevitable that attention should be paid to the transfer of the various community work elements of the different departments to the Community Development Section to be established. The Local Government Act which brought into existence the new local authority structure in 1973 required that committee meetings should be held in public. I welcomed this as a necessary first step towards the operation of a participatory democracy. Open committees were welcomed by the Liberals for the same reason, and also because they felt it was desirable to ensure that the arrangements for local government should be, as far as possible, compatible with the effective management of city affairs, and illustrative of an open government approach to Council work. The Labour and Conservative Parties were not as keen on the new arrangement in Liverpool, believing that there were two significant in-built dangers. First, councillors might tend to play to the gallery occupied by the press and public, and, second, opportunities would increase for individuals and groups to exert undue pressure on elected members. Throughout the spring and summer of 1973 the Liberal Party had a small working party of selected individuals from the political and community work fields discussing possible arrangements for the future. The outcome of these deliberations was made public after each meeting and, although I was not party to the discussions, my views were sought on the proposals as they emerged. I was not anxious to see the Community Development Section, when established, become directly involved in community work, believing that its crucial advisory and monitoring role would thereby be threatened. Nevertheless, in August 1973, the CDC considered a resolution moved by the Chairman

> that proposals for the establishment of a Community Development Section be submitted as soon as possible after the appointment of the Community Development Officer, such proposals to include the transfer to the Community Development Section of the Social Work Liaison Officers in the Social Services Department and the staff engaged on youth and community service work in the Education Department.

In the course of debate an amendment, moved and seconded by Labour members, was accepted by the Committee. This amendment read: 'that consideration of this matter be deferred pending the appointment of a Community Development Officer, and the submission of reports by the Directors of Education, Social Services and Housing and the Community Development Officer to be appointed, on the proposed appointment of a Community Development Section.' I was appointed by the District Council to continue in my post as CDO at the end of August 1973.

During the summer and autumn the debate on how best to establish a Community Development Section continued. The City Council had previously determined that it wished to see a section without any fieldwork responsibilities. However, in the light of the new District Council's review of the entire range of community work and community development work, the City Council (politically) relinquished its interest in the CDO's work. Autumn 1973 was a difficult time. Clearly the Liberal Group wished to see the Community Development Section emerge as the tool for implementing its policies of community politics. The combined strength of Conserative and Labour members was sufficient to frustate this objective. The strongly expressed views of the voluntary organisations and professional staff engaged in community work were against the Liberals' intention. They feared the inevitable centralised and party political control of what was neighbourhood-based organic community work. Additionally, the close identification of CDOs with a party platform was seen to be unhelpful at a time when the open relationship between the statutory and voluntary interests was becoming recognised. Further, any moves towards a party political identity for the Community Development Section was seen as a very real potential threat to the independence of voluntary organisations at that time in receipt of local government grant-aid.

At its meeting on 6 December 1973 the CDC received and accepted my report, concluding that it would not be to the advantage of voluntary organisations or the local authority if the community work staff of the different departments of the authority were transferred to the Community Development Section. It was argued that transferring such staff from the Social Services, Housing and Education Departments would remove essential community links from the departments. It was further pointed out that the Secretaries of State for Social Services and Education would have been obliged to agree to such transfers, and to see such agreement would have caused delays and uncertainty which would have been bound adversely to affect the services.

By the end of 1973 the District Council had agreed to the creation of a Community Development Section comprising a CDO, Principal Assistant CDO, four Area CDOs, Secretary, Administrative Assistant and Clerical Assistant. The CDC had been constituted, and its terms of reference, inherited from the now defunct Joint Advisory Committee on Community Development, agreed. When appointing staff to fill the professional posts the aim was to create a multi-disciplinary team. A disagreement which arose at this time was over the role of community workers and CDOs vis-à-vis elected members. The disagreement was fundamental and continued throughout 1974 and into 1975.

It is necessary to understand the political nature of the disagreement. I saw the primary tasks of members of the Community Development Section as being to assist local groups and departments of the City Council in identifying issues and needs and enabling progress to be made through participatory and consultative exercises. Sometimes this required the creation of new machinery. More often it called for attitude changes and the encouragement of groups to look beyond unemptied dustbins and delays in housing repairs to social and political goals which questioned policies and priorities. The strength of much community development work was to be measured in the confidence and awareness of groups and their ability to tackle political issues, alone or with politicians. The leadership of the Liberal Council, on the other hand, saw the principal task of CDOs as being the identification and assessment of environmental and social issues for the benefit of elected councillors who, armed with further information, could take political decisions. Whereas such work might have improved the service delivery in the short run, it would have done nothing to change the relationship and balance of political power between councillors and residents. Community Development Officers, community workers in the field and activists in community groups were anxiously exploring together ways of helping voluntary organisations to base their day-to-day tactics and action upon an understanding of the need to think and plan well ahead. Short-term ameliorative measures would have little effect on long-term political thinking and involvement unless the context was understood by all involved. Throughout this period many meetings were held, courses organised for voluntary organisation activists, and community newspapers and broadsheets produced to progress social and political thinking in the localities. Many groups required support and advice to enable them to take up current issues (repairs, lighting, cleansing, etc.) within the broader strategy of long-term planning being undertaken by group members.

In February 1974 the Council agreed to allocate a budget to the CDC, the money to be granted to voluntary organisations for certain specified work. Throughout the late 1960s and early 1970s grants had been made available to voluntary organisations in Liverpool involved in community work. In addition to grants through the Urban Programme, CDP and trusts and foundations, some money was allocated by the City Council through the Education and Social Services Committees. I was not anxious to have a budget at the disposal of the CDC; first, because it would be likely to lead to other committees relinquishing their responsibilities in community work fields on the pretext that the CDC would fund all community work; second, because the CDOs' opportunities to comment upon proposals and advise other committees on the allocation of funds would be severely limited.

The essential advisory and developmental roles would be jeopardised because of the increasing importance of the administrative role. In addition to an assurance that grant aid would continue to organisations already in receipt of Council money, the Council allocated a further £93,000 for the year 1974—5:

Community transport	£5,000
Neighbourbood festivals	£3,000
Part-time and full-time staff for neighbourhood community work	£30,000
Up-grading of premises used by neighbourhood organisations	£40,000
Running costs, equipment and projects	£10,000
Work with the elderly	£5,000

There was no doubt that most voluntary organisations welcomed the availability of more money, and many gave early and urgent attention to the submission of applications. It soon became obvious that the terms of reference of the Committee were so wide as to encompass areas of work which were the responsibility of the Social Services, Housing and Education Committees. This did not necessarily cause problems for voluntary organisations but it made relationships difficult between the CDOs and colleagues in other departments of the City Council.

The Chairman of the Committee was very anxious to ensure that the deliberations and decisions of the Committee were public and, as far as practicable, interested and informed members of voluntary organisations participated in Committee meetings. I wholeheartedly supported the Chairman's wishes both because I believed it was necessary to explore various ways of moving from a representative democracy to a participatory democracy and also because it was necessary to make sure that the CDC was seen to be a different type of committee. The Committee comprised Liberal, Labour and Conservative members in the same ratios as existed on other Council committees. There were, in addition, co-opted members of the Committee representing neighbourhood organisations, youth organisations, University, Community Relations Council and Council of Social Service. The time and dates of meetings were widely publicised, agendas and papers were circulated in advance, press and radio were encouraged to attend all meetings and people concerned with any item on the agenda were given the opportunity to speak. Additionally, the public were not separated physically from the elected members in the meeting room. Thus the large gathering at the six-weekly meetings, often exceeding sixty, formed a valuable forum for considering community work issues. Tea or coffee was served to all, and everyone who attended, regardless of status, had all the necessary committee papers.

The consequences of this arrangement were many. For a large number of people, the mystique of local government was removed: information was equally available. Lobbying and pressure-group politics was taken into the meeting of the Committee. Demands were forthcoming for an equally open approach at other commit-tees and, when these demands were not met, it became increasingly clear that opportunities were taken by community work activists and voluntary organisation representatives to raise a wide range of issues at the meetings of the CDC. In other words, the open CDC was used as a forum for issues more appropriately the concern of the Education, Social Services or Housing, Building and Planning Committees. It is my contention that the openness of the CDC strengthened the positions of the elected members of the Commit-tee and the officers serving it. This strengthening derived from a closer awareness of many of the current issues and a clearer under-standing of the pressures and needs evident in the City. However, if there was strengthening on one Committee there was a weakening on the others, which made no organisational concession to the establishment of a system of open and participatory government.

Other committees and officers tended to withdraw behind invisible but none the less real barriers, and exhibited exaggerated postures of remoteness. Questions were asked about the closed nature of other committees but were never answered to the satis-faction of the questioners from community groups, who began to accuse the City Council of 'window-dressing' with an open CDC which had little power in the City Council as a whole. The real gain from this period was the appreciation that the traditional organisational and administrative arrangements for a Council committee are not beyond change and that moves towards a participatory democracy are possible within the existing local government structure. The preoccupation of 1974 was the con-sideration of applications for grant aid from the Committee and subsequent administration of grants. I felt that a disproportionate amount of time and effort was spent on dispersing a comparatively small sum of money. Indeed, by the end of the year, some volun-tary organisations came to share this view and agreed that so long as the main services and procedures of the Council remained unchanged the very small CDC budget could be only a sop.

In July 1974 the Department of Environment issued a consultation circular on Neighbourhood Councils in England, and the Council established a small working party to consider Liverpool's position and viewpoint. The Liberal view was strongly in favour of directly elected neighbourhood councils throughout Liverpool which would have a structured formal relationship with the City Council and would, on behalf of the City Council, perform certain delegated local functions. During 1974 the Liberal Party was encouraging officers of the Council and local voluntary organisations to consider ways in which there could be greater public involvement in decision-making in the management of council housing, the management of schools and environmental improvements. However, at the same time, the Party Group on the City Council was very concerned about the pressure and influence which well-organised and staffed community groups could display in Liverpool. The Labour and Conservative Parties both opposed the introduction of formal neighbourhood councils, but for different reasons. The Labour view was that a further tier of local government, which directly elected and publicly financed neighbourhood councils would inevitably become, would make for delays and problems of remoteness. It was also the view of the Labour Party that such an arrangement would threaten the public position of City councillors as representatives of the electors. The Conservative Party was of the opinion that the effectiveness and efficiency of City Council services would be weakened by extra consultative machinery and that the concept of formal statutory neighbourhood councils was damaging to the local government structure as recently reorganised.

The Department of the Environment Consultation paper was widely discussed amongst the community groups and by the community workers in Liverpool. The strong majority view of the groups and the workers was that the creation of a formal network would inevitably damage the organic community groups and break down the relationships which were developing between groups and City Council members and officers. My opinion, expressed at the time, was that directly elected, officially recognised and publicly financed neighbourhood councils would create an even wider gulf between the City Council and the people of Liverpool and would prove to be the negation of a participatory democracy. To a great degree the potential of community work and community development initiatives in the City rested on the many varied local groupings of people pursuing specific or general objectives which they determined for themselves from time to time.

Eventually the City Council agreed to reject the proposals for formal statutory neighbourhood councils and to pursue a community development policy based on the thesis that the City Council and voluntary organisations can work in partnership towards the betterment of life in Liverpool.

Early in 1975 the conflict between the controlling Liberal Group on the City Council and the community groups became greater and my position as CDO became untenable. The Council opposed the concept of grants going to groups with 'no strings attached', and wished the staff of the Community Development Section to ensure that no group in receipt of public money acted or campaigned against the policies of the Council. This I could not do.

The validity of a community development policy depended upon the freedom of groups to pursue objectives which they set for themselves and, consequently, the freedom of CDOs to furnish groups with needed advice and information. The Community Development Section had to be seen to be able to serve the groups as well as the Council. Therefore, it came as no surprise to those involved in community work in Liverpool when the Leader of the Council proposed that the Community Development Section be disbanded and the Committee be wound up. After much debate the Committee was wound up, the budget was dispersed to the main spending committees of the Council and the Community Development Section was required to confine its work to advising the departments of the City Council and voluntary organisations in the field of community work. The opportunity to encourage policy and practice changes or significantly alter the balance of power between the Council and the people was reduced.

In retrospect, it may well be claimed that the work of the Community Development Section of the City Council from 1972 to 1975 had heightened expectations among community groups and community workers. Perhaps too much was expected from a changed arrangement which lasted only for a brief period. If one expectation had been a perceptible move of power from the City Council to the community, this was not achieved. The City Council's structure and political attitudes in 1975 were centralist and opposed to public involvement and participation. This, in a short three years, was a dramatic change from 1972. Not only were many voluntary organisations encouraged by the newly elected Liberal Council in 1973 to look towards a transfer of resources and power from the City Council to the community but they were also encouraged to look foward to a time in the not too distant future when the community would enjoy a wider use of City Council facilities. Expectations were raised only to be dashed very quickly. Certainly it is true that more money was put into community work, many groups were strengthened through advice and support and were thus more capable of presenting their views and exerting political pressure, and the procedure and policies of the City Council were more open to public scrutiny than hitherto. Nevertheless, achievements during this period were modest and, when an objective and close study is made of the consequences of the CDP in Vauxhall, the Inner Area Study in Liverpool 8, and the general work of the Community Development Section is written, although I am convinced that the work of the Section will be seen to have had the greater impact in the light of the marginal changes in City Council policies and practices, that impact will be seen to be slight. The experience in Liverpool during these three years has shown that it is very difficult for a City Council to put a progressive community development policy into practice. I think it has also shown that essential co-ordination and professional 'boat-rocking' can be done only from within the local authority structure. Finally, it has also shown that voluntary community organisations will be happy to work with local government offices whose terms of reference are understood and whose everyday community work is open to public gaze.

The views expressed in this chapter are those of the author. Neither Liverpool City Council nor the Inner London Education Authority have been consulted about the content or opinions contained within it.

10 Politics, conflict and community action in Northern Ireland

Tom Lovett and Robin Percival

Over the past eight years, since the onset of the present conflict, there has been a tremendous growth in community action in Northern Ireland. Over 500 community organisations in both Protestant and Catholic areas have been established.

Many of the problems community activists have to face here stem directly from the troubles: the collapse of government authority at certain critical times, as in 1971 and 1974; the rivalry between political parties and para-military organisations for power and influence within communities; and, of course, the sectarian divisions between Protestant and Catholic. Nevertheless, community groups have made significant contributions to the resolution of these problems.

However, community activists also face the sorts of social and economic problems found in working-class communities throughout western society. Their internal problems are also very similiar: the existence within community groups of sharp differences as to the function of community action; the dangers of co-option by political bureaucracies; the pressure towards greater 'professionalism'; the failure to develop a coherent analysis by which to measure success or within which to build a radical politics as an alternative to both conventional and para-military politics.

Thus, although community action in Northern Ireland is in some degree a response to, and operates against a background of, violence, it does in fact highlight many of the problems, issues and contradictions facing those involved in community action in more peaceful settings.

Historical developments

Community action is not a new phenomenon in Northern Ireland.

In the 1930s there was widespread resistance in many working-class areas to the imposition of a major rent increase. Similarly, in the mid-1960s there was a further rent strike, though this met with little success. A variety of community organisations have also existed for a considerable time. Tenant leagues and associations were established in many of the new Belfast housing estates, such as Finaghy and Ballymurphy, in the late 1940s. In the 1950s two important self-help projects were initiated in Londonderry. One was the Derry Housing Aid Society, which began its own house-building programme to offset, in part, the lack of new houses being built by the Unionist Corporation. The other was the Credit Union, a financial co-operative movement which assists people on low incomes to pool their financial resources so that they can borrow at cheap rates of interest. This was formed in 1959 and grew into the largest of its type in the world. Later Credit Unions have been widely established in many Catholic areas of the province. In Belfast itself there were other forms of self-generated economic activity. Workers' co-operatives were formed in the Whiterock/Ballymurphy districts and today they are among the major work providers in that area.

Thus an important tradition of community action and mutual aid was established in Ulster in the twenty years before the present political conflict began. It is a tradition which, for some at least, affirmed the possibility of change without resort to violence or to conservative and sectarian political parties. It is also a tradition which in the turbulence of the past eight years has managed to allow many ordinary people to participate in social and political action on an unprecedented scale. Since 1968, the year in which the political unrest began, at least 500 permanent community organisations have been established in all parts of the province, roughly one group per 3,000 head of population.[1]

It is not our intention to analyse in detail the many reasons for this rapid and widespread growth in community action. It is important to note, however, that the style and content of much of it has been intimately linked with the origins and progress of the disturbances. In 1967, for instance, the Derry Housing Action Group was formed, which, in contrast to the self-help-orientated strategies of the Credit Union and Housing Aid Society, pursued more militant tactics with a campaign of direct action.[2] It was the Housing Action Group which, with the N. Ireland Civil Rights Association (NICRA), organised the first civil rights march in

Derry in October 1969 which triggered off the present unrest. This coalition between a community action group and a politically significant civil rights campaign arose out of the nature of the discriminatory policies of the then Unionist administration. These policies were political in the sense of denying many people the right to vote in local government elections, and social in the way they affected job opportunities and the provision of social services (such as housing) in Catholic areas.

Since then, as the conflict within Northern Ireland has intensified, there have been several occasions when various communities have tried to prevent the normal functioning of many state agencies. These were the 'no-go' areas in Catholic districts, the most famous of which was Free Derry. It is of course impossible to generalise about the no-go areas. After 1971 most of them were dominated by para-military organisations who did little to encourage community action or self-government. But, prior to that, the no-go areas were to some extent experiments in community self-management which many believe is a primary objective of community action.

One of the people who played a part in that experiment in Free Derry had this to say about the organisation involved, the Derry Citizens Action Committee:[3]

> The Derry Citizens Action Committee was notable for one thing. They didn't have a community organisation but they did have street committees. The Derry Citizens Action Committee, after the initial clash in 1969, adopted a social role. They went out into the various streets and got representatives from the streets so that no decision was made by the DCAC unless the street representatives had a say. As well as that it was quite common, after a decision had been made, to go out into the street, have a meeting on a street corner and say that a decision has been made tonight—do you agree with it or not? You had democracy, perhaps a primitive form, but still a democracy which enabled people to feel that they were having a say in what was going on . . . It was amazing how the bureaucrats were able to co-operate with the DCAC, which had declared its intention of overthrowing the government. It was unbelievable. The local bureaucrats and the local officials came and offered their services. Life went on normally. The bins were collected, the roads were swept, the electric power

was left on. It's amazing how society just doesn't fall apart in such circumstances.

This experience has been repeated on a number of occasions over the last eight years in both Protestant and Catholic areas because of the armed conflict in the streets and, on occasions, the effective breakdown of government such as occurred in May 1974 during the Ulster workers' strike. This has meant that community groups have been thrown onto their own resources and forced to undertake much of the day-to-day running of their areas. During the internment crisis of August 1971 many neighbourhoods, particularly in Belfast, had suddenly to cope with major movements in population as people scrambled to get into areas where they could feel relatively safe. This led to the creation of relief centres for the victims of the violence as well as the relatives of the internees. Vigilante groups were also established and, in Catholic areas, an effective and widespread rent and rate strike was organised.

In May 1974 the disruption caused by the Protestant Ulster Workers Council strike was more widespread than the internment crisis of August 1971, though much less costly in terms of human lives. The province faced a situation where electricity was progressively run down, causing a complete industrial stoppage. Gas supplies were cut off so that many government agencies were unable to function as their members were on strike or unable to reach their work. In this situation it was the community groups which had to organise the provision of food and drink and prepare makeshift cooking facilities. They had also to arrange for the immediate care of those sections of the community who are particularly vulnerable at a time of dislocation, such as the old and infirm. They had to establish their own transport systems when fuel was obtainable and, of course, set up the usual relief centres.

One of those actively involved had this to say about that achievement:[4]

> The UWC strike created an emergency and the Area Boards proved unable to handle the problems that arose. Where else in the world would you have had that condition prevailing in Northern Ireland without concurrent waves of looting and lawlessness? The peace that prevailed did so because of the community groups, Protestant and Catholic. These groups were able to do all the things that central and local government bodies are supposed to do in a state of emergency.

Since these events there has been an upsurge of interest in co-operatives in both communities. Whether the latter is the result of the former is difficult to assess. But the experience certainly underlined for many the fact that there are methods, other than private enterprise or state bureaucracies, for resolving some of the problems to be found in working-class communities.

This emphasis on co-operatives has certain historical links with Irish initiatives in this field. However, it also has parallels with the movement for workers' control in industry and with historical traditions in Great Britain, in particular the early emphasis in industrial working-class communities on building their own social and economic institutions.

Such moves can be criticised because they fail to deal with the 'large' issues. Nevertheless, many of those concerned feel that only through such involvement will people begin to see the need to challenge the larger structures with an alternative which isn't simply some form of state socialism. The same point has been made by some radicals involved in community action in Great Britain who criticise the Marxist argument that 'community' as a concept and base for social action is ineffective and irrelevant to the major problems facing the working class.[5] There are serious practical problems for those activists in Northern Ireland who see community action as a potentially radical social movement growing out of this grass-roots involvement. Some of these problems will be discussed in the section below on 'recent developments'.

It would, of course, be misleading to suggest that community action in Northern Ireland deals mainly with such crisis situations. Much of it is prosaic, necessary and time-consuming, concerned with such important issues as housing, planning, supplementary benefits and recreational provision. In this respect the problems community activists face in Northern Ireland do not differ from those in other regions of the United Kingdom except in the extent and degree of deprivation to be found there.

Violence and community action: two case studies

What makes the experience of community action in Northern Ireland important is that it has occurred within a context of political instability and armed conflict. It has taken place at a time when the political situation has given rise to deep and often bitter divisions within communities as well as between the communities.

There are few homogeneous communities in Northern Ireland. Even in working-class districts there exist many significant political differences; differences between those who believe in the necessity of armed struggle or retaliation and those active in formal party politics; differences between those with a conservative political philosophy and those who advocate one form of socialism or another. There are differences also between those who hold to a limited view of community action—that community groups exist to pass on demands and grievances to those in effective power— and those activists who see a more revolutionary potential to it, questioning the assumption that politicians or civil servants have the right to decide the crucial decisions that affect community life. In the heightened tension that violence brings, the struggle between these various groupings within working-class communities can be particularly intense and bitter.

Two community groups which have had to live with the problems that the political violence in Northern Ireland has caused have been the Bogside Community Association in Derry and the Finaghy Community Association in south Belfast.[6] The problems these two associations have had to face in a deeply divided community mirror, to some extent, the problems many such groups face in similar areas throughout Northern Ireland.

The Bogside Community Association

The Bogside is a large Catholic area in the city of Derry and was the location of Ulster's largest and most durable no-go area. Like many Catholic working-class areas in Ulster, it has constantly faced the perennial problems of poor housing, chronic unemployment and poor recreational provision. The Bogside Community Association (BCA) was started in April 1972 when the Bogside was still a 'no-go' area. Those who initiated the association (a young priest and a schoolteacher), after consultation with other community organisations in the area, divided the Bogside into twelve areas and held a ballot in which over 70 per cent of the total adult population participated. As a result twelve people were elected to form the first committee. Their task was to establish the association on a permanent footing and initiate a programme of community action 'to improve the physical environment of the area and utilise and add to the existing recreational facilities and thus provide a fuller social life.'

However, the beginnings of the BCA were fraught with a number of problems which illustrate graphically some of the issues that the very presence of a community group in Northern Ireland can raise and the types of political problems that community activists must face. As we noticed earlier, the BCA was established at a time when the Bogside was still a no-go area. It was an area effectively ruled by the Provisional IRA. However, the continuing violence in Derry was beginning to have a largely divisive effect on the Bogside community. The division was particularly deep between those who supported armed resistance to the British military presence and those who did not. Attitudes had been polarised on the one hand by the dreadful events of 30 January 1972 (Bloody Sunday) when thirteen civilians were shot dead by paratroopers during a civil rights demonstration, and on the other hand by the suspension of Stormont in March of the same year by the British government.

It was not to be expected that the BCA would escape from being involved in these divisions. On the one hand many within the Provisional IRA saw the BCA as a threat to their position within the Bogside. They were themselves in the process of creating their own civilian grouping to run the Bogside, which would be known as the Free Derry Council. They feared that the BCA would be a rival organisation; a front for 'moderates', which would eventually seek to negotiate the return of the RUC back into the Bogside. It was for this reason that the group of men who were organising the first BCA election were asked to drop one of their basic aims, which was to 'set up a body of citizens who will discourage anti-social behaviour, vandalism, robbery, etc. in the Bogside', a week before the elections took place.

But the IRA was not alone in regarding the BCA with some scepticism. Within the Social Democratic and Labour Party (SDLP), the largest political party in Catholic areas, there were those who saw the attempt to create a representative structure for the Bogside as pre-empting their own discussions for the reform of local government with the new Whitelaw administration. Such was the position of John Hume, Deputy Leader of the SDLP, who declined to serve on the new association even though he had been elected by a considerable majority to its first committee. Other non-IRA elements within the city and the Bogside feared the BCA for different reasons. Many people, possibly confusing the BCA with the Free Derry Council, thought that it would be controlled by para-military groups. Such views persist to this day, as we shall see. It is enough, however, to see why members of the BCA have felt the real need to be certain of their 'mandate', at least in the initial stages of the development of the association. Indeed in the first four elections from 1972 to 1975, members of the BCA were elected by polls in which everyone over the age of eighteen could participate.

The question of the structure of the Bogside Community Association was one to which a good deal of thought and discussion was given. At the time of Free Derry, many groups had been claiming to speak on behalf of the people, but none of them had ever tested their support directly. The creation of the BCA was the first attempt to do so, though it should be noted that most, if not all, of the twelve people elected to the BCA committee in 1972 and 1973 were chosen on the basis of their involvement in youth groups or tenant associations rather than of their political affiliations.

In 1974 it was decided by the outgoing Executive Committee to make some far-reaching changes in the structure of the association in order to encourage a higher participation in its affairs. A two-tier system was devised and the Bogside area re-divided into thirty neighbourhoods which then elected up to five people as members of the new Council of the association. The person with the most votes in each neighbourhood was elected onto the Executive Committee.

It was an important change for the association. It brought into the decision-making processes of the BCA up to 150 people, whereas previously the number was around 20. Yet it also marked an important change in attitude towards the community association by one political grouping in Derry—Provisional Sinn Fein, the political wing of the IRA. They put forward a slate of candidates for election in most of the Bogside area and about forty of their members were elected. Shortly after the results were announced, *Volunteer*, the IRA's local paper, described the BCA as the authentic voice of the Bogside people and printed in full the names of all those people who had been elected to the new Council.

Not everyone was happy with this new development, including many of those who had also been elected to the new Council. They argued that because of the electoral procedure used, no longer based strictly on proportional representation, the Republican influence within the BCA was more than their actual support within the Bogside and that Provisional Sinn Fein had attempted a 'take-over'. Such a view was not shared by all the non-Provisional Sinn Fein members of the new council. Some argued that Republicans, like anyone else, are members of the community and had a right to participate in the work of the association as indeed did others of different political persuasion. They pointed out that members of the SDLP and Alliance Party had also been elected, some of whom had used their involvement in the BCA as a stepping-stone to a seat on the City Council.

The issue of the involvement within the BCA of supporters of a para-military organisation came to a head in the ensuing year. A priest nominated to the BCA Council by the Catholic Bishop of Derry proposed a motion calling upon the Provisional IRA to declare a cessation of hostilities in Derry. It was defeated, principally on the grounds that it was too one-sided as it left unmentioned the military activities of the British army in the Bogside. However, the failure to carry the motion resulted in a number of members permanently leaving the association. Subsequently, the BCA organised a referendum within the Bogside on the contentious issue of policing. Did the people of the Bogside want to see a return of the RUC to the area or, if not, did they want the BCA to establish a community police service? The decision to hold a referendum quickly became a controversial one. It was condemned almost universally by the Northern Ireland press and, much more important, by the SDLP, whose attitude was that the issue of policing could be solved only within the context of a solution to Ulster's political problems. They advised the people of the Bogside to boycott the poll, as did the Republican Clubs, the political wing of the Official IRA. In the event, up to 40 per cent of the Bogside electorate voted: overwhelmingly against a return of the RUC and marginally in favour of a community police force.

The Bogside Community Association involvement in the policing issue in Northern Ireland illustrates very clearly the problems community groups have to face when they attempt to involve themselves in broader political questions. The BCA as an association had no particular position on the issue of policing and saw the referendum as a mechanism whereby ordinary people could express their views as well as politicians. But, that said, it is clearly difficult for a community group to be seen as being 'above party politics' when it seeks to involve itself in problems that deeply divide the community it represents, however democratic the procedures it may follow. This is particularly true where community groups co-exist with other political organisations who are attempting to build up or maintain their own power base within the community, independent and distinct from that of the community group.

The Finaghy Community Association

Finaghy is located in the south of Belfast and is a very different area from that of the Bogside. To begin with, it is a Protestant housing estate built shortly after World War II. It is also a relatively when prosperous working-class area, at least compared with the Bogside. It has a high employment rate, both male and female, and most of the working men on the estate are skilled or semi-skilled.

The origins of the Community Association of Finaghy (FCA) go back to 1947 when the first tenants' group was established to deal exclusively with housing repairs and rates. It is significant to note, however, that this group by 1967 existed in name only. It needed, like so many other community groups in Northern Ireland, the catalyst of the troubles and the special community problems that they brought with them before a viable association could be built. In fact, the more immediate beginnings of the Community Association were to be found in another group which came together in late 1968 and 1969: the vigilantes.

Finaghy is situated very close to the Catholic stronghold of Andersonstown. With the start of the present political unrest, many people in Finaghy felt vulnerable to an attack by groups coming over from Andersonstown. It was to prevent this that the vigilante group was established, and the streets patrolled, especially at night. (As such, the FCA shares a common origin with many community groups in Belfast, especially in Loyalist areas.) It would be true to say as well that the evidence, such as it is, showed that the early vigilante patrols in Finaghy operated with a large measure of popular support. This was to change significantly, though, when in 1971–2 many of the vigilante groups came together to form the Ulster Defence Association (UDA)–the largest of the several Loyalist para-military groups. At this point popular attitudes towards the vigilantes were divided between those who supported the UDA and those who felt that illegal activity of any kind was wrong and that security should be left in the hands of the police (RUC) and the British army. This division was eventually to be reflected in popular attitudes towards the Finaghy Community Association, as we shall see.

When people begin to act together for limited purposes it very often happens, as in Northern Ireland, that they see the need to tackle other social problems. This occurred to the Finaghy vigilantes, who became in 1970 the Finaghy Tenants Action Group—though, despite the name, their primary concern was to provide entertainment on the estate rather than to deal with housing issues. This shift in emphasis brought with it many new members who were concerned primarily with community issues rather than defending the area from outside attack. This emphasis has continued to the present day, to the extent that now the Finaghy Community Association is almost solely concerned with what can be broadly regarded as community or social issues: the running of a permanent community centre, organising social activities for old and young people, negotiating with statutory authorities to improve facilities in the locality.

The structure and intentions of the Finaghy Community Association are in some important respects very different from those of the Bogside Community Association. The FCA has not attempted to involve itself in the broader questions of Northern Ireland politics, as has the BCA. Its membership comprises those members of the community who join and attend the AGM at which the Parent Committee and its officers are elected, whereas in the Bogside everybody over the age of eighteen is technically a member of the association. If this attempt by the BCA to build a representative structure has created for itself the problems that go with paramilitary involvement, the same is true of Finaghy. Interviews on the estate showed that the reason many people would not involve themselves in the work of the FCA was because they felt it was a 'clique' which was dominated by the UDA. Of course it is difficult to assess how true this is, though the members of the Parent Committee very strenuously denied it. Nevertheless members of the Community Association did accept that they had a communication problem between themselves and those members of the housing estate who would have nothing to do with the association.

The experience of both the Bogside and Finaghy shows that in a community that is already deeply divided politically and where rival political (and military) organisations are seeking to win some measure of popular support, many people will be genuinely suspicious of the reasons why members of political or para-military groups should want to be involved in community groups. The disagreements that such groups engender can often hinder a community group from initiating community action as they try and cope with their political differences. Equally, if a community association is thought to be dominated by one group to the exclusion of others, that too can limit the ability of that association to initiate *community* action as opposed to *sectional* action.

At the same time, it must be said that many of those within community groups who have links with para-military groups are involved in community action because they regard community action as a strategy which offers the possibility of a bridge between the communities and an alternative to violence. Members of para-military organisations on both sides have initiated worthwhile community projects, such as the Andersonstown Co-operative in West Belfast. They have also suffered from their own hardliners because of their involvement. It must be remembered, too, that not all those who raised the issue of para-military involvement in community groups do so because of disinterested motives, as we shall attempt to show later when we give some account of the problems that community groups have had to face from politicians.

We have noted earlier that for a variety of reasons members of para-military organisations often become involved in community action. This has meant, sometimes unintentionally and sometimes quite deliberately, that the meetings of community leaders at conferences and seminars have provided the means and the opportunity for members of rival para-military organisations to meet and establish lines of communication. This resulted in several meetings between para-militaries (in the Republic of Ireland and in the Netherlands) where they exchanged ideas about community development and co-operatives and were able, as well, to discuss their political differences. This groundwork culminated in the Feakle peace talks between members of the IRA and Protestant clerics which established the 1975 ceasefire.

The role of government

The first important official recognition of the role that community groups could play in combating sectarianism and social deprivation came from a government-appointed body, the Northern Ireland Community Relations Commission. The CRC was established in 1969 by the O'Neill administration with the intent of fostering better community relations. The Commission, however, decided to pursue a community development strategy: that good community relations would grow from a common awareness among Protestants and Catholics of social problems and through initiating common action to deal with these problems.[7]

The Commission, through its field staff, was extremely successful in establishing and assisting community groups in both Protestant and Catholic areas through Northern Ireland. Whereas in the early days of the troubles community action to redress social and economic grievances played an important part in the Civil Rights Movement. largely because of the economic and social conditions in Catholic areas (the concept of 'relative deprivation' has been offered as one explanation for the growth of community action in Catholic areas[8]), changes in the locally-based structure of the Northern Ireland economy have played their part in widening the base of community action. Efforts by the O'Neill administration in the 1960s to attract foreign capital to redress the decline in the locally controlled industrial base resulted in massive redevelopment and an emphasis on road transport and redeployment of labour in new 'growth' areas, such as Craigavon, working for multinational companies. These changes in turn have weakened the old relationship between the Protestant working class and the Orange small business bourgeoisie, undermining the traditional Unionist coalition of capital and labour. Community action thus became a feature of Protestant, as well as Catholic, reaction to the changes and conditions in working-class areas, particularly in Belfast.[9]

This growth in community action was also assisted by other factors, e.g. those occasions (discussed above) when local communities had to manage their own affairs, the increased importance of the physical community itself because of the dangers involved in going out of it, and the centralisation of housing, welfare and educational services as a result of local government reorganisation. *Both* communities reacted unfavourably to this latter development, although part of the reason for the reorganisation was the sectarian policies of many local councils as well as the need to produce a centralised, co-ordinated welfare service to meet the needs of a planned economy.

However, both the civil service and the power-sharing executive viewed this growth of community groups with some suspicion. The civil servants, as in other countries, did not respond positively to the information and advice offered by the Commission. They did not react to the call for the co-ordination of government agencies and departments to tackle the problems of social and economic deprivation found throughout the north, emphasising its position as the most deprived region in the United Kingdom. The Commission was in fact seen as a threat to the well-ordered function of government agencies, even though it pursued what was essentially a consensus approach.

Politicians, on all sides, saw dangers in the growing community action movement. They did not see the necessity for it once the short-lived power-sharing executive was functioning and people had their MPs and local councillors to take up their grievances (a view not unique to Northern Ireland but found in many British towns and cities). They were quite unaware of the tremendous social and economic changes which had occurred while they attempted to resolve the 'national' question. 'Governments may go and governments may come, but the civil service goes on for ever'; and it did in Northern Ireland, pursuing policies laid down in the early 1960s. The result was, as in England and elsewhere, a growing gap between politicians and the working class, even at local constituency level.[10]

They also felt that community groups were too radical and that they were infiltrated and controlled in some instances by paramilitaries, ignoring the complexities of that involvement pointed out in the case studies above. The end result was, in 1974, the disbandment of the Community Relations Commission, an example of agency conflict with many parallels with the American and British experience of government initiatives in the field of community development.[11]

Both politicians and civil servants viewed community development as essentially a system of self-help which could assist the statutory authorities and agencies, but should remain non-political. One Minister, Lord Donaldson, put it thus:[12]

> The Commission and the Department realised that the need on the ground required a practical response to what were essentially social problems and that real progress could best be made through local groups and associations which were working to improve their local environment. The government is determined that this progress should be maintained and given new emphasis. In particular it is impressed by the contribution that local groups are making by mobilising the

resources of the community to improve social conditions within the community.

Recent developments

The decision to disband the Commission drew the community groups together, united in their opposition to all politicians, and determined to set up, if not a new independent agency, then a province-wide organisation. A number of community conferences were held in 1974 and 1975 at which it became obvious that the government would not sanction a new independent agency, and a decision was taken to set up a community organisation, CONI (Community Organisations Northern Ireland), to assist community groups throughout Northern Ireland and to act, when requested, on their behalf.[13]

This radical development was assisted by a number of factors. One was the opposition of government and civil service to any new independent agency. Paradoxically, another was the UWC strike and the fall of the Executive. The latter did a great deal for the self-confidence of the Protestant working class, restoring some of their self-respect lost as a result of the fall of Stormont and the years of what they saw as IRA Republican and Catholic gains at their expense. It was in fact possible for Protestants to come together with Catholics with some degree of confidence in the quality of strength of both parties. This coming together, as pointed out above, resulted in meetings between para-militaries because of their connection with community groups, and played its part in the 1975 ceasefire.

However, despite the creation of a province-wide federation and the experiences (detailed above) gained during the troubles, community action in Northern Ireland is, unlike the Civil Rights Movement, lacking in any agreed clearly defined, and publicly stated, social philosophy or any in-depth class analysis of the situation facing community groups in the province.

There are a number of reasons for the state of affairs. One is the differing views about the nature of community action among both Catholics and Protestants, and an inherent suspicion of those who 'preach' socialism. Another is the fear, particularly amongst Protestant community activists, of any explicit public involvement with a radical community action *movement*, as distinct from community *work*, because of the potential connection, in the minds of many Protestants, with the Civil Rights *Movement*, still regarded as a vehicle used by the IRA to destroy Stormont. Protestants are justifiably fearful of the reaction in their own communities to any widely known involvement with Catholics. A number of community workers have been murdered in recent years. This is much more of a real fear on the Protestant than on the Catholic side, where such involvement is not viewed with suspicion. Finally, and most important, because of the emphasis on 'practical' community involvement, there is a great suspicion on both sides of 'ideology' or theorising and, as a result, a reluctance to become involved in any reflective, as distinct from practical, education.

These factors have tended to offset the radicalising effects of the experiences described earlier, gained in the no-go areas and during the internment crises and the UWC strike. So that, despite the creation of a province-wide federation, community activists have been drawn into a situation in which community action increasingly has become a means whereby the existing social and political system can be made to work more effectively through community pressure and local involvement.

This situation has made it relatively easy for the new British administration in Stormont to support community activity along the lines outlined by Lord Donaldson and quickly to co-opt leading members onto a Standing Advisory Council of Community Groups to oversee voluntary community work in the province. Because of the absence of formal political structures since direct rule, community groups thus have had, unlike their counterparts in Great Britain, direct access to government departments and ministers, although this is something of a colonial situation with various groups waiting in the ante-chambers at Stormont Castle to meet the 'Colonial' Secretary.

Those concerned did feel that they could exercise some influence over the new ministry, but they quickly found that their own lack of a shared philosophy, and the difficulties outlined above, weakened their role as a pressure group. As a result, the ministry was able to hand over responsibility for community work to the local authorities, despite the opposition of community groups. The carrot of a new Community Studies Centre was held out to them, but that again proved an illusion. The strategies of education, negotiation and pressure had, as elsewhere, proved a failure in dealing with structured organisations and political bureaucracies.

In fact the minister had provided financial support for the conferences held to set up CONI because he wanted to deal with an organised pressure group!

The experience of community groups is in fact a striking example of the British genius for taking the radical edge off local community initiatives by creating some form of co-optive machinery. Granted the obvious divisions within and between community groups outlined above, this government policy has still managed to play a considerable role in undermining any moves towards the creation of a dynamic social movement among community activists in Northern Ireland.

The experience in England among the coloured population is somewhat similar. One American commentator on the racial problem in England remarked: 'This country's positive genius for "co-opting" fledgling black leadership, smothering it with kindness, may be one of the reasons there is so little likelihood of a major, politically significant civil rights movement developing here.'[14]

Community work is now financed through, and thus to some extent controlled by, local authorities, and the latter are closely involved in helping community groups to set up local community controlled 'resource' centres. However, because of the financial strings, these resource centres are in danger of becoming concerned mainly with stimulating 'self-help' and co-ordinating welfare provision at a local level, complementing the job of established welfare agencies and confining their activities to non-controversial matters and adopting non-controversial tactics. (This move is contrary to the views of many community activists who see resource centres in a broad educational role, i.e. meeting practical educational needs but also stimulating a larger social and political awareness.)

This development has also had the effect, as in Great Britain, of formalising the structure of community groups emphasising the need for formal procedures and constitutions and channelling popular initiatives through safe and well-tested mechanisms which meet the needs of local bureaucracies rather than those of community groups.[15]

Thus many community groups in the North of Ireland, despite having gone through stages leading up to successful conflict action strategies in the early years of the troubles and successfully managing their own communities in periods of crises, are in danger of becoming part of the state social welfare system. Obviously they are hampered by the conflict between the two main religious groups and the suspicions arising out of that conflict regarding the future of the state. This in turn has taken them away from joint direct action strategies into negotiation and direct involvement with government, creating a situation which is not in the best interests of the Protestant or Catholic working class and hinders the growth of a radical social movement. Many of those involved believe that, despite their differences, only by working together on common social and economic problems will Protestants and Catholics see the need for a united working-class movement and more radical community action strategies.

There is some evidence that this belief is justified. For instance, community groups are increasingly dissatisfied with the conservative role that local authorities have laid down for the resource centres referred to above. There are moves to set up a province-wide organisation of resource centres with an educational emphasis, to become in fact the educational 'arm' of community action in Northern Ireland.

Another illustration is the rent strike begun in 1976 by tenants on the Protestant Shankill Road as part of their campaign against rent increases and the general financing of local authority housing. Emergency legislation introduced in 1971 to claw back arrears from Catholics involved in the Civil Rights rents and rates strike is now being used against Protestants involved in less 'political' community action. This is done directly, at source, from unemployment and welfare benefits, a situation which does not as yet exist in Great Britain.[16]

The recent emergence of the Ulster Community Action Group is another example of Protestant militancy in the community action field. This is a Protestant group located mainly in East Belfast and backed by the UDA. It is seen by some observers as a means whereby the UDA can gain access to the political arena and cut across the existing Protestant political parties, many of which, like their Catholic counterparts, are divorced from the practical problems faced by the Protestant working class, despite their ability to attract votes when the large political issues are at stake. Last year's local authority elections did, in fact, see the emergence of community candidates from both communities although, as in the other activities described above, they lack any agreed social philosophy or strategy other than opposition to traditional politicians.

There is also some evidence that existing political parties sensing this danger will, as with the Liberals in England, present themselves as community politicians, again hindering the growth of a genuine working-class political movement arising out of community action. This danger is enhanced because the existing trade union movement in Northern Ireland is regarded with grave suspicison by Protestants since the UWC strike, and an alliance of community groups and trade unions is difficult to visualise. There is also the additional problem, emphasised above, that many people involved in community work in Northern Ireland, like their counterparts in Great Britain, do not see themselves in the radical working-class tradition and do not align themselves with the trade union movement. For them community action is seen as a means of involving *all* the community. This again is not altogether a situation unique to Northern Ireland but reflects the extent to which the 'Orange' system, the lack of large-scale industrialisation and the 'traditional' nature of many Protestant and Catholic communities in the North of Ireland has resulted, as Margaret Stacey's study of Banbury illustrated, in a deference by the working class to middle-class leadership and a lack of class consciousness.[17] Trade unions for their part have not been particularly noticeable in their involvement in, or awareness of, the problems faced by working-class communities at neighbourhood level.

Given the political vacuum in Northern Ireland, the role of the community worker highlights many of the problems raised in the United Kingdom and the United States of America as to whether or not his (or her) role is that of a professional or as a member of a social movement,[18] a social work task or an educational one.[19] There is obviously a real sense in which in Northern Ireland community action is a social movement which, despite all its weaknesses, offers the only radical alternative to para-military action on the one hand and traditional politics on the other. The last seven years have, despite the problems and difficulties referred to earlier, provided community groups with experiences and opportunities not available in other western countries.

As we have argued above, these opportunities are weakened by the conflicts *within* Catholic and Protestant communities, by the differences within community groups about the nature of community action, by the conflict *between* the two communities, by the policy of co-option, and last, but by no means least, by the lack of a clearly defined social philosophy. These difficulties have to some extent been overcome where community workers have seen a broader social and political dimension to their work and have encouraged community activists to engage in political as well as social welfare activity. However, it is no coincidence that these workers are independently financed and their activities are not controlled by professional or government agencies.

The greatest danger is that community work will be seen as a 'professional activity', thus undermining its radical possibilities. Already training courses are being set up for community workers employed by the various government agencies and some people active in their own communities are drawn towards the idea of a professional qualification.

The universities and other educational establishments are assisting this process and, although a certain amount of educational assistance is given to community groups, too much is made of the need to provide them with a professionally oriented training. This is not, in fact, what many of them either want or need. What is required, even more than it is in Great Britain, is a process of practical political education where the day-to-day educational needs of community activists are met, but within a broad social and political framework which relates everyday experience to the broader structural questions of how decisions are made and resources allocated. It is in answering these questions that a radical social philosophy can be formed and strategies decided. This, for many involved in community action in Northern Ireland, is the next, necessary, step towards the creation of a social movement.

There are parallels here with the work of the Highlander Folk School in Tennessee which played a vital educational role in the formation of trade unions in that part of the USA in the 1930s, and in the Civil Rights Movement in the 1960s.[20] Its axioms were:

(a) To learn from the people and start education where they are;
(b) To educate people away from the trap of individualism and to reinforce those instincts amongst individuals which lead to co-operative and collective solutions to problems.

Highlander avoided narrow ideology and indoctrination because it learnt that ideology, no matter how firmly grounded in objective reality, was of no value if it was separated from a social movement of struggling people. As a result of community action there are the beginnings of such a movement of struggling people across the religious divide in Northern Ireland.

Conclusion

However, despite all the community activity outlined above, recent reports have underlined the extent to which Northern Ireland is still the most deprived region in the United Kingdom.[21] *New Society* commented on this state of affairs:[22]

> It is debatable how many of Northern Ireland's problems are caused by politics, race and religion, or by economic and social malaise. What is indisputable is that the violence and destruction of the past six years have been endured by a society with 2·8% of the United Kingdom's total population which is demonstrably one of the most underprivileged.

That final fact underlines the extent to which community action in Northern Ireland, as in Great Britain and the United States of America, has obvious limitations when confronted with basic structural problems. Nevertheless, having said that, 'community' remains a dynamic and potentially radical, social concept for a large section of the Northern Irish working class and, as the American sociologist W. I. Thomas said, 'If people define a situation as real, it is real in its consequences.'[23] Community is real in Northern Ireland. It is real as a divisive force but it is also real in the opportunities it affords for the creation of a radical social movement cutting across religious divisions amongst the working class.

The situation was aptly summed up by a community activist from the Bogside:[24]

> I don't think there's any future in simply changing jockeys unless we are prepared to try and change the system, and whether it happens to be a Unionist or a Nationalist or an SDLP up there riding a horse, if the horse itself is not worth flogging to the post then I am not for it . . . even if they do solve the national problem . . . the community struggle goes on.

References

1   This figure is based on the findings of a research project done by the staff of the Department of Social Administration, the New Universtiy of Ulster. See Frances Duffy and Robin Percival, *Community Action and Community Perceptions of the Social Services in Northern Ireland*, The New University of Ulster, 1975.

2   See Eamonn McCann, *War in an Irish Town*, Penguin Books, 1974

3   P. Doherty, 'Community Action, Local Authorities and Government' (paper given at conference on Politics and Community Action held at the New University of Ulster, Institute of Continuing Education, Londonderry, in July 1974).

4   Samuel Smyth, 'Effective Community Action—Reality or Myth?' (paper given at conference on Politics and Community Action).

5   J. Radford, 'The Community Movement', in *Community Politics*, ed. Peter Hain, John Calder, 1976.

6   See Duffy and Percival, op. cit.

7   See Northern Ireland Community Relations Commission, First Annual Report, 1971.

8   W. D. Birrell, 'Relative Deprivation as a Factor in Conflict in Northern Ireland', *Sociological Review*, 20 (3), August 1972.

9   See Ron Wiener, *The Rape and Plunder of the Shankill: Community Action: the Belfast Experience*, Notaems Press, Belfast, 1975.

10 B. Hindess, *The Decline of Working-Class Politics*, Paladin, 1971.

11 Hywel Griffiths, *Community Development in Northern Ireland: a Case Study in Agency Conflict*, Occasional Paper in Social Administration, New University of Ulster, 1974.

12 Northern Ireland Office, Press Notice, 30 August 1974.

13 *Community Action: The Way Forward* (report of Conference of Community Groups published by the Greater West Belfast Community Association, 1974).

14 W. Raspberry, 'Why Britain's Blacks Have no Leaders', *Observer*, 19 September 1976.

15 See John Dearlove, 'The Control of Change and the Regulation of Community Action', in D. Jones and M. Mayo (eds), *Community Work One*, Routledge & Kegan Paul, 1974.

16 See Tom Hadden, 'Open Space', *Fortnight*, no. 135, 22 October 1976.

17 M. Stacey, *Tradition and Change: a Study of Banbury*, Oxford University Press, 1960.

18 H. Specht, *Community Development in the United Kingdom*, Association of Community Workers (London Council of Social Service), 1975.

19 *The Teaching of Community Work*, Central Council for Education and Training in Social Work, 1975.

20 Frank Adams, *Unearthing Seeds of Fire: The Story of Highlander*, John F. Blair, Winston-Salem, North Carolina, 1975.

21 Eileen Evason, *Poverty: The Facts in N. Ireland*, Child Poverty Action Group, 1976.

22 'Northern Ireland Trends', *New Society*, 24 July 1975.

23 Quoted in P. L. Berger and B. Berger, *Sociology: a Biographical Approach*, Penguin Books, 1976, p. 239.

24 P. Doherty, op. cit.

Part III Three Perspectives for Development

11   Joint union-resident action

Jack Mundey and Gary Craig

Introduction

Jack Mundey is an Australian trades unionist. He was brought up on a small farm in Queensland and, after leaving school early, went to Sydney to play Australian football as a professional. He gave this up fairly quickly and has worked in the building industry ever since. The Builders Labourers' Federation (BLF), of which he is a member, was controlled by rather shady elements from the 1930s on and Jack Mundey took part in the struggle to democratise the union. Some of the changes which were won after long and bitter battles are described in the interview below.

Building workers are more highly organised in Australia than in Britain, and the 'lump' there is much less of a problem. However, although this theoretically gives the BLF a much stronger influence than the Union of Construction Allied Trades and Technicians (UCATT), its British counterpart, the Australian union has, until recently, been reluctant to use its industrial power for purposes other than securing better wages and conditions. This situation changed dramatically in the late 1960s and early 1970s, as Jack Mundey describes.

His major interest now is in the question of the social usefulness of labour—that is, the sort of work that trades unionists ought to be doing and the sorts of products they ought to be making. Throughout the world, trades unionists struggle for better wages and conditions for their members. More progressive sections of the trades union movement are now thinking about the question of workers' control of production. However, as Jack himself says, 'production of what? Workers should be gaining control of the means of production in order to produce things that are useful—kidney machines, not Concordes; hospitals, not office blocks'. He

199

feels that this kind of debate has hardly started in Britain, with the notable exception of the Lucas Aerospace workers.[1]

Jack Mundey spent three months in 1975—6 in Britain on a visit organised by the Centre of Environmental Studies and financed by the Gulbenkian Foundation and the Sainsbury Trust. During that period he was able to visit and talk to a considerable number of trades unions and community groups, and to think about the question of the limits of community action.[2] His view, expressed in the interview below, is that community action as a method cannot achieve very large gains for the working class unless it is linked in to the broader labour movement. It is a limited strategy in at least three ways. First, community groups organising around some issue in a neighbourhood can rarely muster the sort of political muscle that is required to push through significant changes. Second, by limiting participation to those people living in a neighbourhood, it becomes easier for the resource-holders (council, developer, etc.) to play off groups against each other. Most activists are familiar with the sort of council tactic, for example, that offers resources to one neighbourhood by withdrawing them from another, and then exploits the divisions which arise. To a certain extent this can be overcome by making wider alliances across a city on particular issues. Finally, community action as a method can tend to limit the vision and understanding of activists. A group in a neighbourhood may, with reason, be concerned at the delay in demolishing their houses, or a sudden switch from clearance to modernisation or a dramatic rent rise. It is, however, often not enough for groups merely to make demands for 'clearance now' or 'no rent rises'. These demands are easily fobbed off by councillors who can mystify with facts and figures (often being themselves totally mystified by them!). Only by a wider understanding of a government's housing strategy, its economic policy, or the way in which housing is financed, can valid demands be made. Council tenants who understand, for example, that 70 per cent of their rent goes in interest charges are better placed to wage a battle.

Jack's view is that both the muscle, and a wider discussion of the right sorts of issues, can come through a development of links between community activists and the labour movement as a whole. Again, he feels that Britain has barely started along this road, although some hopeful examples are described in a postscript.

The interview was recorded in July 1976 during his brief return to Britain.

The interview

GC: Can you tell us something about the background to the Builders Labourers' Federation in Australia and the power struggle within the union?

JM: I think the starting-point should be that the Builders Labourers' Federation in New South Wales was a union with a real difference. Before the radical left wing came to power in the mid-1960s, the BLF (Australia) was controlled by what could best be described as a USA Teamsters-type union, one that openly worked with the employers, that appointed officials, that black-listed and even bashed militant workers. This meant that the union members had to conduct a very vigorous fight to win control of the union, but in doing so we ensured, by having some in-built guarantees in our rules, that we would not repeat the return to the days of standover tactics and business unionism.

GC: What sorts of changes were made?

JM: Take just a few things we introduced. First of all, to combat entrenched bureaucracy, we limited the power of union officials by saying that all union officials had to be elected, and that elections had to be held triennially. At the same time, no full-time official could serve more than two terms of office, i.e. six years in all. I was the first Secretary of the union to step down after six years. This is a very important issue as it brings the rank and file membership closer to the leadership. I found in case after case, throughout the world, that militant leaders became union officials and then, after one or two decades had passed, these officials mellowed—they tended to get away from the grass roots and lost contact with workers on the job, moving in the process closer to the employer. If they were not openly corrupt, they were entrenched in their position and lost real touch with the workers they represented. The introduction of limited tenure of office was very important and broke the inner cynicism in the union, that the leaders were out to entrench their own position, and would use the leadership as a stepping-stone to other political appointments in Parliament, councils, boards and so on.

We also fought for the right of women to work in all-male industry. This was a hard struggle, too, against not only the employers but the more chauvinist male workers. We won this fight and we raised the credit of the union amongst the women's movement generally. There were also many migrants—over 50 per cent of the membership were migrant workers—and together with

the Aborigines, who were treated badly, we fought for them to
have equal rights. Finally the three largest groups—Italians, Spanish
and Yugoslavs—all got their own full-time organisers, and this gave
the migrant workers greater confidence.

We also set out to reduce inequalities in wages, to narrow the
gap between the building tradesmen and the builders labourers,
having in mind that our union covered all workers who do the
most arduous, least congenial, work in the building industry, like
erecting scaffolding down to jackhammer work, pouring concrete,
and so on, which is skilled and difficult. When we came into office
the gap was very large: we narrowed it from labourers getting
55 per cent of the tradesmen's rate, to top labourers getting
100 per cent of the tradesmen's rate and unskilled labourers
getting 90 per cent. We had a bitter five-week strike to enforce
that, with the employers using scab labour to try to suppress it,
the union having to use flying pickets under the direction of the
Strike Committee. The following year we had another dispute
with employers to force them to improve safety conditions on
site. We were involved in supporting the improvement of the
conditions of blacks in our country, and several union members
were amongst the first to be arrested in the mass protests against
the Vietnam War which our government, without any consultation
with the people of Australia, got us involved in. We were among
the most militant unions in organising workers to shut down
particular works and call for an end to the war. Finally, when the
streets of Melbourne and Sydney were blocked by protesters
against the war, we managed to get nearly all the union's members
to walk off their sites in support.

Getting involved in this sort of struggle and fighting to civilise
the building industry gave our members the feeling that we were
sincerely fighting for their rights.

GC: Where did the union go from here? How did it get
involved with residents' groups?

JM: It was at a builders labourers' conference that I put
forward the view that the union should have a broader vision. It
should be concerned not only with wages and conditions, important as they were, but with social issues. There were wider issues
over which the union should consider using its industrial and
political muscle. Following this contribution, which was reported
in the press, a group of women came to the union after a number
of programmes which their residents' action group had carried out

had resulted in failure. Ironically this was a well-to-do group of women from the fashionable suburb of Hunter's Hill. They were fighting for the retention of a piece of land called Kelly's Bush the last piece of bushland (an area of natural, uncultivated countryside) within miles of Sydney Harbour, which in 1968 A. V. Jennings, Sydney's biggest developer, proposed to 'develop' for the erection of luxury flats. Having read my view that unions should be concerned with broader issues, they came and more or less appealed for us to carry that view through.

They pointed out that in the early 1970s they had gone through all the motions of protesting to the Municipal Council and to the State government, which had the final say. After this had failed they physically stood in front of a bulldozer which was coming in to knock down the bushland. They wanted us to ban the destruction of the bushland. We replied that we would consider it, provided that a sizeable demonstration was held which genuinely showed that the people of Hunter's Hill wanted such a ban.

The following Sunday over 700 people assembled in a park in Kelly's Bush and we acceded to the request that a ban be imposed on the destruction of the bushland. This would give the protesters more time to mount their protest, and to lobby further parliamentarians and bureaucrats in the State planning authority in New South Wales. It would also give much more real meaning to the question of public participation. As you often find in the UK, and more so in Australia, there is a sort of tokenism about public participation within the minds of bureaucrats, governments and developers. As a result of our ban, there was a line-up between the developers and others hostile to us: the more conservative papers ran articles criticising the ban; the developers said they would ignore the ban and use non-union labour. In Australia, about 80 per cent of building workers are in the building union, which is higher than the national average, and certainly much higher than England, where only about 44 per cent of building workers are unionised and there is much difficulty with the 'lump'. That would make it difficult for UCATT to take similar action in Britain unless more workers were unionised.

We then went on to hold a meeting at the site where A. V. Jennings was building a 40-storey office block in the middle of Sydney. The workers there gave support to the demands of the leaders that if one blade of grass was touched on Kelly's Bush, they would walk off the site for ever, leaving the half-finished block as a monument to Kelly's Bush. This certainly had the desired effect and put the cat amongst the pigeons. The press editorials and the media turned their attention fully to the question of the ban.

We said on our part that we, the union, weren't setting ourselves up as arbiters of what should or should not be done but we felt that ordinary people should have the right to determine what happened in their neighbourhood. We also believed that we had a responsibility, as a responsible union, to see that this public park should be kept not only for the present generation but for future generations. And why, we argued, should this beautiful parkland be destroyed so that a privileged few could have luxurious apartments with a view over Sydney Harbour?

GC: Is this where the notion of 'Green Bans' first started?

JM: Yes, we decided at this stage to call the ban a 'Green Ban'. In Australia there had been certain connotations about unions using their industrial muscle for 'black bans'; that is, unions refusing to do particular kinds of work until the employer agreed to an improvement in wages and conditions. The gains in those campaigns were for a particular group of workers in their own struggle. We thought the word 'green' was particularly apt because it wasn't for the benefit of the workers concerned—in fact they were denying themselves labour—but was seen as an important social expression of what the workers did with their labour. In addition we were supporting residents who wanted a pleasant environment for themselves and others who might want to go there. Thus a broader, and more noble, new dimension of a union engaging in social affairs came into being, and the Green Ban movement was launched.

GC: You mentioned that a lot of hostility was generated by this campaign among certain groups, especially government and big business. Did you get much support from anyone?

JM: In general, television, radio and journalists were quite favourable to the union's action, but the big guns—the captains of industry, the big developers, the Tory State government—were all against the unions, and said things like 'this is usurping the rule of the government, it's anarchy, it's building labourers setting themselves up as proletarian town planners'. We even had a most hypocritical editorial in the *Sydney Morning Herald*, our main morning paper, and the oldest conservative paper in Australia, which said that 'Mundey should be told that his job is to win better wages and conditions for his members.' What hypocrisy that was when, during the bitter five-week strike to civilise the building industry two years earlier, which tried to improve wages and conditions, this same paper attacked us for too much militancy. Yet when we took the broader step of involving ourselves on a wider plane with people many of whom actually supported the Conservatives, the *Sydney Morning Herald* said we should confine ourselves to wages and conditions. That in itself was an expression of the fear the Establishment has when unions go beyond the normal confines that it thinks the union should limit itself to.

At the same time we saw the more conservative elements on both sides reacting to it in different ways, and polarising. I spoke about collusion where you would expect it, between developers, the Tory government and the newspaper editors who were opposed to the action of the union. Ironically, however, we had some of the more conservative right-wing unions, and even some of the supposed more left-wing unions, also voicing much the same thing— that the union's going too far, it's treading on dangerous ground, and the like. On the other hand, we had progressive Conservatives, people who had voted for the Tories all their lives, writing letters to the press, for example, to say that normally they were opposed to unions, or not pro-union, but on this occasion they thought the action of the BLF was correct. Therefore they supported the Green Ban as a means of allowing those people to have a greater say about what happened in their area. So the great debate on Green Bans had well and truly commenced.

GC: What form of organisation and liaison occurred between the union and residents' groups?

JM: In talking about this, it should be made clear that they were quite separate. The residents' movement was formed in a period when the government and the developers were making a property killing in the major cities in Australia, and there was a notion that turning Sydney into a mini-New York was desirable. When this had been going on for a while, and people became aware that there were 10 million square feet of unlet office-block space in Sydney, there was a certain revulsion. People said that the city was being destroyed, a city that had a lot of charm and colour was suddenly being overwhelmed by blocks 600, 700, 800 feet high around mere bullet-tracks. There were these concrete monstrosities, and between them the canyons with thousands of cars pouring into the central business district.

So Kelly's Bush was but a beginning, and the thing that gave the union a starting-point, together with the unions that joined us later on. This is having in mind that by 1974, the third year of this campaign, we had fourteen unions all over Australia involved in some sort of social or environmental struggle. The strength of the union was that it never set itself up to make decisions. It was always the people making decisions and then coming to the union, and convincing the union that the request for support was a genuine expression of the people of the area (and not of just a small group of selfish people who might get some personal advantage such as a better view of a leafy area). Having been convinced, we would have to depend on those residents participating and making decisions about what happened in their neighbourhood. So while there was a strong liaison and strong ties, for example when laws were introduced to stop unions and residents occupying buildings, we went out together, but organisationally we were separated. On one job we had people aged between eight and eighty being arrested and taken off by the police from a site where a building was surrounded by the police while a developer tried to use scab labour to knock it down. We warned them on that occasion that while they might be able to guard it while it came down, they couldn't have police around it for eight or ten months while a new building went up, and so it would remain a park, which it did!

GC: Could you describe some of the union's campaigns after Kelly's Bush?

JM: Well, there were forty-two Green Bans won in Sydney alone. Even though the recession had set in, and the main cities of Australia have changed a lot under Burn, all of these bans are still holding with the exception of Victoria Street, where there was a compromise. This was to be a 45-storey complex and, with the residents' consent, we agreed to limit it to 9. After Kelly's Bush, there was The Rocks, where convicts had cut into the sandstone 200 years ago to build some of the oldest houses and cottages in Australia, which are architecturally famous. It is occupied by working-class people who service the city, working on the docks and on the ferries, who had lived there for generations. The idea in 1971 was that this would all be demolished and $A500m (about £300m) of high-rise buildings, luxury hotels and expensive flats would be put up. This would have meant an extension of the concrete jungle of the central business district right down to the harbour's edge under the bridge. The residents rose up against this, and over 500 people attended a meeting. We now saw the wide variety of the people who were coming to us for support. At that meeting we had the small businessmen of the area who would be put out of business, the local Catholic and Anglican leaders, a whole range of social groups such as the Mission for Seamen arguing why it should be retained, and the residents themselves. The residents argued that they weren't opposed to medium-density housing, to infills where there were some derelict houses or even to some more commercial buildings, as long as the existing residential structure remained and low-income groups could continue to live in the area, and as long as the area was not allowed to become 'trendy', as often happens when inner city areas become rehabilitated.

So The Rocks remains The Rocks today. Not only that, but the people drew up a People's Plan for The Rocks. That is, the ban wasn't just a negative action, since it allowed the residents more time to discuss the project with the State government, and more important still, the people, by using sympathetic town planners and architects, were able to draw up their own plans. We in turn said we would supply labour to conform with the wishes of the residents but would not do so to demolish their houses or build further high-rise blocks.

At the same time the National Trust, a very conservative body interested in preserving old buildings, came to us. In Australia the law protecting old and historic buildings is quite weak, and Australia is such a young country that there are few such buildings, which makes it all the more important that they should be retained. We agreed with the Trust that we would impose a Green Ban on any building they felt to be worthy of preservation, and at the same time we called on State governments to enact legislation to save such buildings so that it wouldn't be necessary for unions to use their muscle to refuse to demolish them. So 127 buildings that otherwise would have been razed to the ground in all Australian State capitals and provincial cities now stand because of that action, and many State governments have been forced to pass laws to make it more or less impossible for owners of such buildings to demolish them willy-nilly.

GC: When did you develop the idea of the social nature of labour?

JM: Our co-operation with The Rocks people gave us impetus in this direction; while the papers were saying that the union was denying members the right to work, we were able to answer by saying that while we would not build according to the ghastly State government plan, we were prepared to build the People's Plan. We developed this answer to the accusation by saying we wanted to build *socially useful* buildings, ones that are of concern and need to the people—hospitals, schools, kindergartens, flats and homes for workers who were ill housed. This was where the resources of concrete, metal and sand should be going. This was the beginning of raising our consciousness in the union movement about this most important question of all, the social nature of labour, the social consequences of labour, and we started to insist that we had a say in what we did with our labour. The yardstick was to be whether the work would be socially beneficial to the community at large. It seems to me this is the most neglected issue throughout the entire union movement in the world. Unions, certainly throughout the Western world, are still mainly concerned with wages and conditions and give very little thought about broader matters of concern: transport, the quality of housing, the quality of life within the area in which they live. Obviously, the economic issues of wages and conditions have to be struggled over, and will be important as long as capital opposes labour under capitalism. Even when, as I hope, we get a suitable form of socialism with a human face, workers will still need to argue about what sort of wages they should get. But workers will have to become increasingly involved in these social issues.

So The Rocks remains The Rocks, the hundreds of thousands of people go to see the area of 'White Australia' which they wouldn't have been able to do if they had been covered with high-rise blocks.

GC: What happened next in the development of the campaigns?

JM: We were inundated with requests from people who were frustrated, and felt helpless against bureaucratic power and State government working in the interests of the developers. Two of the other requests we dealt with were the Botanical Gardens and Centennial Park, which again illustrates how the States and developers work together.

The Botanical Gardens is near the Opera House. $A120m had been spent on a fine Opera House and we didn't criticise that, as workers should be building cultural centres instead of office blocks for insurance companies. But they then proposed to destroy the Gardens with their 140-year-old fig-trees to provide a car-park for the God car. A wide section of people at a public meeting called on us to prevent this, which we did. No one now in Sydney would support the car-park being built on the Gardens, and a shuttle service from another car-park to the Opera House has been quite adequate.

Then we had Centennial Park, a bit like Hyde Park in London. Despite councillors, MPs and developers trying to rape open land, Centennial Park remained our biggest park. Yet, in the faint hope that Sydney might hold the 1988 Olympic games, a group of politicians and city councillors almost unbelievably decided to build a huge sports complex in the park, to celebrate 200 years of lovely 'White Australian' rule. The people living round this beautiful park were part middle class, part lower middle class, and partly working class. They organised a meeting of 2,500 angry residents in the park and requested the BLF to introduce a Green Ban. There really was a broad spectrum from Patrick White, Nobel prizewinning novelist who was normally a recluse but came out fighting on this issue, the Catholic Cardinal Gilroy of Sydney, Vincent Savant, a well-known Australian naturalist, the girls of Sydney High School, and a host of other people. We imposed a ban and, as the protests mounted on Centennial Park, the government lay low and quietly announced six months later it had abandoned its plan for desecrating the park.

GC: You implied widespread corruption. Were *you* ever approached?

JM: The Green Bans stopped the destruction of working-class housing, the desecration of parks, the building of luxury hotels and homes. Of course we were not only opposed openly by much of the press and the State machinery, but we also had to contend with attempts at buying us off. In one case, for example, a developer had plans for a $A400m high-rise building. He offered me 10 per cent of the total proceeds if I could get the residents to agree to allow a $A200m-worth to go ahead and even gave me a rationale for the residents along the lines that if they accepted $A200m-worth, it would be acceptable to him, but if they stuck out for no building, they might lose the lot. We told him we supported the residents and he would have to talk to them. But that gives you some idea of the corruption when there is so much money at stake. In the four-year period 1971–4 we held up

$A3,000m of work on forty-two projects in Sydney alone. Another one which illustrated corruption of a different kind was where people were duped into buying flats overlooking a park which was a big attraction for their children, only to find developers moving into the park six months later to build on it. They announced that the residents had been 'misled' by salesmen, and that it wasn't a park. We were asked to intervene, and it remains a park.

GC: In Britain we've recently had a spate of motorway protests, generally by means of direct disruptions of public inquiries. Were you and the BLF involved in action on roads and motorway construction?

JM: Yes, Sydney was rapidly becoming like Los Angeles, spreading forty miles inland from the sea, with almost unbroken housing stretching to the Blue Mountains. Public transport was decreasing and there was more and more reliance on the private car. The State government proposed to knock down many of the inner city areas, 25,000 homes in all, so as to enable people to race away on a network of motorways from the overbuilt central business district. They were nearly all perfectly good homes and, not surprisingly, largely working-class areas, for it's these which always suffer from freeways and motorways. A ban was imposed after a huge meeting in Sydney. We said we would not knock down any homes in the proposed path of the motorway and so the motorways have been held up.

This shows the difference between Australia and Britain, where most of the struggle about motorways seems to have been by the 'enlightened' middle class. It's essential, incidentally, when talking about 'which way for community action in Britain?' that the working class are brought into this kind of struggle.

GC: Where do you see the trades union movement going now?

JM: You have to explode two myths. One, that the working class shouldn't be interested in environmental issues as they are only for the enlightened middle class. That's a terrible myth, and it suits the establishment, because it's the working class who live in the worst areas of our cities throughout the world, the noisiest, the dirtiest, the least leafy suburbs. Many of the unions fall for this myth, though. I see no contradiction at all between working class and middle class on this sort of issue; between them they can constitute an almost irresistible force. So the unions must broaden out from their concern with the shop floor. The other myth is that if unions become too involved in environmental issues, this means worsening unemployment. We can see now throughout the whole capitalist world the deepening of the crisis in cities, where the environment has been completely ignored and where much of the city has been destroyed. We've got to stand things the right way up. You have to go back to the social nature of labour and say that work that is performed must be in the interests of that city, its people and, more important, the people to come. What's the use of winning control of the means of production if we're not thinking how we are going to use it when we do win control: and that applies under capitalism or socialism. More people, like the Lucas Aerospace people in Britain, are now thinking on these lines. And that's the main ingredient of the Green Ban—that we will build socially useful buildings, and start a debate about what *is* socially useful.

Now, even the most militant unions in the Western world are confining themselves to demands for full employment, but there's no question of 'employment for what'—making millions of extra cars, for example, which can't be sold or which pollute our cities.

When you talk about the environment you have to think about what you mean by your standard of living. For many people this means more and more consumer things. People are brainwashed by our consumer society into buying things which should never be made, let alone sold; things that are often injurious to health. Sure, everyone must have the right to work, but it should be socially useful work of benefit to the community. So there's a gap here to be bridged between the working class and those organisations such as Friends of the Earth, and so on, which are dominated by the middle class.

GC: You said something earlier about the future for community action in Britain. Could you enlarge on this?

JM: People living in a community are restricted in what they can do by community action methods; they can win things only piecemeal. I believe that community activists should involve workers living in the community. Often you will find workers who are strong and militant on the factory floor who live 3 or 4 miles away and who are inactive in their own neighbourhood. They see it as a different struggle. Similarly, workers who get on the council live one life on the factory floor and wear a different hat when they sit on the municipal council. But these struggles must merge. What's the use of winning better wages and conditions if we live in a rapidly worsening environment—in cities without parks or trees, with unbearable noise level? Where one works and where one lives are linked, together with the transportation between them, and the recreation and cultural facilities. Then I think community activists will see that once we involve the working class, and the organised working class, by taking strike action, by forcing governments and authorities by their intervention to take new positions, then we'll get somewhere.

GC: You were accused of usurping the government's role and of being almost anti-democratic. Often community activists are accused, for example by councillors opposed to some action, of not using proper democratic procedures. What are your thoughts on this?

JM: We were told frequently that we were usurping democracy. Our answer was that we have a social responsibility, especially a right to intervene on anything that affects the worker or the worker's family or the people of the future. We have every right to express our social conscience and, if we deem it necessary, to withdraw our labour or use it on things we want to use our labour on. When we say that, we mean every-day democracy, not just once every three years with a ballot-paper thrust in your hands to vote for someone. If this sort of thinking got through the unions, it could revolutionise unions, too. The unions could become vehicles for genuine social change and not just defensive organisations concerned with improving their economic position, which they are now. As I said, the struggle broadened in Australia: it moved from being just the BLF to fourteen other unions, including the Metal Workers' Union, the waterside workers, dockers, seamen and the building tradesmen, which have now taken action over social and environmental issues. So, for example, when the government wanted to build a power station near Melbourne (Australia's second largest city with a population of 3 million), which would have increased the pollution by roughly 50 per cent, all the workers in the Trades and Labor Council of Victoria, a sort of workers' parliament, said 'no', except for a couple of right-wingers. So the whole labour movement said 'No', and the Victorian State Premier had to come to us and say, 'Where will you build it?' This shows the power of the workers organised around issues which have wide public appeal. Again many Tory voters came out and supported us. Similarly in Queensland, the Trades and Labor Council came out against a plan for a huge multinational firm, with permission from the government, to mine a small island for

sand. This island, Fraser Island, was a favourite spot on the
Barrier Reef for bushwalkers and naturalists, and there was an outcry that the ecology of the island would be ruined for ever. The
trades union movement refused to convey the bulldozers and
mining equipment to the island. So Fraser Island was saved.

I don't think either of these campaigns would have been won
but for the widespread discussion about Green Bans and the role
of unions. These were extensions of those early struggles which
came about because of the general lifting of trades union political
and environmental consciousness. From this, things moved to an
even broader plane. The ACTU (equivalent to your TUC) overwhelmingly carried a resolution banning the mining, handling and
export of uranium, even though we have large uranium deposits
and the Japanese are keen to get it. This was in September 1975.
Six months later, a train driver was sacked in Townsville, Queensland, when he saw material going through to the uranium mine
which was supposed to be closed. Immediately rail workers
throughout Australia stopped work and forced his reinstatement.

This opened up the debate again on the political role of unions,
and on all the radio talkback programmes a wide discussion took
place on the unions and the whole nuclear question, too.

GC: What about opposition within the union movement?

JM: The right wing within the unions moved to support the
Tory government. For example, it demanded the rescinding of the
ACTU motion banning the handling of uranium. The inter-State
executive, by 12 votes to 4, ruled that it couldn't overthrow the
ACTU decision, but I'm sure there will be many bitter fights ahead
as the government is determined to sell uranium. This helps us,
though, because it will make many more people think about the
deadly dangers of the proliferation of nuclear weapons and power,
about the use of power for so-called peaceful purposes, the blight
of radiation from nuclear waste dumped in seas and in mineshafts,
and the waste of energy. For example, in 1975 in America over
50 per cent of all energy was wasted at the same time as everyone
was saying that they should go nuclear. So people are really beginning to think about the so-called energy crisis.

In summary, then, if community work is to be effective, it must
strengthen the links between the activists and the workers living
and working in a neighbourhood, and get them to think on a
broader level about the totality of their city and their life. And, of
course, on a global level too, so that people in the Third World are

helped to do what they want and not mimic the worst features of the capitalist system.

GC: Do you see any hopeful signs in Britain of his happening?

JM: In the next year I would like to see the more advanced community activists and the more advanced trades unions starting a discussion on the social nature of work, with the involvement of environmental groups too. It's mainly in the unions now that a better level of understanding and action is needed, but some people are needed from outside the unions. Already Clive Jenkins (ASTMS), Ernie Roberts (AUEW Assistant General Secretary) and others have shown some interest in this, and the Institute of Workers' Control may take it up by organising conferences and the like. In Canada, which is much more economistic than here, trades unions are organising a conference on Employment and the Environment, so Britain can do it, too. And as capitalism gets into more difficulties and the ecological crisis worsens there are a myriad of issues which are building up. But until these wider issues are taken up, I can't see the working-class and community groups making much progress.

GC: There has been some action, though, in Birmingham, which followed a visit you made there some months ago. Do you see hopeful signs there?

JM: First of all, although action has been confined to Birmingham so far, there has been a lot of interest throughout the country in the subject matters I've raised at various talks, particularly about the success of the Green Bans, which wasn't just a theoretical point but something which actually happened.

The Birmingham Post Office campaign (see the Postscript) has gone well, and attracted attention and this needs looking at. A public meeting was called in Birmingham and about 150 people came along: they were very diverse, too, rather as I mentioned in Australia—a wide variety of people, politically and socially. I had discussions with the building union (UCATT) and found that they were well organised. They were able to link up with and support those who wanted to retain the building. This was not seen just as a question of retaining the building, which again is often seen as a middle-class issue. (This has to be debunked because it implies that the workers haven't got any respect for our older buildings, or interest in preserving some of our past for future generations.) Not only did they want to preserve this old building—considering so much of the city had been destroyed—but also they urged that the resources which would have been used for new buildings on the site of the Post Office, had it been destroyed, should be diverted to urgently required housing in Birmingham. This was an important point: when we come out with bans, we recommend tangible alternatives as to what should happen. This was good and it won not only the support of the building workers but also the whole Midlands, where the union movement has come in behind it, with many parliamentarians including some right-wing Birmingham MPs such as Roy Jenkins supporting the notion of a Green Ban. Peter Carter, the UCATT secretary, is now getting letters from people all over the UK (as a result of a BBC feature) asking if they could place a Green Ban in their particular area on some project. So the same possibilities do exist here for joint union-resident action if the union is strong enough to support that position, and can hold against the 'lump'.

This shows, I think, despite the vicious anti-union posture of the press generally, how a union can enhance its position and win broader allies in this very important struggle of socialising the unions away from purely wages and conditions and making them more political.

Postscript

Birmingham

In early 1976 Jack Mundey went to Birmingham at the invitation of a local branch of UCATT, the building workers' union. There were at that time several environmental groups fighting to save the Post Office in Victoria Square. The Post Office, built in 1891, is listed by the Department of the Environment as a building of historic and architectural interest, and lies within an officially designated conservation area. Despite this, the Post Office had agreed to its demolition to make way for a complex of high-rise concrete office blocks. The history of the proposed development showed up both the way in which a nationalised industry, the Post Office, had become enmeshed in the drive to make profits above all other considerations, and the close integration of local authority planning procedures with property development.[3]

The Post Office was one of the last Victorian buildings standing in Birmingham at a time when 2 million square feet of office buildings remained unlet in the city. Following Jack Mundey's

visit to the city and discussions with trades unionists, environmental groups and community groups, a Green Ban Action Committee (GBAC) was formed which was broadly representative of
those various interests. The Committee immediately launched the
Post Office Preservation Campaign. Because of the relative weakness of the builders' union vis-à-vis their Australian counterparts,
direct action tactics were not possible, and the campaign to date
has had more of a parliamentary flavour about it. However, local
branches of UCATT, AUEW, TGWU, AUEW-TASS and EEPTU
were among the unions to give early support to the campaign, and
the West Midlands Regional TUC, having pledged its support, led a
delegation to the City Council to demand that the Post Office
should be preserved and improved. Factory committees, ward
Labour Parties, MPs and community groups have also pledged
support, and the West Midlands County Council has come out
strongly in favour of the revocation of planning permission.
Petitions, press releases and a city centre demonstration have also
ensured that the issue is kept in the public eye.

The campaign has, predictably, been attacked as a 'type of
fascism and extreme communism' by Sir Frank Price, the former
Lord Mayor of Birmingham, in a statement reminiscent of the
Australian right-wing reaction to Green Bans. Price is a partner in
Comprehensive Development Associates, the consultancy firm
retained by the Post Office to plan the scheme. At the same time,
the issue has been complicated by the intervention of a former
Liberal City Councillor, Gordon Herringshaw, who has served a
writ on the Post Office claiming that under the Post Office Act of
1969, the Post Office has no right to embark on an essentially
speculative venture without the specific permission of the government minister responsible.

Birmingham's Green Ban campaign has thus developed into a
less clear-cut issue than the Australian Green Bans. To a certain
extent this is inevitable, given the strategies available to the Committee. However, the GBAC has succeeded in starting a debate
which not only goes beyond the question of the Post Office to a
consideration of the built environment as a whole, and has spread
beyond the confines of Birmingham. It also has raised the possibility of joint action between residents, environmentalists and trades
unionists in a practical way.

London

In the five dockland boroughs of East and South-East London, trades unionists have become increasingly involved with community groups in struggles concerned with the redevelopment plans for the area. Formally, the trades unions and the Trades Councils have been represented on the public participation machinery ('the Forum') right from the start of the present phase of consultation in 1974.

With the exception of certain notable individual trade unionists, however, this official representation has not, until the last year or so, been backed up by any very lively involvement at the level of the local trades union branches and beyond. Now the situation has been developing rapidly and the trades union movement has become far more actively concerned. Symptomatic of this trend, a trades union representative has been elected chairman of the Forum. He is also, ex-officio, the Forum's representative on the official planning body itself, the Docklands Joint Committee (composed of representatives from the GLC and the five boroughs).

The growth of trades union interest in planning can be explained by two major factors. First, London's industrial decline has hit the old industrial areas such as docklands particularly hard. As a result, unemployment is up to three times the national average. In the face of such a crisis, trades unionists are inevitably more concerned to maintain manufacturing employment. They have therefore been increasingly interested in the potential of developing new industrial estates in docklands. Second, the plan itself (unlike the previous plan) emphasises the importance of resolving the employment crisis if the overall strategy for regenerating the area is to have any success.

As a result, demands for jobs in docklands have now gained an important place in the wider trade union programme for East and South-East London. Each of the boroughs has set up some trades union machinery for organising around these demands, ranging from a sub-committee of the Trades Council to a joint action committee based on representation from the Trades Council' trades union branches and community groups (as in Tower Hamlets). In addition, these borough-wide organisations have also set up a working party which arose from a successful joint conference in December 1976.

So far, apart from the formal participation process, the focus of activity has been twofold. There has been pressure on central and local government to make policy changes to assist the industrial redevelopment of East and South-East London (via lobbies, deputations, public meetings and demonstrations). In one borough a working party on employment has been established by the borough with representatives from central government and employers, as well as trade unionists. There have also been direct campaigns to save existing jobs; for instance the West India Dock was saved from closure in 1976 as a result of trades union action backed by the wider trades union movement and the local community groups. Action on both fronts can be expected to increase as the situation develops and the Strategy Plan begins to be implemented.

Notes

1 The Lucas Aerospace combined shop stewards' committee has been active for the last two years in promoting a discussion about the alternative products their factories might make. The initial spur to this discussion was the realisation that their traditional products, dependent on aircraft construction and defence contracts, were likely to be less in demand. However, since this debate has begun in the seventeen Lucas plants in Britain, the notion of socially useful work has caught on and been developed. Workers have realised that they have the skills to develop kidney machines, for example, but that they are not asked to make them because they are not profitable. Among the articles and pamphlets to which reference can be made for a further discussion of the Lucas initiative are the following: Counter Information Services, *Anti-Report on Lucas*, autumn 1975, available from CIS, 9 Poland Street, London W1; *Guardian* articles, 12 December 1975 and 23 January 1976; Labour Research article, March 1976, available from LRD, 78 Blackfriars Road, London SE1 8HF; *Undercurrents*, nos 14 and 18, available at 45p from 11 Shadwell, Iley, Dursley, Glos.; *Jobs and the Environment*, available at 12p from SERA, Tidy's Cottage, School Lane, West Kingsdown, Kent.

2 Other articles and interviews featuring Jack Mundey include the following: *Undercurrents*, nos 14 and 18 (see above); *Community Action*, no. 24, available at 18p from P.O. Box 665, London SW1X 8DE; *Guardian* article, 28 January 1976; *Labour Weekly* article, 12 December 1975; *Town and Country Planning* article, January 1976; *New Society* article, 31 October 1974; *Trade Unions, Community Groups and the Environment* (report of a meeting addressed by Jack Mundey), available at 15p from LCSS, 68 Chalton Street, NW1.

3 For detailed history of the Birmingham campaign contact Val Stevens, Green Ban Action Committee, 77 School Road, Hall Green, Birmingham B28 8JQ.

12 Class, culture and community work

Laurence J. Tasker

One thing that has become familiar in the community development business is the enthusiasm felt by many in the trade for the political elements of community work. The sooner communities show signs of taking action and learning the ability and eagerness to organise for their own self-protection, the happier workers become. This is a highly creditable goal. The ability to assert oneself and organise is basic to the self-interest and dignity of anyone, and a democracy has no value if people don't know how to operate within its formal framework. But the process of moving towards that kind of ability seems to be inadequately understood by many in the community work business and very often so where the enthusiasm to see political processes develop is at its greatest. Community development is supposed to bring about political development, self confidence, social awareness and cohesion, but so often, in contrast, it produces sporadic organisation, discontinuity, disinterest and inactivity. There is, of course, standard professional lore to cope with all such phenomena: 'community work is a long term process', 'it takes one and a half years to get to know your area', etc.

It seems timely after such a cynical comment to make it absolutely plain for whom the article is written or, more precisely, *to* whom it is written. This is a polemic to those in the participation industry—not necessarily community workers, but planners, educationalists, social workers: various professionals who do some community work for whom the state of mind of those people with whom they are dealing often is inadequately understood. This is illustrated at one level by the legislation facilitating community development, e.g. the Town and Country Planning Acts,[1] and at a lower level by the often discussed failure of projects to survive after the worker 'withdraws'. This is not to say that there is not already an extensive and useful amount of literature on working-class politics.[2] The problem seems to be to take the lessons from this for a particular purpose: the idea of community development. The gulf already noted between hope and understanding on the subject of political development in community work is an indication of social characteristics of people engaged professionally in this field of work by comparison with those among whom they are working. If the paper were to be read by enthusiasts indigenous to those communities with such problems as those with which community development is mainly concerned, then apologies would need to be presented each time these readers felt obliged to say 'that's not new', 'that's stating the obvious' and so on. But it can't escape notice that people coming into paid community development work, e.g. from community work, social work and similar courses, still come predominantly from educationally and socially elite backgrounds. Those from areas where community workers are generally occupied don't need telling such things as will be under discussion in the present argument—at least, not in the same terms. In any case they don't read books such as *Political Issues and Community Work*. Community workers—or related professionals—presumably do, and it is to them that this paper is directed.

This is not an invitation to middle-class community workers to start applying the scourge, but it is worth while reminding oneself of the circumstances in which such papers are written and subsequently read. Somebody needs telling about somebody else. Much has been attempted already through the anthropological tradition of British sociology which seems to be for people who do not know what class is about. A great deal of attention has been paid in literature to describing life-styles of working-class people—i.e. those people whose income, or whose family's income, derives mainly from manual or physical work as opposed to administrative, professional or related work. The reasons why the latter, the minority, need to devote research and educational resources to understanding what is commonplace among the majority—the manually employed—is a political point *per se*, and writing papers in social work and community work in the same academic tradition might be deemed to perpetuate the division—if the assumption is that the intervener doesn't know already and is therefore from a socially different group. To achieve enlightenment in an issue which professionalism tends to obscure, we need to ask the questions: 'how much political development can we hope for?' 'How much involvement in locally organised projects can the community worker expect?' When this is very little, as it so often is, patience is needed, plus sympathy, respect and possibly a revised approach to the community work task. The reasons people do not get involved politically or at community level are complex and not nearly as obvious as many would make out.

The notion of a class tends to include in it many definitions and usages. Thus for example the notion that certain experiences are peculiar to certain occupational categories and being born into circumstances where these form the means of livelihood means a tendency to experience this life-style through one's own life and pass it on to one's progeny. Thus manual workers' sons *tend* to become workers and lead the way of life which separates them so significantly from office workers. The differences in relation to politics are often inadequately treated from a sociological point of view, tending to focus on voting behaviour, but a more sophisticated examination is vital if the community worker is not going to become as crudely administrative in his approach to cultural differences as were his professional forebears.

The term must not be used, however, without paying due attention to the distinctions between various sections of the population whose income is based on manual work. Apart from differences of status, income and other material factors there are cultural differences: for example, differences in leisure pursuits between northern and southern England and educational traditions between the British nationalities; and more clearly political differences such as the job mobility in London compared with the relative restriction in one-industry communities of North and South Wales. The breadth of this diversity can be faced from the community work point of view because of the trend in manual work experience to bring with it attendant experiences, or lack of them, which are of consequence to local politics and community affairs. However, one aspect of the differentiation in working class life needs special mention, on account of its special relevance to community work. This is the position of women. In the authority system of working-class ways of life, the woman occupies a peculiar and subtle position.[3] Her apparent subservience to the male and her lack of involvement in formal politics and the sorts of experience which support it, such as trade union activity, can make her a very difficult person to work with. On the other hand, when the chips are down and the case is for direct action, the woman's role can be an extremely influential one. Thus the expensive modifications to the Carbon Black work to protect the near-by environment came almost entirely as a result of women's action.[4] The influential Wapping Parents Action Group decided to 'let the dads play in the Action Group's band' and have persisted satisfactorily at a political level without them for several years.[5] There are probably many such examples from around the country. The action of women in this kind of role has been of particular interest and importance in Northern Ireland, where in numerous reported incidents the women have taken action in protecting the rights and liberties of local people against the possibility of their infringement by the occupying army. In more conventional community work women's roles are also very significant, for example in Women's Aid and the playgroups movement.[6] All in all, the woman's role in community work is an extremely interesting and important one and the phenomenon of women's authority relationships and their consequence in community work needs careful examination. The discussion has been greatly helped by the earlier book in this series, edited by Marjorie Mayo.[7]

The experience of authority in working-class life is almost complete, and this seems the single most important factor overlooked or underestimated by people brought up in homes based on incomes from professional or administrative work. The experience of *receiving*, not applying authority, that is. If a boy is born into a household on a council housing estate in an industrial town, his pattern for life in terms of administrative relationships is predictable. The house will be owned by the local council; it will also be rented out by them—having earlier been 'planned' by them and designed by them. In certain circumstances, usually decided by the council, they can even re-possess the house. They organise and do the repairs and fix and collect the rent. Thus the simple factor of housing as a basic provision of life is subject to a great many decisions which are well detached from the individual residents of the particular household. The clinical services which a child undergoes, for another example, are as remote from him as the housing administration already mentioned. The authority of medical personnel adds a dimension derived from a body of knowledge and professional status which sets them apart from and above other jobs. These are all unfamiliar phenomena to a working-class person, in terms of the experience of his own life. Social contact with medical or other 'professional' personnel will never be closer than the other side of a desk. The experience of authority is one-dimensional. It is one way.

Schooling is the most sustained experience of administration which a child undergoes, and is the most substantially researched[8] in terms of academic sociology. The difference between the working-class boy and the middle-class boy is perhaps most important—from the point of view of this paper—the contact with his teacher. The latter is recognised as better off, 'someone whom your Mum and Dad don't mix with' and probably wouldn't want to. He doesn't live in your area, and wouldn't, given the chance. The social separation—the sense of detachment and inferiority—couldn't be better put than by John Lennon, in a well-written popular song:[9]

> They hurt you at home and hit you at school,
> They hate you if you're clever and despise a fool,
> Till you're so f—ing crazy you follow the rules.

Note the effect of accent and the ability to brow beat through 'extended' verbal ability as researched by Bernstein et al.[10] There are many other points of irrelevance: for example the fact that the curriculum may have no occupational or recreational relevance at all to a working-class boy. This point has been the subject of much discussion in recent literature.[11]

It may be argued that the true nature of involvement by working-class people in the administration of their own lives is misrepresented by this argument; i.e. that local government is based on a democratic, electoral process and much of what is discussed here is subject to the direction of democratically elected local representatives. This rests on two theoretical propositions which frankly are too crude to validate such a benevolent view of our democractic system, although the conventional wisdom of the local authority structure demands this. First, locally elected representatives are supposed to 'represent' satisfactorily the people concerned. Second, theirs, as elected representatives, is the real power in policy-making at the local level. Local councillors all too frequently do not live in the wards they represent—when these happen to be the poorer or council-owned areas of a town. Moreover, they appear on the ballot slips often by the workings of a very tight-knit exclusive organisation: the local party and its selection committee. This results in the public being minimally involved in choosing a representative, particularly where there is a long-established 'safe' local seat. Moreover, the ability of the councillor to represent the locality is usually severely attenuated once he is returned, because of the all-embracing power of the party group to which he belongs.

The other point about the councillor's ability to represent concerns the balance of power existing between a council committee and the officers of the local government department concerned. A representative, particularly a newly elected one, may not serve on a particular departmental committee, but even if he does, he may find that the tradition of the committee may give great power and initiative to the officers so that his scope to exercise influence may be limited. Moreover there is no rule to indicate the relative power of chairmen and officials, as this tends to vary according to personalities and local traditions. The professional distance is again unlikely to be overcome by social contacts. Local government officers are no more likely than councillors to live cheek by jowl with their working-class citizenry and probably less likely to meet them socially.

The issue of local government is extremely important in discussing the role of administration in the lives of the people concerned. Parks, recreation, public health, social services, planning, as well as those subjects mentioned above, affect profoundly the environment and day-to-day lives of people who, socially and politically, are widely detached from them. But to portray the lives of manually employed people in terms of the experience of administration, in local government and various branches of domestic life is none the less to avoid a factor which probably has more influence in this respect than all those other local influences put together. This is an easy oversight for community workers to make, as they are preoccupied particularly with local affairs and various branches of local government administration. The factor, of course, is the experience of authority in the work-place. It scarcely needs re-emphasising that the working life of manually employed people consists of being in the situation of receiving instructions to an almost total extent. The foreman is the king, and discussion with him or possibly a shop steward is the nearest most men will get to participating in running their own working lives. But the point is that such experience contrasts directly with that of 'white collar' personnel. In their case the working life *is* administration. It is their calling, so instead of responsibility being disseminated through the work-force it is, through them, professionalised. A minority of the British working population are thus collectively responsible for making and implementing professional and administrative decisions for the rest. The experience of administration and responsibility is made exclusive to the few.[12]

It could be added, of course, that longer working hours, shift work and other such mundane phenomena of manual workers' lives equally prevent them from getting involved in organising at local level—a factor which community workers soon learn. As one person, unwilling to get involved in one of Alinsky's programmes, is said apocryphally to have explained: 'You know why we won't go to your meetings? We're too f—ing tired'.

The working lad born into the council house can therefore move through home, school, job and the environment generally without himself ever having to take responsibility for anything and remaining pretty well socially detached from the people who do. Moreover, his recreational and sporting life may produce a very similar set of experiences. This may be something of a caricature to many people in manual occupations but the basic presuppositions are unavoidable: in general one can go through life without making any decisions or having any responsibility to speak of beyond the internal affairs of one's own home.

This may not appear as a revelation in the sociology of class, but the details and their consequences in terms of political behaviour need to be very closely examined by the community worker if he expects people to emerge from a lifetime of such experience and suddenly begin to 'participate'. Before we consider in detail the mental background behind these differences we should remember that there are material deficiencies which obstruct the participatory process that are far more tangible. It is quite clear that the educational, social and family aspects of such a career are going to give little grounding in some of the basic attributes which form the stuff of politics at the local level. People who work at shop-floor level will have little experience of how things are organised by post or telephone. Typing facilities, telephones and franking machines are relatively unavailable to them. The know-how connection with the production of circulars, designing or filling out forms, composing letters or writing press releases is not fostered among working-class people on the basis of work experience.[13] One tenants' association chairman, who has played a considerable part in community politics in his part of the country, reflected on his reluctance to write letters on behalf of his group, then confided: 'I normally write a letter only once a year—to my sister at Christmas.' To put it at its simplest level, many people leave school with comparatively undeveloped literary skills.[14] More to the point, many more let them fall into decay through the lack of demand made in domestic and working life. While this is happening among the manually employed population, written and formal verbal skills in administrative and related jobs are being developed to a point where they give the personnel considerable advantage in the basic conduct of administrative and organisational behaviour.

Verbal ability, too, is unevenly distributed from a conventional apolitical point of view. One housewife was totally unwilling to speak in early public meetings attended by local government officers, but has since become a vociferous leader of her action group and confidante to her fellow tenants on official matters. The council official, the public health inspector or other local authority professional or administrative officer cannot be matched in formal eloquence or negotiating skill by the manual worker who has perhaps never attended more than the occasional union meeting or—even more seriously—by the housewife whose activities and social contacts are centred on her own home. Measured, skilful discourse is the bread and butter of the administrator's work—even at a relatively low level—but to the manual worker or his family the procedure of a committee, or the wording of an official letter, could be as mystifying and confusing as a foreign language. Negotiations or meetings between the two in the community work situation, no less than at the work-place, are therefore never on equal terms.

Meetings as tasks of participation or preparation require a particular kind of ability, experience of which is general in the day-to-day life of administrative work. A well-organised social life may also feature committee work and responsibility and produce the kinds of skills which this requires. They can thus become an important learning process. However, this is typically not the recreational pattern—club and society based—which people from manual occupations choose. Working-class people don't *like* meetings while middle-class people often do. One has only to turn to the field of voluntary social work to be reminded of the well-respected core of middle-class regulars who often make up the mainstay of voluntary activity in a town, thus appearing to approach committee-going not just as an instrumental activity but as something of a pleasure in itself.

There is a persistence, however, in community approaches to local services and community-orientated projects where participation is a conscious aim to remain surprised at the reluctance and sluggishness with which local participation actually evolves. Community workers themselves are often over-optimistic about results when too preoccupied with the apparent worth of the programmes they have to offer. The Housing Act 1974[15] and the Town and Country Planning Acts legislation[16] contain procedures for extensive public participation which are probably warmly embraced and sincerely implemented by many local authorities, yet the written reports of their effectively stimulating widespread participation are rare. Community workers can find the same problem through inadequately researching a project. Mitton and Morrison's book[17] shows how a large budget and several years' work could not adequately keep a small project alive without the direct support of the worker. Expectations of people in community development programmes are often quite unrealistic where large-scale changes are hoped for on the basis of a limited range of input. The most conspicuous and most immediate needs of working-class people are undoubtedly material, and these shortcomings are as consequential in the community work field as elsewhere. However, it is useless to tackle community development problems in these terms without recognising the extent and gravity of the consequences of such aspects of a life-style as those described above. This needs a thorough analysis in terms of a person's propensity to respond to a community worker's initiative if a fair-minded approach is to be developed towards community and general local participation.

To summarise: the facilities of organisation and locally-based community activity are not easily available to the sections of the population whose livelihood is based on manual employment and who live in areas where that section of the work-force became concentrated. Moreover, jobs and more general life experiences in such situations give very little training or experience that is relevant to successful participation in local activities such as the community worker might wish to encourage. These are fairly tangible factors against which those interested in community work can construct a strategy. But to do so without considering deeper factors—the underlying beliefs and thought-processes of the population concerned—is to do so without sufficiently taking account of the extent of the problem. Living in the type of circumstances referred to above does not only inhibit a person through lack of facilities available and abilities developed at a pragmatic level, but produces in time a state of mind which itself inhibits the kind of activity which the community worker would like to see non-involved residents participate in. This factor itself, the nature of the thought which lies behind the activity—or inactivity—seems to have two main problematic characteristics. The first concerns morale.

For a person to *believe* that he is not particularly capable of organising aspects of his own life—when he has persistently through his experience to date been subject to the decisions made by other people on his behalf—seems perfectly reasonable. The issue of differential intelligence is well ingrained in the perceptions of jobs and careers or role differences and general ability. Others supposedly have positions of power because they are bright, and if one does not have such a position oneself one supposedly is not bright. Such is the effect of educational differentiation and its pervasion of many status systems throughout the economy and the rest of society. Having been subject to decision-making by other people in so many areas of life for so long, people on the wrong side of this differentiation quite understandably come to the conclusion that this is because the others are good at it and they are not. *Inherently* this is not the case, although through the passage of time and all the attendant experiences such as those described above it could in effect become so. The effect of recurrent experience on morale eventually must become profound. Inherent ability is what concerns the community worker, and this is what he is nurturing despite the effects of the morale barrier which intervenes.

Local residents are never going to challenge local authorities successfully unless they *believe* their own decisions to be as valid as those of the officials. Yet too often self-depreciation rather than self-assertion is exhibited when the two sides meet. Every community worker has seen such instances; for example when a tenants' delegation is rendered almost mute through the overawing effect of the conference table and walnut panelling of the town hall. One remembers another instance, which is probably familiar to those in the field, when a community worker attempted to begin devolving responsibility when organising a playgroup. No parent would accept the responsibility for minding the key to the premises between meetings, and the worker had to resume the organising role to keep the group going temporarily. Another case featured a mother who was reluctant to commit to paper her enormous experience of the playground movement because she felt she 'couldn't spell'. Extroverts among the local leadership survive these situations. The discussion, however, is not about extroverts or exceptions; it is about average members of a community and what prevents them from taking part in public life on the same basis as other average citizens, particularly those from the white collar classes who are permanently involved. Generally, only anger and crisis suffice to overcome such inhibitions among the non-involved population, but it is not anger that solves long term problems, it is organisation and skilled, continuing involvement. If the highly centralised and class-based administrative structure which is a feature of our country's urban way of life is to be tackled by those in the field of community work, they must start with a belief, not coloured by impatience or incomplete understanding, that ability is basic to a person in respect of decision-making, and rate the effect of negative socialisation as carefully as they do the positive contributions to their own lives. There is little evidence to oppose such a view, but there is a lifetime of personal experiences and traditions which provide an impression of what is normal, and these can have a far more searching influence than scientific evidence in an argument, and a far more shattering effect on all-important individual morale. It is not just the lack of material resources and experience which cause disadvantage, it is the necessity of convincing the competent—even the gifted—leader that he's as capable of playing a role in the community as the next man. Inducing this basic *belief* has got to be the task of community workers in addition to the transfer of resources and opportunities. Without the former, the latter will have limited meaning and effect.

If morale were the only element involved in this question of belief, the problem would be a relatively simple one—at least in concept. The tradition of unequal distribution of administrative resources in our community has, however, far more complex and profound effects. In addition to what people believe they *can* do about the system as discussed above there is the far less tractable problem of what they think they *ought* to do. The tradition of administrative hierarchy—so firmly ingrained in British society—not only results in feelings on the part of the underprivileged person as to what he can do about it, but what in addition is the right and proper way of organising things. Those who receive the greatest array of administrative influences impinging upon their lives tend to believe more than any that this is the 'right' way to build an organisation, whether this is a local association, a local government department or a nation-state: one small sector makes the decisions, organises everybody else and takes general administrative responsibility for the majority. The situation is 'normal', i.e. 'correct'. This is not to say that tradition is a straightforward factor in influencing what is regarded in organisations and society as normal. The phenomenon works in subtle ways. For example 'citizen participation', a common concept in much recent legislation, suggests that what citizens are supposed to participate in is something distinct from them. Government or authority is one thing, citizens are another. There is an acceptance of the separateness of the two sides, e.g. 'participation in the firm' recognises that there are two sides: the participators and the firm. Thus the workers, by implicit definition, are not the firm. Their rights implicitly are therefore secondary. Another example illustrating the assumptions about authority and the rights accruing to it is in the reporting of 'disruption' in industry. This is generally described as arising from 'strikes' or 'labour problems'. 'Whose problem?' is a question which is never seriously applied. 'Management problems' or 'management disputes' would seem an equally reasonable description where there is dispassionate comment on a conflict involving two sides. However, impartiality is never really complete, and the situation referred to in such terms becomes less than a fair fight. To take a similar example, 'absenteeism' is the epithet used to describe a situation where workers prefer extra leisure to extra cash. Likewise 'wasted votes' is the expression used to refer to those cases where people consider the electoral process relatively unimportant to them, representing to them perhaps a negligible political involvement rather than the essence of democracy which in the mythology of western systems it is meant to represent. A vote that is referred to as a duty is not a very convincing form of popular franchise. Where authority equals power, it can still be said of our system that 'might equals right'. The 'normal' is biased on the side of those in power. This is of course inconsistent in a society where redistributive ideals are so prevalent and so proudly championed, for example by the Labour Party. One might expect that the radical would be normal, but that is not the case, even at local government level. The language of the media and the legislating institutions describe the innovator in such a way as to present the existing order of authority and administration in the aura of normality and thereby propriety. The effects on the receiver of that authority and what he accepts as proper can be reckoned—in the face of such a prevailing ethos—to be deep and enduring, and have consequences for the community worker and his aims.

Steeped in such an ideology, it is not surprising that the individual should believe in the idea that one section of the community will always make the decisions and the other have a duty as good citizens to obey them. Thus we are faced with a perfectly consistent attitude on the part of someone who reacts in such a way in the community work situation. A woman who is perfectly happy to let other people organise her children's schooling, even to let the council bulldoze her house down and 're-locate' her as part of a development plan, or re-route buses to her inconvenience —even though she might hate the prospect or be very distressed by the event—is in her own terms acting consistently with the accepted rules regarding the exercise of authority in the community. Passive responses by people in crises are quite familiar to community workers in the field. They are often incredulous when people don't or won't 'fight'. Often, unfortunately, such passiveness is regarded as weakness. This view is quite misplaced when the consistency with life experiences and normality is so great, and the community workers' incredulity merely a sign of social distance. It is not just a question of the viability but the morality of taking on council officials by those who live in the administered section of the population, a morality which has subtle and deep-seated origins.

But even this is likely to leave the matter over-simplified in understanding the structure of political thinking among working class people and the disadvantage it produces vis-à-vis the established institutions of authority. Ability and the resources it depends upon have been listed, plus the issue of morale and personal potential and, last, the question of belief in the morality of one person exercising authority over another. There seems, however, to be another level of this phenomenon. It is not only the belief that it is simply right to respond to those who have been put in authority over one but that this is somehow underpinned by a natural order of things, so that there is a division between

ruler and ruled based on an ineradicable feature of the relationship
of man to man. This is reflected in the subsequent maldistribution
of authority and responsibility throughout the community. Thus
hierarchy and domination are seen as part of society, as though it
were itself an organic being with basic unalterable characteristics.
The Church of England could not have supported this impression
better and with such moral force than with a verse only recently
eliminated from 'All things bright and beautiful' (*Hymns Ancient
and Modern*):[18]

> The rich man in his castle,
> The poor man at his gate,
> He made them high and lowly,
> And ordered their estate.

Recently the endorsement of inequality seemed to figure in the
opening prayers of the Queen Elizabeth II Jubilee Service:[19]

> Almighty God who rulest over all the kingdoms of the
> world, and dost order them according to thy good pleasure
> . . .

The sentiment is presented in many subtle forms in our
approaches to hierarchy, e.g. in the concept of authority in
schools and in education generally. Thus legislation for working-
class people, whether it be in the general field of housing, or at a
local level such as in the canteen and toilet facilities within a
factory, seems to assert that class is something inherent and therefore treated as permanent. Moreover it involves not only the distribution of material goods, but the distribution of responsible and
administrative tasks in society. The important ideological consequences of this—affecting the way people see themselves—is when
this is perceived not as circumstantial—a temporary feature of the
particular kind of society in which we live—but as a natural condition of the species, thus meaning that the position one has in the
hierarchy is something born to and to be accepted. Such a belief is
a widely spread feature of the working classes' attitudes to their
position in the economic world, the result of a complexity of life
experiences such as those previously described and the inter-
generational consistency with which these recur. There can be
no better example of this self-image than the hesitancy which
has interlaced shop-floor discussions in the recent months over
the Bullock proposals,[20] not necessarily regarding this scheme

specifically, for it has many features that belie any real intention to represent democratic interests of manual workers, but in the hesitancy with which industrial democracy itself has been approached among manual workers. It appears that the working man does not see it as his role to take command.

Considerable space in this paper has been devoted to the question of the reluctance or resistance on the part of the residents in poor communities to become involved in the projects that professional workers seek to promote. The nature of their experience of administration and authority and their access to the means of organising is argued to pre-determine various attitudes of relevance to politics and community work. In the analysis of these ideological and attitudinal factors, morale could be said to be the single most important aspect in relation to community action. To this, what a man *thinks* he can do, is added the issue of what he *can actually* do in terms of resources, plus the question of what he thinks he *ought* to do—the moral question—and the issue of what he thinks in the long run is *normal*, i.e. accords with the natural order of things and is therefore proper and viable.

The effects of a set of attitudes and beliefs on community and political attitudes are no doubt subtle and complex, and in analysing a belief system like this, one is probably raising more questions about ideas and actions than are here answered. But one thing is clear: the complexity of ideas among working-class people concerning notions of authority and the consistency of these with life experiences merit a far more comprehensive understanding and a more sympathetic approach than that given by many of those involved from an outside standpoint. This externalised, professional viewpoint often results in impatient and unsympathetic criticism. The incredulity which accompanies this and the failure to understand another life-style and identify it too much with one's own can result in a patronising or even slightly insulting attitude to the residents who don't respond to situations in accordance with one's own predispositions. Working-class residents often don't or won't get involved. This phenomenon is based on a completely different set of attitudes from those of town-hall-based or university-trained personnel. It is not illogical, unrealistic or unsophisticated, nor is it in any sense an inferior or less intelligent view of political life (by which is meant also community life) than that of the better trained observer. The working-class view of the local political world, as influenced by the tendencies described here, is entirely consistent with the upbringing and the material circumstances which surround it. It is as such, as far as the term can be used in an objective analysis, an entirely consistent ideology supporting a political attitude to the world which is entirely coherent and defensible. The person who uses 'apathy' to refer to non-involvement at local level is not only showing serious misunderstanding of life-styles in the community to which his work is directed, but is being extremely disparaging to a political view of the world as valid and intellectually respectable as his own.

Respect is not the only thing which is required of community workers and their allies in the face of a political culture which squares so badly with their own, though this may be seen as the most important objective of this paper. Apart from moral messages, it is important in community work to examine carefully such points of political argument for their implications in practice. Community work has traditionally been rather atheoretical, but because it is not a discipline in the academic sense, this does not mean that there are not important points of political theory and philosophy underpinning practice and objectives. The long-standing alliance with the social work professional tradition and the consequent confusion of identity could have caused this, and in terms of the argument put forward here the social work identity seems increasingly problematic. Social work could claim on the basis of this that what is implicitly described here as community work practice involves a strong element of traditional social work input; i.e. involving morale (on which great stress is laid in this paper) and which in as far as it is alterable might be seen to employ human relationships, which are traditionally held to be the province of professional social work. The extent to which social work has a monopoly of such skills and to which morale *is* changed in inter-personal relationships remains to be argued, but at least the question is open.

More tangible and more susceptible than morale to outside intervention are some of the other aspects of deprivation mentioned in this paper. These are the lack of organisational facility and ability which could be subject, at least theoretically, to some strategic policy of redress. Stretching a definition of social work to cover this task, however, is hardly helpful. This is not a case for therapy or for dealing with the pathological. This is very much a question of dealing with the normal, and it would seem more helpful at a theoretical level to recognise this as a task falling squarely in the province of compensatory education. This is not to quibble about identities but defined as such, it would seem to involve a better chance of specific tasks being recognised and eventually tackled and the right kind of respect being attributed in the process to the recipients.

Underlying the tangible aspects, however, is an ideological structure so profound and rooted in tradition as to make the task of community work—or 'compensatory education'—imposing, if not staggering, particularly to the solitary community worker. This represents a task of very long term proportions and at the time of writing there seems no chance of the number of community development workers being increased to meet it. Realistically, if any headway is to be made towards the long-term aims of community work, then some other force apart from the efforts of the singly employed community development worker has got to be brought into play.

Redressing the imbalance of power which has been described here does not represent the objectives of this paper. Cultural imbalance of political ability is a vast and complex problem. The aim here is understanding, and some suggestions for broadening the effort to tackle this inequality. This effort, it is held, can and should go beyond the traditional concept of the lone worker or small team approach to community work. Despite expansion in recent years, the number of such workers is small and their distribution patchy. Many of the material resources mentioned here are plentiful and some contribution could be made to community objectives if these were to become more readily available. Several professions now have a stake in the 'participation business' and one wonders if it is merely a matter of predisposition and tradition which prevents resources being made available by them to the communities they serve. Of the many professional groups who consider such a volume as this—and this paper is not directed particularly at full-time community workers—it would appear that social work is in a strong position to consider itself as a contributor rather than a beneficiary or bedfellow of community work. This suggests itself for two main reasons.

First, the histories of both social work and community work are in many aspects closely intertwined. This produces an understanding and sympathy in social work which is probably more widespread than in other professions. There have been dreadful misconceptions, arising from an anxiousness to define community work as 'a part of social work', when the latter was conceived in fundamentally therapeutic and counselling terms, but there is reason to believe this era is past. Community workers, moreover, are often working side by side with social workers—more so than with other professionals—and are therefore known to them. With the decline of professional rivalry, the possibility of co-operation is therefore great. Moreover, social workers through their fieldwork are in a strong position to make contacts involving some of the underprivileged and some of the local issues which concern the community worker.

Second, given the argument earlier, it is apparent that many of the personal skills mentioned are at the disposition of the social worker, his working routine being steeped in office procedure and organisational matters. However, this is perhaps not the most important resource which the profession could bring to bear in the interests of community work. It is fashionable to discuss the school as an under-used resource for the community, but the same kind of argument could be applied to the social services office. This is an institution already frequented in a sense by the under-privileged public, but it does not belong to them as a resource. Many community groups—or would-be groups—founder for want of a meeting place such as a committee room, minor secretarial help, publicity or simple office equipment. That schools close at 5 p.m. represents, fashionably, a scandal to the community-minded. Community workers could regard the closing of social work offices at 5 p.m. likewise. Community work contacts regarded as 'clients' when coming into the office will of course never use the place as a resource in the community-development sense. Social work has a commitment to community work;[21] if the will is there at an individual and organisational level to grasp this, the resources are at hand.

To broaden the effort, to stretch the responsibility for community work's aims—to social workers, teachers, planners, trade unions or whoever might be suggested—is not really to treat the problem of political know-how at its root cause. 'Compensatory education' implies a need for 'education'. People at school are seldom through the curriculum given any guide as to how they might participate in our much-vaunted democratic state. Even instruction on how to use the voting system is rare. Moreover, young people leave school to prospects of unemployment or irregular employment, and are given no instruction in trade union organisation or the principles of the trade union movement, much less the structural reasons for their economic insecurity. Still less likely are pupils, by the time they leave school, to have learnt anything of the complexities of local government administration or anything of the various strands of political thought which go to make up our —or any alternative—brand of democracy.

The political divide in this country is enormous. The factors are not just material but mental—complicatedly so. In facing up to this it might be necessary for us at a strategic level to consider much longer term perspectives and a much wider range of cadres in community work. This almost certainly means going beyond professional boundaries, but until the matter is tackled responsibly and at root, community work is going to remain in a patching-up role for an input which should have been there earlier in the system. But it is important to see how, in the absence of satisfactory political education, our political institutions will have enough effective popular support to remain operable.

Notes

1 See Central Office of Information, *Town and Country Planning in Britain*, 6th ed., HMSO, 1975 (COI pamphlet no. 9) for the best introduction to these.
2 R. McKenzie and A. Silver, *Angels in Marble*, Heinemann, 1968, and B. Hindess *The Decline of Working-Class Politics*, Paladin, 1971, are introductory texts relevant to this paper.
3 See M. Young and P. Willmott, *Family and Kinship in East London*, rev. ed., Penguin Books, 1962, for a preliminary account of matrilocalism.
4 See *Solidarity, North London*, summer 1971, for a good account of this dispute.
5 BBC 'Open Door', 3 November 1974.
6 R. Mitton and E. Morrison portray the different contributions of men and women very well in their book, *A Community Project in Notting Dale*, Allen Lane, 1972.
7 *Women in the Community*, Routledge & Kegan Paul, 1977.
8 See Olive Banks, *The Sociology of Education*, Batsford, 3rd ed., 1976, for a useful review of this research.
9 John Lennon, 'Working Class Hero', Apple R 6009, EMI/UK 1970, verse 2.
10 Reviewed well by D. Lawton in *Social Class, Language and Education*, Routledge & Kegan Paul, 1968.
11 Eric Midwinter, *Education and the Community*, Allen & Unwin, 1975.
12 See Central Statistical Office, 'Social Commentary: Social Class', *Social Trends*, no. 6, HMSO, 1976.

13 In reporting the Southwark Community Project, David Thomas writes: '. . . the substantive reality of the project (to local residents) was that given by its telephone, typewriter, and sympathetic and helpful attitude of the people to team members and local users' (*Organising for Social Change*, Allen & Unwin, 1976, p. 134).

14 The British Association of Settlements Report, *The Right to Read*, 1974, estimated the adult non-reading population of the United Kingdom at 2,000,000.

15 See Housing Act 1974, Cmnd 44, HMSO, 1974, Section 37.

16 *Town and Country Planning in Britain*, e.g. pp. 6—7.

17 Op. cit.

18 For example *Hymns Ancient and Modern*, W. Clowes, 1916, p. 166.

19 BBC, 'Queen Elizabeth II, XXV Jubilee Service', St Paul's Cathedral, London, 7 June 1977.

20 Report of the Committee of Enquiry on Industrial Democracy, Cmnd 6706, HMSO, 1977.

21 See, in particular, Report on the Committee on Local Authority and Allied Personal Social Services (Seebohm Report), Cmnd 3703, HMSO, 1968, ch. 16.

13 Community work, social change and social planning

David N. Thomas

As a way of *describing* what they do, community workers will mention a number of varied activities that range from organising volunteers, to play provision, to slum clearance. When we ask community workers to *conceptualise* their work, many are eager to talk about bringing power to the powerless, overcoming poverty and deprivation, building caring and supportive communities, fighting for more facilities for neighbourhoods, increasing political and social participation, and so forth. Workers may also mention the educative component of what they do—helping to develop the confidence and competence of those in community groups. These educational or process goals are a concern both of workers who follow on in the traditions of people like the Battens and the Biddles, and of those who seek to raise political awareness amongst the deprived and the powerless. This latter group of workers may see themselves either as 'community activists' offering a radical alternative to trade unions, local political parties and forms of establishment help such as social work, or as progressive adult educators influenced by people like Paulo Friere.[1]

Common to most descriptions and conceptualisations offered by community work practitioners and writers is some notion that community work is a means of inducing or facilitating *change* (though often workers will be working with groups to resist change). Many workers are quite explicit and declare that their goals are those of 'political change', 'social change', 'organisational change' or 'community change'. The fact that community work is concerned with bringing about change of one kind or another does not shake the earth beneath our feet because change is also an interest of many other professions and organisations in the fields of social work, education, planning, health care and trade unionism.

239

The plain, but uninteresting, fact is that most human transactions can be conceptualised as change activities. Unfortunately, phrases like 'social change' and 'political change' have become cover-all words with meanings so elastic that they refer to quite a heterogeneous range of activities and ambitions. As such, they may promote amongst community workers more obfuscation, romanticism and self-deceit than clarity of thought and honesty of purpose. Compared with other forms of planned change such as education and casework, we find in community work more rhetoric and exhortation about change than the technical competence with which to achieve it.

The radical tendency

The rhetoric about social change is especially pronounced amongst those in community work whom Holman[2] describes as 'radicals' and Baine[3] as 'political neighbourhood organisers'. These are the workers who, says Holman, 'question the very structures of society and want a fundamental re-casting of the resources of income, wealth and political power.' Their explanations of poverty, disadvantage and other social problems do not emphasise malfunctioning in individuals or in the welfare services but rather the contradictions and inequities inherent in a capitalist, multinational economy. Warren has discussed this kind of 'diagnostic paradigm', as he calls it, in the context of the Model Cities Program in America;[4] and within the British CDP programme Harry Specht has distinguished between the 'national strategists' (the radicals, stressing structural explanations of social problems) and the 'local strategists', whose focus was on enhancing the capacity of local agencies and resources to improve the lives of those resident in the areas of service of the project.[5]

I shall use the term 'radical tendency' broadly to refer to those in community work who espouse structural explanations of social problems, much in the way defined above by Holman and Specht. However, this definition, which is based upon the thinking and political analyses of these workers rather than upon the work that they actually do, defines only narrowly those in community work who see themselves as radical. Baldock's analysis of the origins of community action indicates that the radicals in community work comprise a very heterogeneous group. It includes, for instance, those who describe their work as community action, which is 'a form of community work whose main features are a support of disadvantaged groups in conflict with authority and an accompanying populist, reformist, marxist or social anarchist perspective of society'.[6]

The fact that his definition embraces both structuralist and reformist perspectives indicates the broadness of the radical church in community work. This may, of course, be a faithful reflection of a situation in which the established order may see any community worker supporting a group as 'radical', regardless of the worker's political views, and the goals and strategies of the community group. Indeed, the difficulties of identifying who and what is radical in community work are compounded by the fact that many workers prefer to define themselves, and be defined by others, as 'radical', 'political organiser' or 'community activist', even though their day-to-day activities are really no different from those of other workers who still refer to themselves as community workers, organisers or developers. 'Action' seems recently to have replaced 'community' as the popular spray-on word that projects an image of radicalism that is too often belied by what workers do in practice.

A factor that complicates the task of differentiating between the various labels and allegiances of community workers is that other more established forms of community work also seek the accolade of being radical. For instance, there is now a model of community development whose goals 'include economic and political objectives, such as the realignment of power resources in the community. The community developer following this model does not fight shy of using negotiation, bargaining, advocacy, protest, noncooperation and other forms of nonviolent social action'.[7] This aggrandisement between the various kinds of community work about what is radical and what is not indicates the need for conceptualisations of community work that are based on what people do, and not simply on their political views and on the ways in which they see themselves and would like to be seen by others.

I wish first to acknowledge the pertinence of the radical analysis in community work, and particularly its contribution to thinking about social policy, but also to deplore some of its influences within, and effects on, the development of thought and practice amongst community workers. The existence of the radical tendency in community work disproportionately influences both the ways in which 'outsiders' perceive community work and the manner in which community workers who are local strategists (Specht) or liberal reformers (Holman) think about and describe their work. The effect of the radical tendency on the liberal reformers is two-fold; first, liberal reformers will often use the language and concepts of the radical tendency to describe their work. For example, a community worker attending a short course was asked what his goals were. He replied: 'to achieve a more equitable distribution of resources and power in society' (radical). When asked to explain this, he said he wanted to get local people more involved in decision-making about their community (liberal reform). Second, the influence of the radical tendency has created a climate in community work in which stigma is attached both to professing a liberal reformist analysis and to carrying out reformist activities in the field. Specht, for example, has noted the pressure on CDP Directors to accept the analysis of the National Strategists.[8]

The radical cosmetic to be found in community workers' language, and the stigmatisation of reformist practice, may inhibit discussion between community workers and thus reduce the possibilities of mutual help between them in the growth of their skills and knowledge.[9] I also believe that the temptation to delineate the politics and values of a radical view has distracted many practitioners and academics from pursuing the equally important task of constructing the elements of a generic practice theory in community work. To this extent, the radical tendency has had a reactionary influence on the development of community work practice and training. There are, too, the dangers noted by Tasker and Wunnam to community work arising from the influence of the radical tendency of intellectual dogmatism, intolerance, self-righteousness, romanticisation of the working class and feelings of moral superiority over reformist practitioners.[10]

Another critique of the radical tendency in community work is that its adherents offer only a radical *analysis* and do not suggest the content or even the parameters of a radical *practice* of community work. To the extent that the radical tendency offers no practice theory or practice paradigms, it is unprogressive and a political and professional distraction. At the very least, analyses without prescription for action are an extravagance both in a political movement and in a human services profession like community work. The irony is that those workers operating from a radical analysis tend to drift in the work that they actually do towards working with groups and providing services that fall well within the social reformist tradition. Warren[11] and Specht[12] have noted this dilemma of the radical tendency. It may be argued, however, that what the radical tendency has contributed is an emphasis on the need to relate neighbourhood activities to broader issues arising at the city, regional and national levels. This is an important perspective, but it may be achieved, as I shall indicate later, through developing one's thinking about one's professional role and responsibilities, and is not contingent upon the nature of one's political views.

It is worth mentioning two other comments on the radical tendency in community work, both of which raise questions about its *authenticity*. Tasker and Wunnam[13] suggest that radical practice and outcomes are less important to the radical tendency in community work than the *moral significance* of their analysis. Why is it, they ask, that in spite of community work having little credibility as an instrument of structural social change, many 'politically-orientated community workers' nevertheless talk about, and evaluate, their work as if it had such credibility and potential? The answer, they suggest, is that

> Although its overall political significance is negligible, the work is technically political in nature and therefore to the worker morally sound. It is often noticeable among radicals who apply for community work training . . . that they are very thoughtful about the political nature of the work, but relatively unrealistic about or uninterested in the scale of its national political effect. Somehow the spirit of the job is more important than its productivity.

A second attack on the authenticity of the radical tendency has come from the direction of the Women's Movement. Elizabeth Wilson suggests that the superficiality of many community workers' political views indicates that they have a lot to learn from the Women's Movement—in particular, 'that *daily life* is political—political in a deeper sense than most community workers understand'.[14] The repressive nature of events and language in everyday life, a repression that works against social structural change, has also been discussed by Pateman;[15] the significance of Wilson's and Pateman's concerns with the politics of everyday life is that they help us to see that the political analysis of the radical tendency in community work is cut off from the reality and experiences of working-class people. This detachment from the working class and from the 'achievement of an empathetic and pragmatic approach to their problems' has also been noted by Tasker and Wunnam[16] and by Specht,[17] and constitutes yet another unprogressive feature of the radical tendency in community work. Not only is their analysis divorced from practice but the analysis itself is detached from a patience and interest in the events and transactions of everyday working-class life.

A further value of the critique from the Women's Movement is that it points to the sexist elements in the ideology and motivations of the radical tendency. Wilson and Gallagher[18] suggest that the concern to make and to project community work as a radical alternative may be an expression of professional male machismo, intent on distinguishing community work from (female) social work.[19]

Finally, it is worth noting that the influence of the radical tendency has persisted through a period in which the radical or 'political' *nature* of community work has been questioned by a number of writers, including contributors to *Case Con*,[20] and by Mayo.[21] A dominant theme in the *Case Con* community work issue is that community work is as much a part of the controlling and co-optive apparatus of the state as is casework and those other aspects of the social services that are so vilified by the radical tendency in community work. Mayo argues that 'if radical social change is the prime objective, community development is not a specially favourable starting point at all: nor does it have any automatic advantage over social work of the casework variety— indeed in some instances it may be, and has been, *more* repressive.' She mentions the vulnerable, divisive and sectional nature of community action, and the fact that it succeeds only in redistributing resources *within* and *between* the poor.

Another kind of critique disputes the *potential* of community work to achieve the kinds of structural changes in capitalist society that are implicit in a structuralist analysis. This critique has been offered by Tasker[22] in an article which carries the most honest appraisal of the potential of community work to make a significant impact on the destiny of millions of working-class people in this country. He suggests that

> the idea that wide-spread social change can be instigated by professional community workers is hopelessly unrealistic.

The profession is more a phenomenon of social change, not a 'movement' directly causally related to social change. Community workers in isolation must therefore retain some modesty in the overall social significance they ascribe to their own role.

Tasker argues that the political development of the working class through community work may be more realistically seen to be achieved through the material and educational benefits that accrue to *individuals* through small-scale change.

The social reformist tendency

The social reformist tendency in community work has had a rather different, but just as limiting, influence. The major weaknesses of this tendency, and thus of community work *practice* as a whole, is the continuing emphasis, first, on the *neighbourhood* and, second, on the *interactional* aspects of the community work role.

The neighbourhood

Direct, face-to-face work with small-sized community groups in local neighbourhoods has been, and is, the predominant mode of community work practice in Britain. The content of this work has been greatly varied, though most of it has involved working with community groups in order to acquire, reject, manage or otherwise influence resources, and decisions about resources.[23] Within the social services, this type of community work (which has rightly addressed itself to the here-and-now difficulties and problems faced by local people) may be counted, together with casework and groupwork, as a *micro* intervention.

There is both a political and professional criticism of allowing community work to continue only within the scheme of micro interventions. The political criticism is that local groups need to relate to, and understand their activities within, structural (i.e. non-local) explanations of the problems they face. The professional criticism suggests that it is the role responsibility of community workers, and of other professionals, to address themselves to *macro* interventions, defined by Whittaker as seeking changes to 'a neighbourhood, an organisation . . . an entire community, or even a total society'.[24] A further critique of neighbourhood work is that it has done little to focus agencies like social services departments on macro forms of interventions; indeed, it may be argued that community workers have made such departments even more micro-centred through concentrating only on efforts to promote patch systems of working, the involvement of caseworkers in neighbourhood work, and the assessment of needs and resources in the community.

Interactional tasks

Partly as a consequence of its micro-orientation, community work practice and training gives more emphasis to the interactional or 'human relations' aspect of the community worker's role than to its technical and analytical requirements. This is especially the case for community workers trained or working within social work and adult education. These interactional tasks refer primarily to the worker's role in identifying and engaging with local people, and working with them in forming and developing an organisation through which they seek to achieve their goals. The limitations of an over-emphasis on interactional tasks and skills are twofold.

First, it inadequately prepares people for neighbourhood work; that is, intending practitioners do not attend to those technical requirements of their role that would make them more effective change agents in the neighbourhood setting. Here are three examples: (a) great stress is put in community work on promoting the participation of local people in decision-making, and ever since the Skeffington and Seebohm Reports, agencies have been exhorted to become more participative. But the torrent of exhortation from community workers is seldom accompanied by advice on how such participation is best achieved. Community workers articulate the value of participation but, on the whole, show little technical competence about its implementation. The techniques are there[25] but receive little consideration in training and practice; (b) entering a neighbourhood for the first time is still too often treated as 'hanging about just chatting to people' with little regard to the techniques of participant observation; and (c) process goals are still largely conceived as either 'increasing people's confidence and competence' or 'raising political consciousness' without much thought to the complex business of how adults learn.

Second, it inadequately prepares people to attempt macro interventions that seek changes in the policies and organisations that affect the well-being of those in territorial and functional communities. Effectiveness in influencing the policies, decisions and procedures of other agencies, and the city, regional and national factors that determine the welfare of community residents, requires technical and analytical competence in *social planning*. Social planning also requires interactional competence because it involves political activity—and by 'political' I mean the process apparent within and between all organisations and interest groups through which staff attempt to promote ideas, influence others, compete for, and acquire, scarce resources, and protect and extend their own and their unit's interests. Bolan[26] provides a good introduction to the interactional tasks of the planner, though, of course, there is a good deal of relevant literature also to be found in the fields of management studies, social psychology, sociology and group behaviour about the matter of organisational change and resistance. A most useful presentation of some of this material has been prepared for community workers by Rothman.[27]

Social planning, of course, has always been acknowledged or claimed as a strand of community work.[28] Kramer and Specht choose 'to define social planning as one of the major modes of community organisation practice, that which focuses on a range of interventions at the level of organisations and institutions, rather than directly on the population groups affected by a social problem.'[29] The major tasks involved in intervening at the level of organisations, institutions and social policies are those of problem analysis and needs assessment, the choice of goals and priorities, and the design, implementation and evaluation of programmes and interventions.

The purposeful and informed participation of community workers in social planning provides, I believe, a way forward from the dilemmas faced by the radical and neighbourhood-centred tendencies in community work. The social planning role provides the *practice* link, much needed by both these tendencies, between micro and macro forms of intervention and change, and, as such, takes us one stage further than purely polemical and normative assertions of the need to establish a micro-macro relationship. However, it will not be an easy matter to establish this social planning role in community work training and practice: community workers will be circumspect about technical skills and technologies that have largely been the monopoly of bureaucratic decision-makers. There are, too, suspicions, notably voiced within the CDP, that social planning is not a political activity; and that isolated, unsupported and perhaps under-trained community workers are exposed to the risks of being either ignored or co-opted by the organisations they seek to influence. These are important matters, and I shall return to some of them later in the paper.

Social planning and social change

(Much of what follows is written within the context of social services departments. This is done largely for the purpose of example. The kind of social planning activities that I describe are highly relevant within a wide range of other statutory and voluntary bodies.)

The *targets* of the social planning efforts of community workers (and, for that matter, other professionals such as social workers, and especially area team managers) are those organisations (whether local, regional or national) whose functions, policies and services affect the well-being of those in the worker's area of service. The *goals* of these planning interventions are:

1 to alter community (and, thereby, individual) conditions by bringing about change in formal organisations. Change is sought
   (a) in the 'amount, the quality, the accessibility, and the range of goods, services, and facilities provided for people',[30]
   (b) in the decision-making and operating procedures for the acquisition, allocation and delivery of those goods and services; and
   (c) in the social and organisational policies that influence decisions and procedures in the organisations.
2 to promote services and programmes that will improve the well-being of communities or lead to the elimination or amelioration of 'adverse social conditions', and to attempt to make some impact upon major social problems that are 'caused' by national and international factors but whose manifestations are local.
3 to ensure that social factors are considered in the design and implementation of agency plans and programmes.
4 to foster linkages, co-ordination and joint planning between organisations.
5 to bring about what Kahn[31] has called a 'migration of concepts'. As social planners, we should be able to bring a new vision and breadth to agencies, and help release agency workers, especially in the social services, from a narrowness of approach caused

both by their own specialist training and the burdens of their daily routines and responsibilities. Besides new concepts and perspectives, the social planner may also introduce alternative technologies to agencies.

Why do it?

Why should community workers and others pursue these goals? One answer has already been given: it is through these social planning interventions that community work and the social services can move away from being concerned only with small-scale, face-to-face work with small numbers of people. There are, however, more pressing considerations and they are all related to the single fact that formal public sector organisations at local and national levels are acquiring more and more influence over (a) the living and working activities of most of the population; and (b) the working opportunities of a large number of professional groups, including community workers. I shall look at each of these issues separately, but they are related.

Organisations and people

It is very fashionable in some community work circles both to be highly critical of organisations such as local authority departments and the DHSS *and* to dismiss them as targets for change. Of course, they are changed through the activities of community groups, but workers tend not to regard them as proper objects for a direct intervention on the part of the worker and his/her colleagues. This reluctance is sometimes ideological ('we're not in business to tinker with the system, but to smash it') but mainly pragmatic—in most cases, community workers believe they have neither the training, the skills nor the influence with which to achieve substantial agency change. The possibilities are not as limited as this statement suggests, however, and there is a good, but neglected, literature which discusses the potentialities and techniques for low-level employees to wield power and influence within their organisations.[32] Community workers are also rightly wary of not undermining community groups by appearing to speak for them within their organisations.

The *legitimisation* for community workers and other staff in the human services professions to confront the issues of organisational change has been clearly stated by Patti and Resnick:[33]

> Intraorganisational change refers to the systematic efforts of practitioners to effect changes in policies or programs from within their agencies when they have no administrative sanction for these activities. The legitimation for these efforts is derived from the practitioner's ethical obligation to place professional values above organisational allegiance, i.e. he has the responsibility to become actively engaged in promoting an organisational environment that enhances the welfare of the agency's clients and staff.

Legitimacy for such change activities also comes from the worker's relations with, and mandate from, community groups. One of the special contributions that the community worker can bring to social planning is precisely his commitment to, and identification with, consumer populations.

The *necessity*, even the urgency, of the practitioner's role in inter- and intra-organisational change comes from consideration of the role and influence of welfare bureaucracies in British society today. These welfare bureaucracies (in the fields of housing, social services, health care, education, planning and income maintenance) may be seen to constitute one of the greatest influences on the interest and fortunes of the population, especially the working class, and such influence, of course, is all the more in times and areas of economic depression, unemployment and poverty. The need for community work to take account of this factor has been brought to our attention by the Women's Movement in a paper by Elizabeth Wilson,[34] who writes:

> The reality of community life, as opposed to the confused and romantic dream-image, is women living in a direct relationship to the State as mediated through housing departments, schools and the State welfare system which supports the family. The divison of labour within the family usually means that it is women who go to the rent office, women who attempt to grapple with the schools, women who are interviewed by the social worker.

This insight from the Women's Movement is timely because the trend in community work at the moment is to go in another direction, and to call for links between community groups and

trade unions. I am not suggesting that these links are not important, but that they should not be forged at the expense of neglect-
ing the issues presented by the hold of welfare bureaucracies over
working-class life. For many working-class, and other, families the
most real, and perhaps influential, face of capitalism is not that of
a cigar-smoking capitalist but that of a file-sorting functionary in
the local offices of a welfare bureaucracy or institution. The forces
that mould and control the lives of community residents come not
only directly through the work-place but also as they are mediated
through social welfare organisations and their personnel. The performance and impact of these organisations ought to be a matter
for scrutiny and concern, especially in the present decade when
Britain has been involved in a number of simultaneous major
experiments involving the reorganisation and redefinition of its
health, education, social services and local government structures.

What I am suggesting is that, as part of their professional role,
community workers and others in the social services bring to
bear on local and national organisations that same vigilance for
the rights and well-being of individuals and classes that once
characterised the efforts of those who sought to protect and
extend the interests of employees at their place of work, and to
reduce the arbitrary power of employers and business over the
lives of workers and their families. If we accept the extent of the
influence of welfare bureaucracies, then we should professionally
intervene (through, for example, the social planning role) to
ensure that their policies, procedures and services are in the
interests of consumers. This does not imply an acceptance of an
'individual deficiency' view of social problems, but only that
formal organisations tend to deteriorate as service-giving systems
(they become out of touch, ossified, too big, remote, centralised,
arbitrary and so forth) and we must intervene at an operations and
policy level to counter their adverse effects on people's lives.

I am aware of the counter-arguments that pose as radical
perspectives. Palmer,[35] for instance, writes: 'Public dissatisfaction
with government and public services is most felt at their point of
contact. Therefore piecemeal reform at the periphery of public
contact—the local level—neutralises the demand for more fundamental structural changes.' The trouble with this statement, as
with so many of the offerings of the radical tendency, is that,
first, no evidence is offered to support the contention that work
at the local level neutralises or pre-empts more fundamental

protest; and, second, no advice is given on how the practitioner, as part of his working role, should work in order to help people, if that is what they want, to make the 'demand for more fundamental structural changes'. Palmer's statement exemplifies the vacuity of an analysis that is unaccompanied by a consideration of the related practice or action initiatives.

My final point is to make clear that in calling for more involvement by community workers in organisational and policy change through a social planning role, I am not advocating a decline in neighbourhood work. On the contrary, I have already suggested that part of the legitimacy for community workers to be involved in social planning is their links with consumers and community groups, and these groups and links need to be created and sustained through neighbourhood work interventions. The community worker as social planner will also experience a tension and conflict between his own goals and values, those of his agency and those of community groups. These tensions, however, are very familiar to the neighbourhood worker, and thus experience in neighbourhood work may be seen as an appropriate preparation for social planning roles. Indeed, it may be essential that the community worker as planner has been involved in direct work with community groups and consumers.

I do not believe that professionals have the only or the best expertise in community problem-solving, and the social planner must conceive of his role alongside the interests and responsibilities of residents and elected members. The crucial involvement of residents in social planning has been emphasised by Musick and Hooyman:[36]

> citizens are assumed to have the capabilities to carry out tasks which do not necessarily require trained expertise or large scale resources: to identify community needs, to set goals and standards for community achievement, to participate in formulating public policy, to gather information on community issues, to be involved in overseeing the performances of community institutions and to delegate . . . the authority to perform the tasks best accomplished by them. In other words, citizens can oftentimes decide *what* is to be done; professionals can then be charged with the responsibility for deciding *how* it will be done.

One of the challenges facing community work in thinking about this division of labour over policy and implementation is how to prepare mechanisms of participation for citizens, politicians and professionals that avoid the risks of tokenism, placation and co-option identified by Arnstein.[37] The group process model of Delbecq and Van de Ven referred to earlier is a useful starting point in this task.

Organisations and professionals

Local and central government are significant employers of a number of professional groups. The great majority of community workers are employed by local government departments, notably by the social services. It is these departments which also have at their disposal the money and other resources that community groups and community workers often need in order to carry out their plans.

The involvement of local government departments with community work will deepen as funds for voluntary, once-off, projects become scarcer. Not only will these departments have most of the jobs to dispose of, but they also offer to community workers the opportunities for advancement and promotion. As funds dry up, it becomes less possible for experienced workers to step sideways into either a voluntary project or teaching or a student unit. Consequently, many workers, especially those with a social work training, are now looking, somewhat tentatively and self-consciously, at the possibilities of moving upwards, perhaps into some management role, within the local authority.

I want to suggest two reasons why this strengthening of the employee-employer relationship between community workers and local authority departments should be approached by workers with a resolve to gain familiarity with the skills and knowledge of the social planning process.

First, I believe that community work employers are becoming more knowledgeable and exacting in their expectations of community workers, and that the period of experimentation and of a laissez-faire attitude to community workers is coming to an end. In other words, agencies are becoming interested in the productivity and outcomes of the work, whereas in the first half of this decade community work has thrived in many agencies partly because of its expressive value. In particular, community workers have been as important for what they *represented* as for what they achieved in their work. And what they have especially represented is a value called participation, a value about open, inclusive democratic practices that has been in the ascendent in this country for the last ten years or so.

Gilbert and Specht[38] state: 'There is a continuing cycle of competition among three values (participation, leadership, expertise) that govern the management of community affairs . . . Each value when it is maximised, contains the seed of its own undoing.' If they are correct, then we should be anticipating the waning of participation as the governing value, and the waxing of expertise of leadership. My view is that because of the complexity of social issues that face local authorities, and the scarcity of resources available to deal with them, the value of *expertise* will gain ascendency in the second half of the 1970s. If this is the case, then I believe that one of the most appropriate forms of expertise that community workers (and other staff in voluntary and statutory agencies) can bring to their work is that of the social planner.

My second reason for stressing the utility of social planning to the community worker in his role as local government employee has to do with the nature of organisations, and their influence upon the work, motivations and purposes of the employees. Organisations are inherently political systems, with individuals and sub-groups sensitised to the acquisition of scarce resources, rewards and advancements within the organisation. Local authority departments can be seen in this light, composed of a number of administrative and professional sub-groups in disagreement and conflict about the appropriate values, goals and means either of the sub-groups or of the department as a whole.

Organisations are also systems of control and direction:[39]

> the point of organisation is to limit the number of behavioural alternatives available to individual members of the system so that performance is more predictable. To this end, roles with expectations supported by a system of rewards and punishments are elaborated, and rules for the interaction of role incumbents are set down.

What effect, then, does this system of role expectations, rules and sanctions have on the motivation and aspirations of those, including many community workers, who seek to innovate in a local authority department, and to change and modify what they see as its unhelpful procedures and practices?

What we know or suspect, and what is at the root of many community workers' reluctance directly to intervene to change organisational behaviour, is that such people are either co-opted by the organisation or sapped by the inertia, red tape and opposition encountered in trying to promote ideas within a complex administrative and political system such as a local authority department. Frustration, demoralisation and then cynicism set in, and the worker proceeds to reduce his aspirations and vision comfortably to fit within the narrowly-circumscribed expectations held by others of his role.

My contention is that community workers and others need a level of technical and interactional competence within their organisations in order (a) to compete effectively in the political process of organisations; and (b) to withstand the enervating effects of the bureaucracy on their idealism and change ambitions. I believe that that competence is within the reach of practitioners through the social planning role.

Social planning activities

In this final section, I want to review the major aspects of the *practice activities* of the worker who takes on a social planning role. That is, I want to give some indication, though not the details, of how such a worker would conceptualise the phases of his work, and structure and order his activities. I will also consider briefly the kinds of knowledge and skills needed to carry out effectively some of these activities.

Planning is a purposeful, conscious and deliberate process of exploration and anticipation, whose major phases are as follows:[40]

1   Value exploration and orientation.
2   Preliminary identification and definition of problems.
3   Decision to act, the definition of the tasks to be carried out, and by whom.
4   Assessment of needs and resources for a specified territory and/or group.
5   Definition of goals and targets.
6   Deciding on priorities amongst goals.
7   Designing a programme of services and interventions.
8   Mobilising resources, especially finance and support.
9   Implementation and delivery of the programme.
10   Evaluation.

This is, of course, only one of many ways to describe and order the planning process,[41] and depending on the circumstances, practitioners may find themselves having to enter the planning process at different points. The process is also best seen as a circular activity with evaluation leading on to further insights about 'new' needs and resources. It must be emphasised that each stage in this process comprises a number of technical and interactional tasks, and for each of these tasks there are a variety of linked roles, skills, knowledge and technologies for carrying them out. It is, however, possible to build in some of the interactional tasks as specific phases in the planning process, so that it becomes less rationalistic and technically-orientated than that presented above. Gilbert and Specht, for example, do this with their planning model, and include 'Informing the Public' and 'Building Public Support and Legitimation' as two distinct phases.[42]

Planning processes of the kind I have presented above are a form of control and guidance over the practitioner's activities because he can use such a process as a check-list to ensure that he has carried out or delegated the main activities and operations involved in planning. The process is also a device to raise consciousness—a planning process is designed to make decision-makers more aware of the nature of the problems that require examination, and more alert to alternative solutions, and their likely costs and benefits. Finally, the process may act as a politicising device in so far as it sensitises practitioners to (a) evaluating the political and financial feasibility of alternative solutions; (b) recognising the value- and preference-laden nature of decision-making, and to the fact that the values and choices of those with little access to, or power over, decision-making ought to be recognised; and (c) the need to cultivate agency and community support for preferred solutions and programmes.

The planning process that I have outlined is a generic process because it can be used for thinking about and performing work by staff at all levels of an organisation. The process can also be used for the tasks of both intra- and inter-organisational change (the practitioner uses the process to analyse and understand the organisation, decide on what future organisational behaviours are desirable, and to design, implement and evaluate the strategies likely to achieve the proposed changes) and of community change. It is competence in the skills, knowledge and techniques associated with the tasks at each part of the process that gives to practitioners the possibilities of achieving these changes.

It is, of course, an 'extraordinary expectation' that any one person could master all the interactional and technical requirements implicit in the planning process, 'and it is no wonder that most planning . . . (has) foundered on the absence of adequate technical knowledge just as often as on the lack of the planner's power to implement.'[43] Kramer and Specht here raise the two important problems of knowledge and power, and I shall deal with that of power first. The community worker, and other field staff, may indeed have insufficient *bureaucratic* or *legitimate* power to effect the changes that they seek through the social planning process; there are, however, other forms of power, including that based on *expertise*,[44] and my suggestion is that field staff in human service organisations can become more powerful change-agents by acquiring some expertise in a social planning role. Patti and Resnick also discuss other sources of power available to low-level workers in an agency where they lack legitimate authority to change intra- and inter-agency politics and procedures.[45] In addition to expertise in social planning, the community worker has a source of power that comes from his relationships with community groups.

I believe that there are two ways to make the problem about knowledge more manageable. First, practitioners should seek to acquire a grasp of the overall content and significance of the planning process, and become 'expert in "casing" a variety of problems and pursuing their policy and program implications'.[46] The notion of 'casing' indicates that training programmes in social planning of community workers and other staff would seek to provide students with generic skills and techniques that would help them become more knowledgeable about a range of social and organisational problems that they might meet in their work. Second, it might be appropriate for students to develop a particular competence in one or more of the broad categories of planning activity that can be derived from the ten-stage planning process presented previously. These activities are social analysis, programme design, programme implementation and programme evaluation.

Social analysis

This involves activity primarily in stages 1 to 4 of the planning process. Social analysis is concerned to investigate and better understand social conditions, social policies and agency services.

(a) Social conditions—the social analyst focuses on the socio-economic conditions and problems that affect the welfare of the community and individuals that his organisation serves. The analyst needs to understand the nature and scope of major social problems in the fields of housing, employment, education, health care, income maintenance and so forth, and particularly their impact at the local level. Problem analysis at a local level requires workers to define the problem and explicate its key concepts, to understand how the problem is defined and labelled by relevant others (e.g. politicians, consumers), to determine the size and scope of the problem, and to gather evidence, theories and hypotheses that may help to explain the causes and persistence of the problem.

(b) Social policies—here the objects of analysis are the local and national policies that help to determine community conditions and agency responses.

(c) Agency services—the agencies which deliver services to communities are also targets for social analysis, not least because an understanding of the authority structure and procedure of an agency may illuminate questions about the nature of the agency's services, and the ways in which it attempts to provide them.

It is clear from this brief account that the knowledge and skills required in social analysis include those in research methods, the collection, analysis and presentation of data, the assessment of needs and resources (including the use of social indicators and official sources of statistics) and the ability to 'get inside' and understand organisations.

Programme design

Within this social planning activity, the practitioner is involved in the setting of goals and priorities, the design of a service programme and the mobilisation of appropriate resources such as money, staff and support.

To design a programme is to translate agreed goals and priorities about a community condition or client group into a plan of action that specifies who is to benefit from the intervention and what form the intervention is to take. It might be a programme of services to a group in the community, or a programme of interventions designed to influence some aspect of the work of another agency. The design must specify the organisational form of the intervention, its financing, duration, staffing and other administrative arrangements. The programme designer must be skilled in relating back the design to the original problem analysis, and be able to specify and choose between various programme alternatives on the basis of their respective costs and benefits. The design phase also requires an awareness of how various programme alternatives would be welcomed or resisted by relevant others like elected members, staff and consumer and community groups. Yelaja[47] has suggested that the design phase also includes *advocacy* of the alternative chosen by the practitioner:

> advocacy takes into consideration the fact that a social policy practitioner does not work to produce an alternative just to see it gather dust in a politician's office or a bureaucrat's desk but actively seeks its advocacy by using *appropriate ways and means* with due regard to professional ethics.

Besides specifying the resources needed for an intervention, the programme design phase must also pay attention to the process of acquiring these resources from within or outside the agency. At the very least, this requires competence in the written and oral presentation of requests for finance and other resources like office space and equipment.

Programme implementation

The concern in the implementation phase is to ensure that the programme gets into the field, and that it has an impact on the specified targets as was intended in the programme design. Implementation has a large administrative component, but it also includes responsibility for attending to those factors that may frustrate the successful implementation of a programme. These factors include:

— resistance on the part of those (whether clients, groups or agencies) that the programme seeks to influence.

— difficulty and resistance amongst field staff operating the programme in understanding and applying the programme measures.

— failure or reluctance amongst front-line managers adequately to support, train and supervise the field workers, and to provide an administrative structure compatible with the demands of the programme.

— bureaucratic and political factors that 'represent the main near-term deterrents to more effective implementation'.[48]

Programme evaluation

The purpose of evaluation is to assess the extent to which a programme has achieved its goals. Such evaluation may be used both to decide on whether or not to continue or modify the programme and to illuminate further needs and problems revealed during the programme's operation. Such evaluation requires skill in data collection and analysis, and in research methods, though evaluation is also a political activity, particularly where bureaucrats and politicians have established vested interests in the running of a programme.

I am aware that I have left unstated in the above account of social planning roles (because of considerations of space) much of the knowledge and skills needed to carry them out. For example, I wrote under programme design of the need to evaluate the likely costs and benefits of different types of interventions. It is implicit in this statement that the practitioner would need to be familiar with contemporary methods, such as cost-benefit analysis, of assessing and predicting outcomes.

There are, however, certain generic areas of knowledge and skills that are relevant to all four social planning activities. For example, effectiveness as a social planner from within the kinds of agencies in which most community workers and social workers operate, is contingent, almost above all else, on the practitioner having a sound understanding of the political and administrative dimensions of his and other organisations. This involves general and local knowledge about legislative and political processes within the practitioner's agency and local authority. Knowledge is also required of the principles and reality of organisational design and structure, and, in particular, of those factors and techniques that facilitate or hinder the diffusion and adaptation of ideas through an organisation. The nature of decision-making in organisations should also be a focus of study, and the practitioner will need knowledge of different approaches to decision-making ranging, on the one hand, from the synoptic, to, on the other, the incrementalist.[49]

The skills needed to effect change within an organisation include the ability to develop, articulate, advocate and gain support for ideas and programmes through:

— the clear portrayal of ideas and proposals in written and verbal forms.

— the effective use of self in persuasion, compromise, bargaining and conflict situations.

— mediating between different interest groups and communicating across different hierarchical levels, and between organisations.

Segal[50] has also developed a list of such organisational skills, including lobbying and building support and influence, mapping out strategies to support a particular proposal, working with committees and changing them into productive units and writing strategic letters and memoranda.

Conclusions

I have suggested in this paper that the radical and the social reformist tendencies in community work do not encourage, for different reasons, the development of an awareness and expertise that would enable community workers (and other staff) to make an impact on the organisations and policies that play such a large part in determining the well being of individuals, families, groups and communities in this country today. I have further suggested that such an impact may be possible through developing an expertise in social planning.

My purpose has not been to present social planning as a panacea for the ills of society, the social services or of community work. Rather, I believe that familiarity with the problem-solving skills and techniques of social planning is one way in which community workers will attain the kind of technical competence commensurate with many of their ambitious change objectives. I am thinking, of course, of the emergence of an expertise in social planning that reinforces and is reinforced by the continuing development of neighbourhood work. What is required is the integration of the cognitive and technical skills of planning with the organising, interactional and advocacy skills associated with neighbourhood work.[51]

At a more abstract level, the attempt to achieve a synthesis between neighbourhood work and social planning may be conceived as an attempt to achieve a better fit between, on the one hand, theoretical or analytical activities, and, on the other, practice and action. The present relationship in community work between action and analysis is rather disjointed because of an over-emphasis on both local, neighbourhood action, and on 'grand' political analyses that have little utility and potential for application by

the practitioner. What social planning seems to offer is an opportunity to complement neighbourhood action with a concern for
social and organisational reform, and to stiffen political analysis
with an effectiveness in technical analysis.

Note: I am grateful to Jacki Reason for her help with this paper.

Notes

1 For a discussion of process changes in community work, see
   D. N. Thomas, 'Journey into the Acting Community: Experiences of
   Change and Learning in Community Groups', in *Group Work, Learning
   and Practice*, ed. N. McCaughan, Allen & Unwin, 1977.
2 R. Holman, 'Change or Short Change for Social Needs?', *Municipal
   Review*, February 1975.
3 S. Baine, 'The Political Community', in *Community Work One*, ed.
   D. Jones and M. Mayo, Routledge & Kegan Paul, 1974.
4 R. L. Warren, 'The Sociology of Knowledge and the Problems of the
   Inner Cities', in *Perspectives on the American Community*, ed.
   R. L. Warren, Rand McNally, New York, 1973.
5 H. Specht, *The Community Development Project: National and Local
   Strategies for Improving the Delivery of Services*, National Institute for
   Social Work, London, 1976.
6 P. Baldock, 'Why Community Action? the Historical Origins of the
   Radical Trend in Community Work', *Community Development Journal*,
   April 1977, p. 68.
7 S. K. Khinduka, 'Community Development: Potential and Limitations',
   in *Readings in Community Organisation Practice*, ed. R. Kramer and
   H. Specht, 2nd ed., Prentice-Hall, Englewood Cliffs, 1975, pp. 181–2.
8 op. cit., p. 19.
9 For a further discussion of the training potential of community workers'
   groups, see P. Baldock, 'The Community Workers' Group and Training',
   in *Community Work: Learning and Supervision*, ed. C. Briscoe and
   D. N. Thomas, Allen & Unwin, 1977. See also D. N. Thomas and
   R. W. Warburton, *Community Workers in a Social Services Department:
   a Case Study*, NISW/PSSC, London, 1977.
10 L. Tasker and A. Wunnam, 'The Ethos of Radical Social Workers and
   Community Workers', *Social Work Today*, 15 March 1977.
11 op. cit., pp. 335–6.
12 op. cit., pp. 31 ff.
13 op. cit., p. 12.
14 E. Wilson, 'Women in the Community', in *Women in the Community*,
   ed. M. Mayo, Routledge & Kegan Paul, 1977, p. 9 (my emphasis).
15 T. Pateman, *Language, Truth and Politics*, Stroud and Pateman, Sidmouth,
   1975.
16 Tasker and Wunnam, op. cit., p. 12.
17 op. cit., p. 36.

18 Wilson, op. cit.; A. Gallagher, 'Women and Community Work', in *Women in the Community*.

19 These insights from the Women's Movement help to resolve some of Harry Specht's puzzlement about why the CDP Directors were so fired by an anti-social work ideology when it was not practically required by their working briefs and situations. See Specht, op. cit., pp. 26–32. The CDP Directorate and their action teams were predominantly male; and 61 per cent (166) of the 273 whole-time community workers in social services departments in England and Wales were male (data from DHSS Feedback Document S/S76/3. Figures for September 1975).

20 Community Work issue, September 1975.

21 M. Mayo, 'Community Development: a Radical Alternative?', in *Radical Social Work*, ed. R. Bailey and M. Brake, Arnold, 1975.

22 L. Tasker, 'Politics, Theory and Community Work', in *Community Work Two*, ed. D. Jones and M. Mayo, Routledge & Kegan Paul, 1975. See also Mayo, op. cit.; Tasker and Wunnam, op. cit.; P. Ambrose and R. Colenutt, *The Property Machine*, Penguin Books, 1975, pp. 181–3.

23 D. N. Thomas, 'Said Alice: "The Great Question Certainly Was, What?" ', *Social Work Today*, 27 November 1975.

24 J. K. Whittaker, *Social Treatment: an Approach to Interpersonal Helping*, Aldine, Chicago, 1974, p. 44.

25 See, for example, A. L. Delbecq and A. H. Van de Ven, 'A Group Process Model for Problem Identification and Program Planning', *Journal of Applied Behavioral Science*, 7 (4), 1971; D. Molnar and M. Kammerad, 'Developing Priorities for Improving the Urban Social Environment: a use of Delphi', *Socio-Economic Planning Science*, 9, 1975.

26 R. Bolan, 'The Social Relations of Planners', *Journal of the American Institute of Planners*, November 1971.

27 J. Rothman, *Planning and Organising for Social Change*, Columbia University Press, 1974; *Promoting Innovation and Change in Organisations and Communities*, Wiley, New York, 1976; *Mastering Systems Intervention Skills: a handbook*, University of Michigan, 1975.

28 The basic texts are J. Rothman, 'Three Models of Community Organisation Practice', in *Strategies of Community Organisation*, ed. F. Cox *et al.*, Peacock, Itasca, 1974; R. Perlman and A. Gurin, *Community Organisation and Social Planning*, Wiley, New York, 1972; *Readings in Community Organisation Practice*, ed. R. Kramer and H. Specht, 2nd ed., Section D.

29 op. cit., p. 216.

30 R. Morris and R. H. Binstock *Feasible Planning for Social Change*, Columbia University Press, 1966, p. 14.

31 A. J. Kahn, *Theory and Practice of Social Planning*, Russell Sage, New York, 1969, p. 10.

32 See, for example, R. J. Patti and H. Resnick, 'Changing the Agency from Within', in *Readings in Community Organisation Practice*, 2nd ed.; R. J. Patti, 'Organisational Resistance and Change: the View from Below', *Social Service Review*, September 1974; D. Mechanic, 'Sources of Power of Lower Participants in Complex Organisations', *Administrative Science Quarterly*, December 1972; H. W. Weissman, *Overcoming Mismanagement in the Human Services Professions*, Jossey-Bass, San Francisco, 1973.

33 op. cit., p. 65.
34 op. cit., p. 4. A similar perspective is found in Jan O'Malley's account of community action in Notting Hill—see *The Politics of Community Action*, Spokesman, 1977.
35 J. Palmer, Introduction to the British edition, R. Goodman, *After the Planners*, Penguin Books, 1972, p. 30.
36 J. Musick and N. Hooyman, 'Toward a Working Model for Community Organising in the 1970s', *Journal of Sociology and Social Welfare*, September 1976, p. 16.
37 S. Arnstein, 'A Ladder of Citizen Participation', *Journal of the American Institute of Planners*, July 1969.
38 N. Gilbert and H. Specht, *Dimensions of Social Welfare Policy*, Prentice-Hall, Englewood Cliffs, 1974, p. 187.
39 R. M. Middleman and G. Goldberg, *Social Service Delivery: a Structural Approach to Social Work Practice*, Columbia University Press, 1974, p. 171.
40 The following model and much of the content of this part of the paper, is based on work done at the National Institute by Paul Henderson, Tony Scott and myself.
41 Other descriptions of the planning process may be found in N. Lichfield *et al.*, *Evaluation in the Planning Process*, Pergamon, 1975, p. 17; Perlman and Gurin, op. cit., p. 62; Gilbert and Specht, op. cit., p. 16; Kahn, op. cit., p. 61.
42 op. cit., p. 16.
43 Kramer and Specht, op. cit., p. 217.
44 J. R. P. French and B. Raven, 'The Bases of Social Power', in *Group Dynamics*, ed. D. Cartwright and A. Zander, 3rd ed., Tavistock, 1968.
45 op. cit.
46 A. E. Melzer, W. C. Richau and J. B. Tuner, 'Analysis of Social Planning Problems: a New Design for a Component of the Community Organisation Curriculum', *Journal of Education for Social Work*, Fall 1967, p. 73.
47 S. Yelaja, 'Social Policy Practice', *Journal of Education for Social Work*, Fall 1975.
48 W. Williams, 'Implementation Analysis and Assessment', *Policy Analysis*, summer 1975, p. 545. See also, on implementation, E. C. Hargrove, *The Missing Link: the Study of the Implementation of Social Policy*, Urban Institute, Washington, 1975.
49 A good introduction of different approaches to decision-making is *Planning for Social Welfare: Issues, Models and Tasks*, ed. N. Gilbert and H. Specht, Prentice-Hall, 1977. See also J. Algie, *Six Ways of Deciding*, British Association of Social Workers, 1976.
50 G. Segal, 'Policy Science and Social Policy: Implications for the Social Work Curriculum', *Journal of Education for Social Work*, spring 1976, p. 41.
51 Two ways of achieving this integration within a curriculum have been described by Melzer *et al.*, op. cit.; F. L. Ahearn, R. S. Bolan and E. M. Burke, 'A Social Action Approach for Planning Education in Social Work', *Journal of Education for Social Work*, Fall 1975.